Pro Arduino

Rick Anderson
Dan Cervo

Apress·

Pro Arduino

ISBN-13 (pbk): 978-1-4302-3939-0

ISBN-13 (electronic): 978-1-4302-3940-6

Trademarked names, logos, and images may appear in this book. Rather than use a trademark symbol with every occurrence of a trademarked name, logo, or image we use the names, logos, and images only in an editorial fashion and to the benefit of the trademark owner, with no intention of infringement of the trademark.

The use in this publication of trade names, trademarks, service marks, and similar terms, even if they are not identified as such, is not to be taken as an expression of opinion as to whether or not they are subject to proprietary rights.

While the advice and information in this book are believed to be true and accurate at the date of publication, neither the authors nor the editors nor the publisher can accept any legal responsibility for any errors or omissions that may be made. The publisher makes no warranty, express or implied, with respect to the material contained herein.

President and Publisher: Paul Manning
Lead Editor: Michelle Lowman
Technical Reviewer: Cliff Wootton
Editorial Board: Steve Anglin, Mark Beckner, Ewan Buckingham, Gary Cornell, Louise Corrigan, Morgan Ertel,
    Jonathan Gennick, Jonathan Hassell, Robert Hutchinson, Michelle Lowman, James Markham,
    Matthew Moodie, Jeff Olson, Jeffrey Pepper, Douglas Pundick, Ben Renow-Clarke, Dominic Shakeshaft,
    Gwenan Spearing, Matt Wade, Tom Welsh
Coordinating Editor: Christine Ricketts
Copy Editor: Damon Larson
Compositor: SPi Global
Indexer: SPi Global
Artist: SPi Global
Cover Designer: Anna Ishchenko

Distributed to the book trade worldwide by Springer Science+Business Media New York, 233 Spring Street, 6th Floor, New York, NY 10013. Phone 1-800-SPRINGER, fax (201) 348-4505, e-mail orders-ny@springer-sbm.com, or visit www.springeronline.com. Apress Media, LLC is a California LLC and the sole member (owner) is Springer Science + Business Media Finance Inc (SSBM Finance Inc). SSBM Finance Inc is a Delaware corporation.

For information on translations, please e-mail rights@apress.com, or visit www.apress.com.

Apress and friends of ED books may be purchased in bulk for academic, corporate, or promotional use. eBook versions and licenses are also available for most titles. For more information, reference our Special Bulk Sales–eBook Licensing web page at www.apress.com/bulk-sales.

Any source code or other supplementary materials referenced by the author in this text is available to readers at www.apress.com/9781430239390. For detailed information about how to locate your book's source code, go to www.apress.com/source-code/. Source code is also available via GitHub, at http://github.com/ProArd.

Contents at a Glance

Contents

About the Authors

Rick Anderson is Director of Virtual Worlds for Rutgers University, Co-Director of NJ Makerspaces, and Trustee of Fair Use Building and Research Labs. He's also a sponsor and judge at Hardware Hacking Hackathons, and a featured speaker at TEDxRutgers 2013. Rick teaches basic electronics, Minecraft Circuits in real life, Arduino, and soldering for people of all ages. He designed the original Arduino Test Suite, and is co-designer of the chipKIT Fubarino. His multiplatform code for Arduino 1.5, cowritten with Mark Sproul, won the Blue Ribbon Editor's Choice award at Maker Faire 2011. Rick is currently working on Morse's Secret Technology, a series of steampunk robotics and Arduino projects.

Dan Cervo (Servo) is a project development director at MAD Fellows LLC, a research and development company started by Doug Bebb and Dan. MAD Fellows has embraced the Arduino and its culture as an essential cornerstone for scientific development and rapid proofs of concept. Dan has worked in ballet, jewelry, and commercial flight management systems. Dan is currently working on research in metamaterials, computational science, iso geometrics, and robotic control theory.

About the Technical Reviewer

Cliff Wootton is a former interactive TV systems architect at BBC News. The News Loops service developed there was nominated for a British Academy of Film and Television Arts (BAFTA) award and won a Royal Television Society Award for Technical Innovation. Cliff has been a speaker on preprocessing for video compression at the Apple WWDC conference, and he has taught postgraduate students about real-world computing, multimedia, video compression, metadata, and researching the deployment of next-generation interactive TV systems based on open standards. He is currently working on R&D projects investigating new interactive TV technologies, he's involved with the MPEG standards working groups, and he's writing more books on the topic.

Acknowledgments

Deepest thanks go to Teri, Craig, Doug, Shane, and other family and friends who supported and helped with this project. Thanks to Cliff Sherrill for providing an excellent foundation in computer science. Miguel, Dr. Ayars, and everyone at Adafruit, SparkFun, and Arduino—thanks for your contributions. Rick, Michelle, and the Apress staff—thanks for the opportunity to work on this project.

—Dan Cervo

First and foremost, thank you with love to my wife, Kristen Abbey. She allowed this book to be the center of our lives until it was done. Many thanks to coauthor Dan Cervo. A giant thank you to all those that helped make this possible, especially Ryan Ostrager. I had so much support from my friends, Mark Sproul, Anjanette Young, Anthony Lioi, and editors Michelle Lowman, Brigid Duffy, Christine Ricketts, and Laura Jo Hess. Thanks Rutgers University for creating such a supportive environment. Thank you David Finegold and Rich Novak, and finally the open source and open hardware communities, without which Arduino, and all of my projects, would not exist. Lastly, thanks to the chipKIT team, which has been responsive and has worked sincerely to achieve the best open source support and vision for multiplatform Arduino.

—Rick Anderson

Introduction

Since its release, Arduino has become more than just a development platform; it has become a culture built around the idea of open source and open hardware, and one that is reimagining computer science and education. Arduino has opened hardware development by making the starting skills easy to obtain, but retaining the complexities of real-world application. This combination makes Arduino a perfect environment for school students, seasoned developers, and designers. This is the first Arduino book to hold the title of "Pro," and demonstrates skills and concepts that are used by developers in a more advanced setting. Going beyond projects, this book provides examples that demonstrate concepts that can be easily integrated into many different projects and provide inspiration for future ones. The focus of this book is as a transition from the intermediate to the professional.

■ ■ ■

## CHAPTER 1

Arduino 1.0.4 Core Changes

If you are writing sketches, creating your own libraries, or making your own Arduino-compatible boards, the Arduino 1.0.4 changes will affect you. Many of the changes optimize the Arduino IDE for improved workflow and customization. Changes to the IDE include the removal of unused buttons, and the placement of the Compile and Upload buttons next to each other. The Arduino IDE is now multilingual; you can pick a custom language for the editor. These changes are only the visible portions—with these updates, the Arduino team took the opportunity to make significant and code-breaking changes in order to deliver a more consistent and complete Arduino API. The core libraries of the Arduino Core API have been overhauled as well. Additional improvements include better support for making your own Arduino variations and the ability to integrate programmable USB devices with Arduino. This chapter will go through these changes, what they mean, and how they will affect your code.

The changes break down into the following categories:

- Arduino IDE

- Sketches

- API Core

- Core libraries

- Variant support for Arduino-derived boards

Changes to the Arduino IDE

The original file extension for Arduino was .pde. This is the Processing application file extension. If you had both programs installed, Arduino files would be opened in the Processing program. Now, after the updates, Arduino sketches have their own extension: .ino. Therefore, mysketch.pde is now named mysketch.ino. Double-click the file name, and Arduino launches. You can change the preferences to support the older PDE extension, but by default, PDE files simply open. Files will not be renamed to .ino unless you change the setting in the preferences.

The Arduino IDE editor now has line numbers in the lower-left corner, as shown in Figure 1-1. Compile is the first button, and the second button is Upload. The lower-right corner shows the selected board and what port it is connected to. These changes make it possible to quickly debug simple errors by identifying the line of code, verifying the correct serial port, and establishing whether the board is connected.

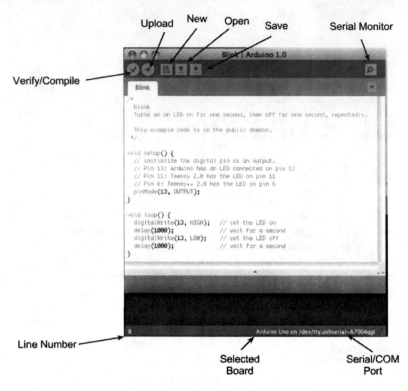

Figure 1-1. *Updated main window for the Arduino 1.0.x environment*

Look now at the Preferences panel (File ➤ Preferences), shown in Figure 1-2. I always use verbose output when I'm looking for errors in the compile process. The verbose-output feature has been moved to the Preferences panel, whereas before it could be triggered by pressing Shift plus the Compile button. The Preferences panel now enables you to resize the compile output for easier reading.

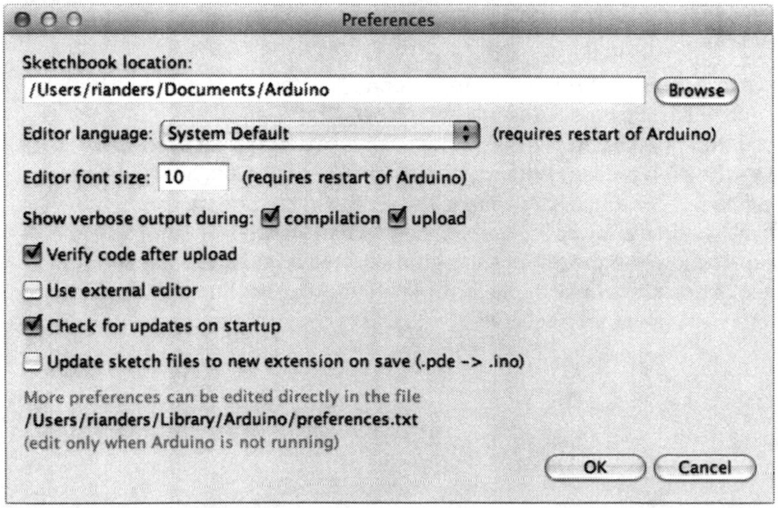

Figure 1-2. *Updated Preferences panel for the Arduino 1.0.x environment*

The location of the preferences.txt file is listed in the Preferences dialog box. It is good to know this because you may need to edit this file.

Changes to Sketches

Whenever you write an Arduino sketch, you are using the core functions and collection of objects that are always accessible, without needing to include external libraries in your sketch. For instance, Serial can be used without having to declare it. The Arduino IDE preprocesses the Arduino sketch before compiling. This process includes the Arduino.h file from core. Some of the files from core have to be included manually, as the Ethernet core does. The Ethernet core features are needed for the Arduino Ethernet board, but because not all Arduino boards have Ethernet, the files are available but not automatically included.

Arduino achieves its simplicity by preprocessing the sketch and automatically generating a basic functional set. So, you never have to worry about including Arduino.h and creating header files for sketches, unless you create your own Arduino libraries. Arduino libraries have to be written in standard C/C++; I will cover their creation later, in Chapter 14.

Here, you will examine how the default core functionality has changed. Then the chapter will cover how these changes have affected the default libraries that come with Arduino.

These default libraries have been replaced by new variants with new features. Also, WProgram.h has been change to Arduino.h.

API Updates

This section will discuss the changes to the API.

pinMode

pinMode has been updated to support INPUT_PULLUP. This adds clean support for creating buttons and switches that are active high by default, and when activated pulled low. Listing 1-1 shows an example.

Listing 1-1. pinMode INPUT_PULLUP Resistor Feature

```
setup()
{
  Serial.begin(9600);
  pinMode(10, INPUT);
  digitalWrite(10, HIGH);
  int  val = digitalRead(10);
  Serial.print(val);
}

In Arduino 1.0.x you can do it this way:
setup()
{
  Serial.begin(9600);
  pinMode(10, INPUT_PULLUP);
  int val = digitalRead(10);
  Serial.print(val);
}
```

3

This approach has the benefit of making the pinMode set the default value as needed. Also, using the internal pull-up resistors removes the need to use external pull-up resistors, allowing you to remove parts from your project.

Return Types

Return types have been updated to return the size of data using size_t, which is an unsigned integer that is platform dependent. size_t is included from stdio.h in the Print.h header. This returns a size type for the data printed. You can use this to check the quantity of data returned for iterating. When writing your own libraries that print custom data, you would use size_t as the return value.

uint_8

Several functions now take and return uint_8, which is a universal 8-bit integer that allows for cross-platform compatibility.

Arduino API Core 1.0.4

Now let's look at the changes in the Arduino API Core.

Arduino.h

If you are using standard AVR GCC system libraries or writing your own library, it's important to know the Arduino library. Arduino.h now includes all the values from wiring.h. If you are already programming with C/C++, it's good to know which functions are already available, so that you don't include the libraries twice.

Arduino.h includes the libraries shown in Listing 1-2, so you don't need to include them in your own sketches.

Listing 1-2. New Headers Automatically Included in Arduino.h

```
#include <stdlib.h>
#include <string.h>
#include <math.h>
#include <avr/pgmspace.h>
#include <avr/io.h>
#include <avr/interrupt.h>
#include "binary.h"
#include "WCharacter.h"
#include "WString.h"
#include "HardwareSerial.h"
#include "pins_arduino.h"
```

You never have to duplicate the libraries in your own sketches. They are automatically included for your use.

The preprocessing compiles Arduino.h, and then combines the sketch with a file called main.cpp. This file contains the implementation for void setup() and void loop(). In fact, it's short enough to show in Listing 1-3.

Listing 1-3. The New Version of main.cpp

```
#include <Arduino.h>
int main(void)
{
        init();
#if defined(USBCON)
        USBDevice.attach();
#endif
        setup();
        for (;;) {
                loop();
                if (serialEventRun) serialEventRun();
        }

        return 0;
}
```

Looking at the source, there are two interesting items to note. First, `main.cpp` now looks to see if a USB connection is defined and attached. Second, the `void loop()` code runs, and then a serial event is checked for. If the event is found, then the code runs it.

Updated Serial Object

Sending data from serial is now asynchronous. The `serial` object depends on a parent object called `stream`, so it is included automatically with `HardwareSerial.h` in your main sketch.

Updated Stream Class

The `Stream` class has been updated. This is part of the serial object and provides the search, find, and parse value functions that the `HardwareSerial` object uses.

Constructor

The constructor simply sets the timeout for the serial port to a default of 1000 ms.

```
Stream() {_timeout=1000;}
```

Member Functions

The member functions are shown in Table 1-1.

Table 1-1. *Stream Member Functions*

Function	Description
`void setTimeout(unsigned long timeout);`	Sets the timeout value for stream functions. If the process takes too long, it returns. The default is configured for 1000 ms, which is 1 second. The constructor sets this value.
`bool find(char *target);`	Searches the stream for the target string. Returns `true` if found, otherwise `false`. Also, will return as `false` if a timeout occurs.
`bool find(char *target, size_t length);`	Reads the stream until a target string of a specific length is found.
`bool findUntil(char *target, char *terminator);`	Works according to the same logic as `find()`, but returns `true` when a terminator string is found.
`bool findUntil(char *target, size_t targetLen, char *terminate, size_t termLen);`	Within a particular buffer and length, returns `true` if a termination string is found or the length reached.
`long parseInt();`	Searches for the first valid (`long`) integer from the current position. Initial characters that are not digits (0 through 9) or the minus sign are skipped; once a non-digit is found, the value is returned.
`float parseFloat();`	Searches for the first valid `float` from the current position, ignoring characters that are not digits or the minus sign. Once a non-digit is found that is not a period (.), the value is returned.
`size_t readBytes(char *buffer, size_t length);`	Reads characters from the stream into the buffer. If a length or timeout is reached, the function returns either 0 (for no data found) or the number of characters in the buffer.
`size_t readBytesUntil(char terminator, char *buffer, size_t length);`	Reads characters from the stream into the buffer. If a terminator character, length, or timeout is reached, the function returns 0 (for no data found) or the number of characters in the buffer.
`long parseInt(char skipChar);`	Allows for the parsing of integers and for a character (e.g., a comma) to be skipped.
`float parseFloat(char skipChar);`	Works similarly to `parseFloat()`, but ignores the skip character.

Print

The `Print` class has been updated. This affects the `Client` and `Stream` classes directly. The classes that include them are affected as well. The `HardwareSerial` and `UDP` classes use `Stream`. Therefore, you do not specifically have to include `Print` in your main Arduino sketch. Table 1-2 shows some of the more important updates to the public methods.

Table 1-2. *Updated Print Public Methods*

Method	Description
`size_t write(const char *str) { return write((const uint8_t *)str, strlen(str)); }`	Prints the character string at the pointer location. This function automatically finds the length of the character string. It returns number of characters printed.
`virtual size_t write(const uint8_t *buffer, size_t size);`	Writes a constant unit8_t pointer to a buffer of size `size_t`. Prints the bytes of a certain length, and returns the number of characters printed.
`size_t print(const __FlashStringHelper *);`	Prints a constant string stored in flash. Returns the number of character printed.
`size_t print(const String &);`	Prints a constant string object passed as reference. Returns the number of characters printed.
`size_t print(const char[]);`	Prints a constant character array. Returns the number of characters printed.
`size_t print(char);`	Prints a character. Returns the number of characters printed.
`size_t print(unsigned char, int = DEC);`	Prints an unsigned character in decimal format. Returns the number of characters printed.
`size_t print(int, int = DEC);`	Prints an integer with the default decimal format. Returns the number of characters printed.
`size_t print(unsigned int, int = DEC);`	Prints an unsigned integer with the default decimal format. Returns the number of characters printed.
`size_t print(long, int = DEC);`	Prints a long with the default decimal format. Returns the number of characters printed.
`size_t print(unsigned long, int = DEC);`	Prints an unsigned long with the default decimal format. Returns the number of characters printed.
`size_t print(double, int = 2);`	Prints a double with two decimal places. Returns the number of characters printed.
`size_t print(const Printable&);`	Prints a printable object passed as reference. Returns the number of characters printed.
`size_t println(const __FlashStringHelper *);`	Prints a constant string held in flash with a newline character. Returns the number of characters printed.
`size_t println(const String &s);`	Prints a const String passed as reference with a newline character. Returns the number of characters printed.
`size_t println(const char[]);`	Prints a constant character array with a newline character. Returns the number of characters printed.
`size_t println(char);`	Prints a char with a newline. Returns the number of characters printed.
`size_t println(unsigned char, int = DEC);`	Print an unsigned char with the default decimal format with newline. Returns the number of characters printed.
`size_t println(int, int = DEC);`	Prints an integer with a newline with the default decimal format. Returns the number of characters printed.

(continued)

Table 1-2. (*continued*)

Method	Description
`size_t println(unsigned int, int = DEC);`	Prints an unsigned integer with the default decimal format with a newline. Returns the number of characters printed.
`size_t println(long, int = DEC);`	Prints a long as a decimal with a new line. Returns the number of characters printed.
`size_t println(unsigned long, int = DEC);`	Prints an unsigned long as a decimal with a new line. Returns the number of characters printed.
`size_t println(double, int = 2);`	Prints a double with two decimal places with a newline. Returns the number of characters printed.
`size_t println(const Printable&);`	Given a printable object, prints it with a newline. Returns the number of characters printed.
`size_t println(void);`	Prints a new line character. Returns the number of characters printed.

New Printable Class

A new `Printable` class was created to define how new objects would be printed. Listing 1-4 shows an example.

Listing 1-4. Example of Writing Bytes

```
void setup()
{
  Serial.begin(9600);
}

void loop()
{
  byte bb = B101101;
  int bytesSent = Serial.print("byte: println: ");
  Serial.print(bytesSent);
  Serial.print(" : ");
  Serial.print(bb);
  Serial.print(" write: ");
  Serial.write(bb);
  Serial.print("");
  Serial.write(45); // send a byte with the value 45
  Serial.println("");
  bytesSent = Serial.write("A");
}
```

Updated String Library

Storing strings into flash for printing has been made easier by the F() command. Whatever string is placed between quotation marks will be stored in flash, and will reduce the amount of RAM used.

```
Serial.println(F("store in Flash"));
```

Wire Library Updates

The `Wire` library also uses `Stream`, so it has the same features as `Serial`. The function `Wire.send()` has been replaced by `Wire.write()`. `Wire.receive()` has changed to `Wire.read()`.

HardwareSerial Updates

`HardwareSerial` now supports USB by default.

- `Serial.begin()` supports unsigned `long` declaration.

- `Serial.write()` now returns `size_t`.

- `Serial.SerialEvent()` has changed.

- `Serial.SerialEventRun()` is implemented to check for up to four defined serial ports (`Serial`, `Serial1`, `Serial2`, and `Serial3`) and look for available serial data on each.

Physical Board Updates and USB Compatibility

All the new Arduino boards come with 16u2 chips for USB or have USB support built in, as is the case with the Arduino Leonardo 32u4. The core now includes USB serial, keyboard, and joystick. The Arduino Leonardo has the advantage that the USB libraries are accessible in your Arduino sketch, and you can use the new USB libraries to program Arduino Leonardo behaviors. However, the 16u2 chips do not use the same library, and since they are separate chips, they have to be programmed separately. Currently, the most widely developed USB support libraries are from Paul Stoffregen for the Teensy and Teensy++ boards.

Avrdude Update

Avrdude is the uploader that Arduino uses to load program images onto the Arduino boards. The version of Avrdude that comes with Arduino has been updated to 5.11, which supports the `arduino` upload type. This used to be the `stk500` upload type. All the official boards are now programmable by this `arduino` upload type from the 5.11 version. Additionally, custom bootloaders and firmware can be loaded onto Arduino using Avrdude.

You can use this feature to program microcontrollers with the Arduino bootloader, so that they can run Arduino sketches. Programmable microcontrollers include ATtiny85, ATtiny45, chipKIT Uno32, chipKIT Fubarino SD, and user-created and designed Arduino-compatible microcontrollers.

The New Arduino Leonardo Board

Arduino revision 3 boards are already configured and updated. The variant types are defined, and the upload types are configured for "Arduino."

The Arduino Leonardo is based on the Atmel ATmega32u4 chip. The Leonardo board has the following features:

- MCU ATmega32u4

- Operating voltage: 5V

- Recommended input voltage range: 7–12V

- Twenty digital pins

- Seven pulse-width modulation (PWM) pins

- Twelve analog input channels

- Flash memory: 32 KB (but 4 KB is used for the bootloader)

- SRAM: 2.5 KB

- EEPROM: 1 KB

- Clock speed: 16 MHz

A unique feature of the Leonardo is that serial data is normally handled and programmed over USB, but the Leonardo also has pins 0 and 1, which are configured as additional serial pins. These can be used for serial communication, in addition to USB. For instance, you can program and communicate using serial over USB, while a device like a GPS shield can use the onboard serial pins as hardware serial, without the need to use SoftwareSerial. Avoid the conflict generated between SoftwareSerial and the Servo library when they are used at the same time.

The firmware updates allow for the programming of the devices over USB serial. They implement an improved reset feature that allows for a software reset, triggered by the Arduino uploader at programming time. If the Arduino is emulating a keyboard, joystick, or mouse, you need to be able to reset the device so you can reprogram it.

In the new system SPI, however, pins are not broken out into digital pins, and are only available in the 6-pin ICSP header. For example, the Adafruit 32u4 breakout board and the Pro Mini from SparkFun Electronics both use the ATmega32u4 chip, and can be configured to act like an Arduino Leonardo. However, the physical pin mappings might be different, and this is where using a variants file is really helpful.

There are also two sets of I2C pins, but they are connected to the same pins on the ATMEga32u4 chip. They do not have internal pull-up resistors. You will have to confirm whether your shield has onboard pull-up resistors, and if not, you will have to add them. For instance, the Adafruit RFID shield will require that external pull-up resistors be added to the board.

Figure 1-3 is a chart stowing how the pins of the ATmega32u4 chip are mapped to the pins on the Arduino Leonardo.

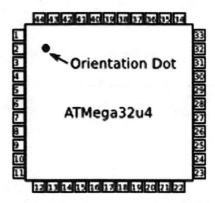

Figure 1-3. *ATmega32u4 pin numbering*

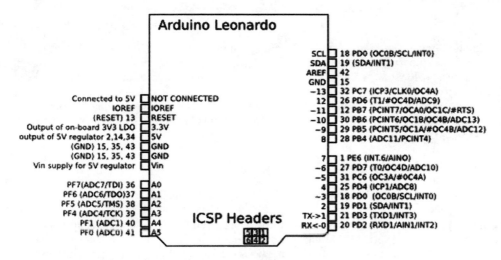

Figure 1-4. *Arduino Leonardo pin and feature layout*

In order to add the Leonard board to the Arduino IDE, they needed to define the boards.txt file, which contains the complete definition of the board. The boards.txt file includes the board name, platform, and upload protocol. Most importantly, the boards.txt file indicates the location of the bootloader file and the variants file to be used. If you make your own board based on this chip, these are the critical files to update. The SparkFun Pro Mini, the Adafruit ATmega32u4 board, and the paper Leonardo are all defined similarly; however, the Leonardo header and the name field need to be changed in the boards.txt file to match each board (see Listing 1-5). If there were a different pin configuration on your custom board, you would need to create your own build.variant file.

Listing 1-5. boards.txt Definition for the Arduino Leonardo

```
leonardo.name=Arduino Leonardo
leonardo.platform=avr
leonardo.upload.protocol=arduino
leonardo.upload.maximum_size=28672
leonardo.upload.speed=1200
leonardo.bootloader.low_fuses=0xde
leonardo.bootloader.high_fuses=0xd8
leonardo.bootloader.extended_fuses=0xcb
leonardo.bootloader.path=diskloader
leonardo.bootloader.file=DiskLoader-Leonardo.hex
leonardo.bootloader.unlock_bits=0x3F
leonardo.bootloader.lock_bits=0x2F
leonardo.build.mcu=atmega32u4
leonardo.build.f_cpu=16000000L
leonardo.build.core=arduino
leonardo.build.variant=leonardo
```

Board Variants

Board variants allow the defining of custom pin mappings for new and custom boards. Originally, all of these features were maintained in a pins_arduino.h file in the core. Now the pin maps have been moved into their own folder, called variants.

Variants Files

The Arduino Leonardo is a good example. The Teensy from Paul Stoffregen and the ATmega32u4 breakout board from Adafruit both contain the same chip as the Leonardo, but have different form factors. The number of pins and locations don't match, so creating a board variants file helps map the pins to the common locations more easily. Like pin 13 used for blink. Pin 7 maps to an LED on the ATmega32u4 breakout board. Adding a variant file causes those mappings to be the same. The variants file makes it much easier to create a custom board that is Arduino compatible.

These variants files are placed into a folder named after the board or the pin layout. Then, inside boards.txt, the variants entry needs to be added to:

```
boardname.build.variant=myboardpins
```

The files can be placed either into the application hardware/arduino/variants folder or in sketches/hardware/myat32u4/variants.

Arduino comes with several predefined variants that support the existing Arduino boards, but this chapter will examine the section specific to the Leonardo variants. Among the other variant folders (mega, micro, standard), there is a new one called Leonardo. That folder contains pins_arduino.h. This is used at compile time as a reference for the pin mappings and board-specific features.

Variant Types and Naming

The Arduino Leonardo has 12 analog inputs, but only 5 are mapped on the silk screen. However, all 12 are defined in the variants file. This means you can use the features—even though they are not labeled—by reading the variants. The SPI pins are not labeled, but can be accessed via the ICSP header. Here is the section where these capabilities are defined:

I2C is defined as pins 2 and 3 on the ATmega32u4 chip, as shown in Listing 1-6.

Listing 1-6. Variant File i2C Mappings

```
static const uint8_t SDA = 2;
static const uint8_t SCL = 3;
```

SPI is defined as pins 17, 16, 14, and 15 on the ICSP header, as shown in Listing 1-7.

Listing 1-7. SPI Pin Mappings

```
// Map SPI port to 'new' pins D14..D17
static const uint8_t SS   = 17;
static const uint8_t MOSI = 16;
static const uint8_t MISO = 14;
static const uint8_t SCK  = 15;
```

The analog pins are defined and mapped on the ATmega32u4 to the pins shown in Listing 1-8.

Listing 1-8. Analog Pin Mappings

```
// Mapping of analog pins as digital I/O
// A6-A11 share with digital pins
static const uint8_t A0 = 18;
static const uint8_t A1 = 19;
static const uint8_t A2 = 20;
static const uint8_t A3 = 21;
```

```
static const uint8_t A4 = 22;
static const uint8_t A5 = 23;
static const uint8_t A6 = 24;    // D4
static const uint8_t A7 = 25;    // D6
static const uint8_t A8 = 26;    // D8
static const uint8_t A9 = 27;    // D9
static const uint8_t A10 = 28;   // D10
static const uint8_t A11 = 29;   // D12
```

The rest of the file configures the ports and other features to support these constants.

Uploader Options Renamed to Programmers

There are several programmers supported in the list. The supported programmers are

- AVR ISP

- AVRISP mkII

- USBtinyISP

- USBasp

- Parallel programmer

- Arduino as ISP

These options make it easier to program devices that don't have serial or USB serial ports. The smaller chips, like the ATtiny 4313, 2313, 85, and 45, can only be programmed via one of these programmers. These programmers can also be used to put new bootloaders onto Arduino boards. Additionally, they set the chip configuration and speed

New Bootloaders

A bootloader is the software on the Arduino board that loads the sketch into memory. The sketch is compiled into a HEX file. The bootloader receives the HEX file from a programmer called Avrdude, and then loads it as the active program on the device. Several new bootloaders come with Arduino 1.0.4:

- *Optiboot*: The bootloader for the Arduino Uno rv3.

- *Diskloader*: The bootloader for the Leonardo and 32u4-based boards.

- *Stk500v2*: The bootloader for the Arduino Mega 2560.

USB Firmware for 16u2

The firmware is for the USB support and VID information for official Arduino boards. The USB firmware for 16u2 also contains the LUFA library, which Arduino licensed for official USB support. This firmware is burnable into the Atmega16u2, the Atmega8u2 for the Arduino Uno, and the Arduino Mega 2560. These are now updated for all the revision 3 boards. Revision 3 also removes the FTDI USB support and replaces it with the Atmega16u2.

You need to use the DFU programmer to program this firmware into those chips. The DFU programmer is available here: http://dfu-programmer.sourceforge.net/.

Additionally, a modification to board needs to be enabled to allow the programmer to communicate with the chip.

To enable programming via the DFU, you need to populate the second ICSP programmer, and in some cases perform a hardware modification described here in order to start working with the 16u2.

This ultimately allows for Arduino to have an onboard USB device separate from the main microcontroller. You will have to work out the communication protocol between the two devices. However, this will add USB device support to the latest family of Arduino boards. I think the Arduino Leonardo offers the best of both worlds, because instead of requiring you to program it separately, it allows you to program it using the Arduino USB API.

Summary

The Arduino 1.0.4 core changes update the built-in command structure for Arduino significantly. The changes to the object hierarchy affect the behavior of the objects that inherit from the parent objects, allowing for a more regular and cleaner API to program. A lot of work has also gone into supporting more boards, and updated boards, from Arduino. The changes to the bootloaders, particularly the addition of board variants, is a significant step toward supporting more Arduino variations. Now, your own Arduino-compatible board is much easier to create and distribute. For example, you can use an Atemga32u4 chip on your own custom board, or even make a Leonardo-derived board like the SparkFun Pro Mini, Adafruit Flora, or Adafruit 32u4 breakout board.

■ ■ ■

## CHAPTER 2

Arduino Development and Social Coding

Improve the world through sharing your code. Participating in a community of coders brings professionalism to your hobby. The Arduino world is a community that values the free flow of knowledge and recognizes the benefit of the community to problem solving.

While sharing code might seem to be an unsolvable puzzle at first, many tools have been used to accomplish the task of code collaboration. In this chapter, you will learn to use the online code-sharing community called GitHub. Along the way, this chapter will also explore how the Arduino open source community uses modern social-coding practices to contribute to projects.

Social coding is the idea that any code you create begins with and contributes to the work of a community of coders and active users who want to assist you as well as to improve their own projects.

Arduino is a fast-changing platform, and its development and best practices are set not by industry standards alone, but also by the emergent interaction between industry makers and an open source community of software and hardware hackers. How you participate in the open source community demonstrates how you are a *professional*. In the field of Arduino and open hardware, *pro* means using emergent techniques in social-coding communities, alongside making and testing in open, entrepreneurial communities. Open hardware, like open source software, even if created by a single person, is used and lives on in communities of use. So contribute your Arduino IDE source code for the good of the world and move along.

Because Arduino is open source, it is always under revision by its community of developers. Your code can undergo quite a bit change when starting a project, and when people begin to work collaboratively with you. The fast pace of change in a project needs to be matched by fast updates to the documentation. You and your collaborators will all need to have the same shared idea, and learn to describe that shared concept via documentation in a collaborative wiki environment. Even if you work alone, documenting your process will enable you to quickly return to projects once set aside, keep track of multiple projects at a time, or publish the software to run a kit you want to sell. To document your project, you need to know how to create pages, and edit a project Wiki using the Markdown syntax. This will be covered in the Documentation section of this chapter.

Components of Social Coding and Project Management

Project description, issue management, code version control, and documentation are the main components of social coding and project management. We will dig into each one, including a description of what each is and how you manage it through GitHub. Instead of these features all being hosted in different systems, they can all be found on GitHub. Centralizing these features in one place helps your community of users and developers keep up to date with the project and automatically watch for changes. The project repositories you host at GitHub can be created as public or private repositories. You choose whether you are hosting a private project for a small team, or a public open source project. On GitHub, you can host as many public open source repositories as you like, but you have to pay for the ability to have a private project.

The first example in this chapter will be a Hello World GitHub example that you can use as a template for structuring typical projects. All the examples for the book will be organized in a GitHub project repository: http://github.com/proard. As we learn the tool, you will be able to not only get your own copy of the code for the book, but you will be able to submit your changes back to the main project.

What Is a Project and How Is It Organized?

A project is the story of what you are working on, and then the hardware and code that make your physical project blink, move, or communicate. You can't put physical electronics on your site, so you have to put the description of the electronics. For our purposes, these files will count as code. and how is it defined?

The basic unit of a project is the *code repository*. This is where the code lives. Every project is required to have a name and a description. A readme file is strongly encouraged as well, as it is commonly used as a quick starting point for people to pick up key concepts and examples of your project. When you use a social-coding tool like GitHub, it derives a starter page for the project and generates the project's own unique URL, so users of the project can find it the project page easily. Hosting a project so that it is public and findable is a good start, but you want to encourage even more usage and participation. When someone watches, stars, or joins a project, GitHub tracks the changes in the repository. These changes are then emailed to them, or listed as part of their main page in GitHub.

There are two common patterns for project directory layouts. If you are creating a plain Arduino sketch, then the folder and the sketch name are the same. So, a sketch called *HelloGithub.ino* would be placed in a directory called *HelloGithub*. As seen in Figure 2-1 for HelloGithub.

Figure 2-1. *Example HelloGithub directory layout from Arduino sketches folder*

That directory would be the repository name. This way, when the project is cloned or downloaded from GitHub, it unpacks as a valid sketch and then can be easily placed in your Arduino *sketches* folder as in Figure 2-1.

The second pattern is for hosting Arduino libraries you create. In Chapter 13 we go over the details for writing libraries. In this case there is a pattern to create a repository for the Arduino library you are writing. If you were to write a library called "HelloLibrary" you would call your repository HelloLibrary. The repository name would automatically be the directory name that the holds the typical files in an Arduino library. However, the name of the project and the directory should not include a "_" because Arduino doesn't allow that in a library name. That way you do not have to change file names when you want to download or clone the library into the Arduino *sketches libraries* folder, like in Figure 2-2.

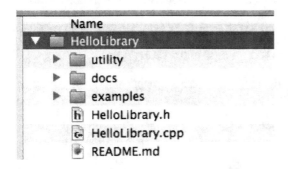

Figure 2-2. *Example HelloLibrary directory layout*

The Hello Library directory layout contains the required header file, implementation file, and the common sub directories for examples, documentation, and utility code.

Once the code is in GitHub it can be accessed in several ways from your GitHub project page. Figure 2-3, the GitHub menu bar, shows that you can download a zip file of the project. "Clone in Mac" triggers the GitHub GUI tool to clone or copy the project to your local computer. This option is also available for Windows and Linux.

Figure 2-3. *GitHub access repository options*

Figure 2-3 also shows you can also do a manual copy or clone of the project via secure Hypertext Transport Protocol (HTTPS), or secure shell (SSH). When you use these secure protocols GitHub will allow you to not just read data from the project, but write your changes back to the project securely. Finally, each of these techniques will allow for your sketches to be in your Arduino sketch folder or in you Arduino sketch libraries folder, where you can use or edit your project code.

In Arduino 1.0.5, there is now a new "Add Library" feature used to install your zipped library projects. This feature allows you to download the zip archive version of the project directly from GitHub, and it will extract, then install, the project into your user sketches libraries folder for you. This is very convenient for those developing Arduino libraries.

Many projects use GitHub for project and code management. There are many projects organized in this fashion. The Arduino project and examples in this chapter are using the same principles.

- *Arduino (*`http://github.com/arduino/arduino`*)*: The Arduino IDE source code.

- *ProArduino TiltSpirit (*`http://github.com/proard/tiltspirit`*)*: A simple Arduino game with LCD and tilt sensors.

- *ProArduino HelloGithub (*`http://github.com/proard/HelloGithub`*)*: The example Hello World GitHub for Pro Arduino.

From these project repositories you can find out the source code status, the current issues, and documentation wiki for a project. Each example represents a project that you can use or help with.

Overview of Version Control

In the code repository is the source code for the project. This code will change depending on project progress, features, and issues. A project that is alive changes and is revised regularly. Version control provides a method for multiple people to use, and edit the code simultaneously, and allows you to track the beginning and growth of a project over time. The basic unit of change in version control is the *commit*, which contains the list of all modified files, plus the code changes inside of them. In our case, version control can be thought of as a list of changes that are committed to the project by yourself or by other collaborators.

Overview of Issue Tracking

Issues are the features, bugs, and change requests for a project. A new project has goals and requirements. These are translated into issues for which the code delivers the functionally. Tracking issues can be quite difficult. For small projects that are about tiny tasks, a programmer can simply remember what needs to be done, but when a project takes you a couple days or more, your community starts giving you feedback and people start wanting to help you. In these cases, issue-tracking becomes critical. When you track issues, you keep a written list of new features and improvements. This public list is critical, in that users of your software can add feature requests or describe a problem in detail. A way to handle this is to assign a unique number, description, and category to each issue; this number can then be tracked from when a new issue is reported to when the issue is closed. Even more importantly, the code changes related to the issue need to be collected together. Every code commit should have a message describing the collection of changes. This way there is accountability for who made the changes and when the changes were made, and you will have a good chance of figuring out why the changes were made the way they were. In order to ensure that the code and issue are hyperlinked together, many users write something like, "This was fixed by *#issue_number*." The good news with GitHub is that every code commit can be connected to the issue it resolves.

When working with issues it is typical to take the following steps.

1. Look for the issue in the issue list.

2. If it does not exist, file a new issue, including a concise subject, a description that includes a way to reproduce the problem, and, if possible, a source code example or test that fails due to the noted issue. Then the issue number is generated.

3. People watching and maintaining the project will get an automatic e-mail when you generate your issue. If you need to discuss the issue, you can send an e-mail to the develop list with the issue number and a hyperlink to the issue.

4. Someone may claim an issue, or you can assign it to a programmer, and that connection between issue and programmer can be seen in the issue list. If not claimed, you can update the code yourself to address the issue, and then create an official request that your code fix be added to the main project. This request is officially called a "pull request."

5. Once the issue is confirmed fixed, the issue can be marked "closed" using either the commit, pull request, or issue manager interface.

6. If for some reason the issue is not truly resolved, you can reopen it.

This pattern helps everyone coordinate their work strategies, and divide up the effort of fixing project issues as well as project feature goals.

Documentation

Project documentation is the identity of your wiki project. It is where code experts, and people who are not source code experts and only want to use the project, go to find out what your project is about. It is like a Wikipedia entry for your project. In fact, the type of documentation we will be looking at is wiki documentation. We will use GitHub's wiki documentation to provide a statement of purpose; a description of assembly; a link to step-by-step images of the project; and a link to the schematics, Eagle, or Fritzing files to the printed circuit boards. Sometimes people check only the wiki documentation and never see the source.

The GitHub wiki uses what is called *Markdown* formatting in order to display the text of the pages. The details of Markdown syntax are found at https://help.github.com/articles/github-flavored-markdown. These pages can be edited online in the wiki interface. Additionally, other people can use the wiki and help you keep information about your project up to date.

Project Management for Social Coding

In this section, I describe one way to set up your development environment using the version control system Git and the online code-sharing repository GitHub. Git is the distributed version control software that GitHub uses as a basis for their social code management website.

Version Control with Git and GitHub

This section will provide one way to set up your development environment using Git and GitHub. It will drill into the details of how to perform project management in a social-coding world. GitHub at its core is the code repository that allows for version control.

Version control, or revision control, tracks every change made to software, including who made the change and when it occurred. This allows for multiple people to work on software simultaneously and merge the changes into the master code base. The tool at the heart of this is Git.

What Is Git?

Git is a powerful version control system that is used with many open source projects, including Linux Kernel, which has thousands of contributors and projects. Among the projects tracked with Git are Arduino software projects and projects from Adafruit Industries. The Git tool, which is a version control system that is completely distributed, allows for a massive amount of code hacking by multiple developers across the world. Everyone with a copy of the repository has a complete copy of the entire project with its entire revision control history. What is really unique with this is that developers are encouraged to fork the project and make their own changes to it.

Each copy of the software is either a clone or a fork. A *clone* is a copy of the master online repository on http://github.com/proard/hellogithub; you will use a clone of your project locally on your computer. A *fork* is an online official copy of the repository, one that you maintain on your own GitHub account, at http://github.com/youraccount/hellogithub. Git allows for a highly trackable and secure communication process between repositories. You can send cryptographically signed changes between you local repository and your remote repository. This supports secure development and accountability for who, where, when, and what changed.

Here, I will cover the basic starting commands and the preferred development process supported by the Arduino community. GitHub provides a nice starting guide at http://help.github.com, as well. The steps presented here will be similar to those from the guide, but they will be geared toward starting your own Arduino projects.

Installing Git

First, you must install Git locally and create an account on GitHub. Check out the "Get Started" section on GitHub, at https://help.github.com/articles/set-up-git. The command-line version of Git can be obtained from http://gitscm.org/ and should be installed as you would any software. I recommend selecting the shell options for Windows. The Git shell makes it easy to access Git on the command line. There is also a GitHub GUI tool for managing Git repositories which is helpful, but not a replacement for all of the features that come with the Git command line software.

One additional feature of Git is that it is cryptographically signed, and every commit and change clearly trackable, and makes programmers accountable for the changes they make. You will need to configure a unique key for your system. To get started, you'll need to do the following:

1. Install Git.

2. Create GitHub account at http://github.com.

3. Generate a key pair to authorize your commits.

    • Mac OS X: Go to https://help.github.com/articles/generating-ssh-keys#platform-mac

    • Linux: Go to https://help.github.com/articles/generating-ssh-keys#platform-linux

    • Windows: Go to https://help.github.com/articles/generating-ssh-keys#platform-windows

4. Set your user and e-mail in Git at http://help.github.com/git-email-settings.

Here is the command-line option for setting your global user information:

```
$ git config --global user.name "Your Name"
$ git config --global user.email you@example.com
```

With these settings in place, your system is ready to start working with the Git repositories, and GitHub. Your system will now properly indicate the code changes you make, and the changes you submit will be cryptographically accountable. This makes working with GitHub seemless.

GitHub Tools

Now that you have Git installed, and a GitHub account, you have your own area for repositories and account management on GitHub. I prefer to install the Git command line software prior to the GitHub GUI tools. That way, there is a command-line tool and GUI access for your project files. This lets you experience the best of both worlds.

Figure 2-4 shows the GitHub GUI configured to display projects on the local system. This shows your repositories and what organizations they belong to, as well as their overall status. It is possible to drill down into each project and examine individual files. Importantly, the Git GUI will generate the security keys for you.

Figure 2-4. *GitHub GUI on Mac OS X*

You are now up and running with GitHub. GitHub GUI will list your repositories on GitHub and synchronize changes from both your local repositories and your GitHub repositories. It provides a nice level of convenience, but learning the command line version of Git will offer better access to the revision control features, and showing the code differences between versions.

Version Control, Basic Workflow

In this section we introduce a basic work process for version control. This starts with creating your own example project in GitHub, then expands to working with projects other people have created, and then reviews the necessary Git commands that allow you to manage a version controlled project. This includes finding out what changed, and moving your code from your local repository to your remote repository on GitHub. It is possible to have more than one remote repository, but for this chapter your repository on GitHub will be the remote repository we use.

Creating Your Own Project

Go to GitHub and select "New repository." Call the repository HelloGithub. Then fill in the new repository information, as shown in Figure 2-5. Once finished, select "Create repository."

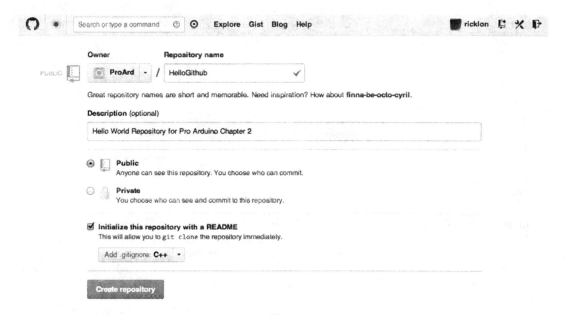

Figure 2-5. *HelloGithub project configuration page*

You want to indicate that this is an Arduino project. All Arduino projects are by default C++ projects. Select the .gitignore option for C++. This automatically keeps Git from tracking temp files and extraneous files common to C++ and text editors. Once you have selected "create repository," you are presented with the default view of the project. the interface should look like Figure 2-6. This view shows you the source code for your project, and links to the many features of GitHub.

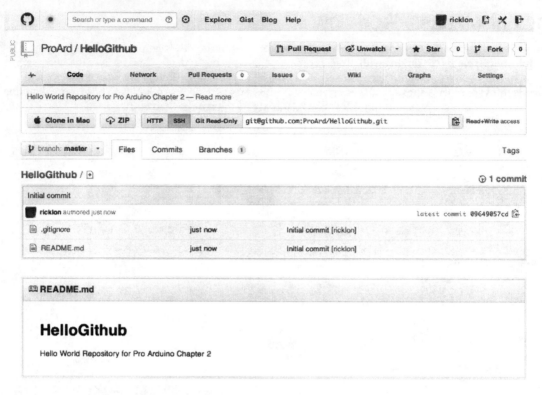

Figure 2-6. *Initial project page after creation*

An initial Readme.md file is created, but you will have to manually edit the `Readme.md` file with a description of your project, and how you would like people to configure the hardware, and modify the code to support different configuration for usage. This edit can be done after you clone your repository to your local machine, or can be done by live editing the file directly on GitHub. GitHub has a feature where you can browse your source code online and select a file for editing. When you save a change it will be saved as a standard code commit. Just click on the file "README. md" in Figure 2-6 to try it.

From Figure 2-6 you can clone the project locally. By cloning the project, you are in fact downloading the repository from GitHub using the "git clone" command. This is your copy of the entire repository on your local computer. Cloning can be done with the GitHub GUI application or on the command line, as follows:

```
$ git clone git@github.com:username/HelloGithub.git
```

In this case the "username" is your username on GitHub, and the command will copy all the files and version control information to your local machine. This is your local repository; all changes stay in the local cloned repository until you push your changes back to your original online repository on GitHub. "Origin" is the official name for your repository on GitHub. Your local code changes do not automatically move to the "origin." You will have to "push" your change to your origin. Also, changes that you edit online directly to your GitHub project or if new code is merged into your GitHub project from other code contributors. Those changes have to be "pulled" to your local repository.

Editing Code and Checking for Changes

Once you now have a complete copy, or local clone, of your project, the process of working with and modifying code begins. Through the work process you will manage the changes to the project, and eventually send those changes back to your remote repository at GitHub. You will need to know how to check to your project for changes, commit those changes, and send them back to you GitHub repository. Then you will want to be able to get new changes form your GitHub repository and add them to your local repository.

Code can be changed in many ways:

```
User git clone git@github.com:username/HelloGithub.git
```

Work process

Make changes to code:

- Use the Arduino IDE to edit a sketch like `HelloGithub.ino`.
- Add or delete files.
- Move files to various places in the project.
- Edit files in libraries with your favorite text editor.

View changes

When you do make changes, you will want to know how to review them. Any time a change is saved, you can issue the following commands to check your work:

```
$ git diff
```

Or show a summary of changes with:

```
$ git diff --stat
```

Saving and committing changes

Once you are ready to commit to the changes you made, you can now commit these changes to your local code repository. Only staged changes are committed without the "-a", to commit all changes, use "-a", like so:

```
$ git commit -a -m "Changed the files and fixed issue #1"
```

To commit only certain changed files list the named files, use the following:

```
$ git commit HelloGithub.ino "Update HelloGithub.ino and changed blink rate for issue #1"
```

Each of these commits are are identified by SHA-1 hash that represents all the changes in the commit. These commits are saved code transferred from one repositoy or another. Also, you can check out different commits and recreate the exact file structure and changes in their code. "HEAD" is an alias for the latest commit you have made. The indicator "~1" is the equivalent of "-1"; they can be combined to read "HEAD~1". It's also possible to say "HEAD~2" which is two commits back from HEAD. For instance, if you want to check out the previous commit you could issue the following command:

```
$git checkout HEAD~1
```

Once that checkout succeeds, the code and files match that exact commit. If you look at the file system, you will see your old files and old changes, but all will precisely match the first commit back form "HEAD". The syntax "HEAD" and "^" can be used with the `diff` command as well. To return to your latest status, issue the command:

```
$git checkout HEAD
```

Now your files and code match the official version.

One extremely useful use case is to check out just one file. You may have make changes you are not happy with, and you will want to only grab an early version or the current version of file. You can use:

```
$git checkout - filename
```

This immediately checks out the previous version of the file. You can checkout the file from two versions ago by using "HEAD~2"

```
$git checkout HEAD~2 filename
```

If the file didn't exists two version back it will complain file is not part of the commit.
You can also checkout what is called a branch:

```
$git branch HelloBranch
```

This command automatically creates a branch called "HelloBranch", but does not switch to it.

```
$git checkout HelloBranch
```

This command will check out that branch. If you want to return to your "master" branch you can use:

```
$git checkout master
```

At some point you will want to know what branches you have. The command is:

```
$git branch
```

The result will list all the branches in your repository.

In our examples we don't cover branching, but you should learn about branching as you use GitHub. A branch allows you to test out new ideas, create different versions of your project, or fix code without making changes in your master branch. In this chapter, I only cover making changes to your "master" branch.

Move changes to your GitHub repository

Now that the changes are committed to the local repository, you need to push them to your GitHub repository, which you can do by using the following command:

```
$ git push
```

If you are working on multiple machines, or multiple people are working with you, then your project on GitHub could have changed. You may have even accepted a "pull request". In this case, you will want to bring those changes, or collection of commits, to your local repository. One method is to "fetch" the changes from GitHub. This grabs the changes as a set, but does not merge them into your code automatically. The command would be as follows:

```
$ git fetch
```

At this point, you have all the changes from the GitHub repository. You do not have to fetch until something changes on Github again. At this point you can use "git diff" and examine the changes that were made on the server from a local copy. Once you are ready, merge the changes from fetch into your local repository. This is the merge command:

```
$ git merge master
```

The "master" key term is for the master branch of the code that was fetched. Most changes can be merged without a conflict. The pull command combines the fetch of changes with a merge. This is a very convenient way to get changes from your GitHub repository. The full command is:

```
$ git pull
```

Once you have successfully pulled your changes to from your GitHub repository. You can immediately begin editing, changing code, and working on your project. As needed, use the above commands to help you complete these common tasks. The options I have outlined are just for getting started with Git; it is a very complex and powerful tool. This chapter should get you started, but for more detail on the commands, see the Apress book called *Pro Git*, which can help you dig in deeper.

Workflow Summary: Creating Your Own Project

We walked through the creation of the HelloGitHub project to demonstrate GitHub's commands, but there is a pattern in the steps we took. Follow these same steps for any project you create and you have workflow that ensures version control for one or multiple creators. Summarizing the steps we already took, we see the common steps for working on any project:

1. Create the project on GitHub.

2. Clone the project to your local machine.

3. Make changes to the code.

4. Add or remove files.

5. Commit changes to your local Git repository.

6. Push those locally committed changes to your "origin" repository on GitHub.

7. Repeat steps 2–6 as needed.

These steps allow you to work locally and keep up to date with your project. You can use git diff, and git diff –stat or any of the many Git commands to check the difference in code version, and the changes over time for the project.

Workflow Summary: Forking Another Project

Frequently there are existing projects that you want to use, but you might want to change the configuration for your hardware, or want to add a feature to the project. Since I work with many different kinds of Arduino compatible boards, not every project is designed to work with one I'm using. For instance, between the Arduino Uno, and the Arduino Mega, the SPI pins are numbered differently. I will typically fork the project, and then make the needed changes to my forked copy of the project. Once I'm sure the code changes are working, I can do a pull request that allows the maintainer of the main project to merge those fixes to their project.

We will use the HelloGithub project at the Pro Arduino GitHub site, https://github.com/ProArd/HelloGithub, and run through the fork process with it. Once you find the HelloGithub project, you can select fork. This copies the project into your own GitHub area. Then you will want to make a copy to your local machine by cloning it.

These are the steps for forking another project:

1. Log into http://github.com.

2. Visit http://github.com/proard/HelloFork. You will find an example of what you'll find there in Figure 2-7.

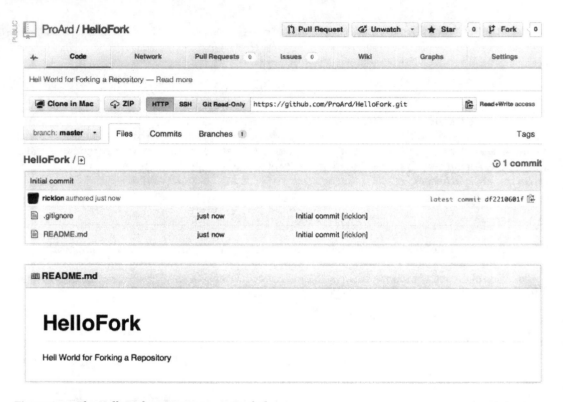

Figure 2-7. The HelloFork project you want to fork

3. Select the "Fork" option, in the list of buttons highlighted by Figure 2-8.

Figure 2-8. The "Fork" button in context

4. GitHub will tell you it is forking the project, with the processing sceen in Figure 2-9.

Figure 2-9. *GitHub's forking page*

5. Go to your fork of the project, as in Figure 2-10.

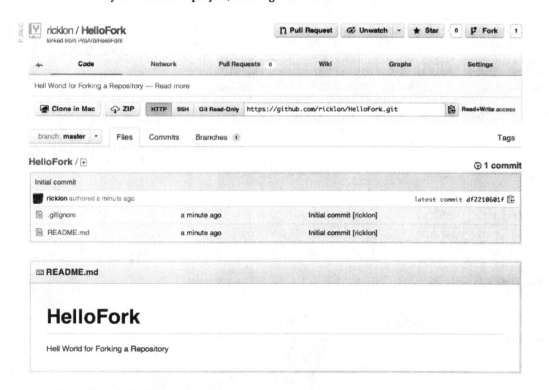

Figure 2-10. *Your fork of the project*

6.   Clone your project with the following:

```
$ git clone git@github.com:YourUsername/HelloFork.git
```

7.   Set the official HelloFork repository as the upstream repository:

```
$ cd HelloFork
$ git remote add upstream git@github.com:proard/HelloFork.git
```

8.   Since you just cloned it there are no changes, but once changes have been made you will want to fetch and merge changes from upstream with these commands:

```
$ git fetch upstream
$ git merge upstream/master
```

9.   You can do a test of the merge by doing a dry run, using the following commands:

```
$ git merge --no-commit --no-ff upstream/master
$ git diff upstream/master -stat
```

If you want to see the difference between the changes that are being made, you can compare your code with the code on your GitHub repository with the "diff" command:

```
$ git diff origin/master
```

You can get a quick summary of the file changes by using "—stat"

```
$ git diff origin/master --stat
```

Given this list, we need to define a couple of new concepts. First, an *upstream repository* is typically the project that you forked into your GitHub repository. Secondly, every so often you will want to go back to the original project and pick up new files and code changes, so that you can synchronize your work with the main project. Your original project on GitHub is called "origin." The latest version of code is called "master." So you can compare the latest versions of "origin/master," or "upstream/master," with your local repository. Over time, projects can get further out of sync. If you fetch the changes from the upstream repository, you can bring the changes to your local machine without clobbering your own code, without breaking existing work by hitting it with a write over. The upstream master code will not automatically update your working area in the local master. After a fetch, you have to take specific action to merge those changes into your own project. git merge defaults to merging the fetched master with your local working master repository. The merge process will combine those changes into your local project.

Creating a Pull Request

In the section we will modify the HelloFork.ino sketch to have your Arduino username and submit the change as a pull request to the official Pro Arduino repository for the HelloFork project. At this point you will already have the forked from Pro Arduino, and cloned to your local system. So now edit the HelloFork.ino sketch to include your GitHub username. The code will look like:

```
/*
* Hello Fork Github Example Arduino Sketch
* Just add your GitHUb account ID and I'll add your pull request to the project.
*/
```

```
void setup() {
  Serial.begin(9600);
}

void loop() {
  Serial.println("Add your GitHub name to the code to test creating a pull request");
  Serial.println("Hello Github from:");
  Serial.println("@Ricklon");
  Serial.println("@ProArd");
  Serial.println("@YourGitHubUsername");
}
```

Once you save this code you can check the repository for the change by issuing the command:

```
$ git status
```

Result:

```
# On branch master
# Changes not staged for commit:
#   (use "git add <file>…" to update what will be committed)
#   (use "git checkout -- <file>…" to discard changes in working directory)
#
#        modified:   HelloFork.ino
```

The status result shows that you modified HelloFork.ino. This change needs to be committed to your local repository with the following command:

```
git commit -m "Added a new username to the HelloFork.ino sketch." HelloFork.ino
Result:
[master f6367cf] Added a new username to the HelloFork.ino sketch.
 1 file changed, 1 insertion(+)
```

The commit uses the "-m" to specify the message. After the message can be a list of files, paths, and or wildcards to specify the file names and directories to include in the commit. If you want to commit all changed, added, and deleted files, you can use the "-a" flag. This flag stands for "all." The message can contain the Markdown shortcuts we described in the documentation section, like @username to mention a user and link to their account. Now that the file is committed, it is time to push the commit to your GitHub repository. That can be done be issue the command:

```
$ git push
```

Result:

```
Counting objects: 5, done.
Delta compression using up to 4 threads.
Compressing objects: 100% (3/3), done.
Writing objects: 100% (3/3), 408 bytes, done.
Total 3 (delta 1), reused 0 (delta 0)
To git@github.com:ricklon/HelloFork.git
   4e28d3f..f6367cf  master -> master
```

The push result summarizes all the changes and commit information that is sent to you GitHub repository. The "To" section. The "4e28d3f..f6367cf" in the result is shorthand for the hash that represents the commit being pushed to your GitHub repository.

Take a look at the HelloFork menu, as in Figure 2-11. Clicking on the file views the file. In our case we want to look at the commit and see what was changed as shown in Figure 2-12.

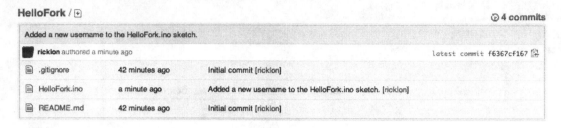

Figure 2-11. *HelloFork.ino changes are now on your GitHub*

Figure 2-12. *View of the changes in the commit*

The "+" indicates the new line of code you added. A minus, "-" represents the removal of code.

Now your project is up to date; all changes between your local repository and your GitHub repository are now synchronized.

Creating a Pull Request

Once all the changes you want to make are bundled in your repository it's time to create a "pull request" that will move your changes to the project you forked your project from. In this case we are using your HelloFork repository. Go to the your GitHub project for HelloFork. It should appear similar to Figure 2-13.

Figure 2-13. *Your fork of the HelloFork project*

The summary shown on Figure 2-13 shows your username, what project is selected, and where the project is from. At the same level are the project options. We are about to use the "pull request" option. You can also "Watch," "Star," or "Fork" the project from this menu. With "Fork" it shows you the number of forks of the project. If anyone wants to make a fork of your project, they can select "Fork." For now just select pull request button, as in Figure 2-14.

Figure 2-14. *Pull Request button*

After the pull request is selected, you are shown the "pull request" management screen as shown in Figure 2-15. Here you can decide the details of the pull request. In our case, we're just going to ask to pull the latest changes from our project in the master branch, to the Pro Arduino master branch.

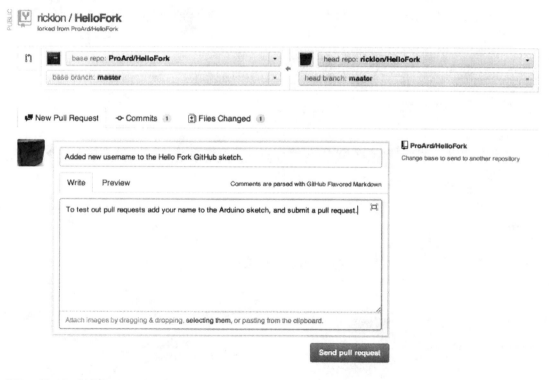

Figure 2-15. *Pull Request screen*

The pull request we created appears in in Figure 2-15, where we give it a title and description. Sometimes the title is descriptive enough, but there are times when you need to explain more about what you are doing, and what issues it addresses, then you can put that information in the main message area. The message area accepts Markdown, as we described in the documentation section of this chapter. Now that you've got your message entered, select the "Send Pull request" button shown in Figure 2-16.

Figure 2-16. *Send pull request button*

Once the pull request is done, it is filed as a request with the maintainer of the project you forked from. So for most purposes, you are finished. You are just waiting for the maintainer to implement your changes, or for the maintainer to ask for more clarification. The good news is that while this process is documented in the GitHub system, the communication between you and the maintainer can be extended in email, and those emails get tracked in GitHub, too, so that nothing is lost.

How To Merge a Pull Request

Now let's look at the flip side: What happens when you get a pull request? Once someone has submitted the pull request, you, as the maintainer, get a message and can immediately check the pull status from the pull request screen as shown in figure 2-17.

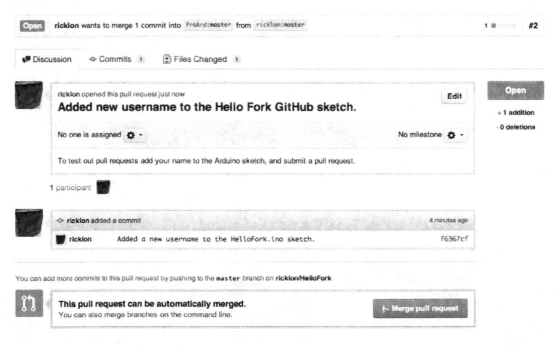

Figure 2-17. *Receiver of the Pull Request screen*

The summary of this pull request identifies who made the request, and identifies the commit that you are being asked to merge into your project. GitHub does a quick check to see if the new code can be added to the original automatically. In our case, the merge request can be automatic. Figure 2-18 shows a close up of that portion of the screen.

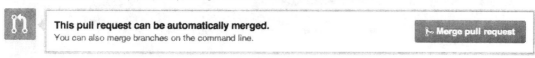

Figure 2-18. *Automatic pull requst merge option*

In this example, the maintainer selects to "merge pull request" and then is presented with confirmation and the opportunity to add a note about the merge as shown in Figure 2-19.

You can add more commits to this pull request by pushing to the **master** branch on **ricklon/HelloFork**

> **Merge pull request #2 from ricklon/master**
>
> Added new username to the Hello Fork GitHub sketch.
>
> **ricklon**
> rick.rickanderson@gmail.com   **Cancel**   **Confirm merge**

Figure 2-19. *Confirm that you want to make this pull request*

Once that merge is confirmed, then a summary screen is show as in Figure 2-20. The entire merge discussion is listed, so that you can review the comments. You can also review the commit status before and after the merge. If there is information about the merge that needs changing, it is possible to edit information about the merge from this screen.

Figure 2-20. *The completed pull request summary showing request closed*

Figure 2-21 shows the summary of the merge. It indicates which repositories were merged, and gives an idea of how much changed, by saying, in this case 1 commit was merged. There are times where multiple commits can be merged at once.

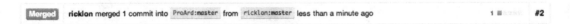

Figure 2-21. *Notification of merged pull request*

Figure 2-20 also shows that the merge is "closed"; this merge was identified as "#2" in the issue system. If you select "#2" you will be sent to the issue system, where you can see that the issue was closed as in Figure 2-21.

Since the HelloFork project currently has two issues, both pull requests that were completed are shown. These pull request are in the Pro Arduino project that accepted your request. In Figure 2-22 the screen from GitHub shows that two closed issues exist, and 0 open issues exist. If you made a pull request earlier to the project, then you would see them as one or more open issues. Since pull requests are integrated into the issue system, it is easy to find out who fixed issues, what issues were resolved, and where the changes came from. This leads us directly to issue management.

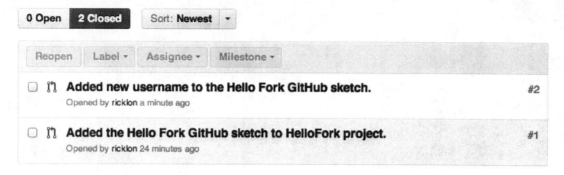

Figure 2-22. *Project issue list shows pull request issue closed*

What is issue management?

GitHub provides an issue-tracking system. Issues include new features, problems with existing code, and code review requests. Each issue is classified in detail by this issue-tracking system. An issue can either be open or closed. It's possible to comment on open and closed issues, as well as to reopen a closed issue.

When working with a forked project, the official issue list is maintained on the project you forked your copy from, not your forked copy.

Watching a project gives you all project updates and information. Starring a project only shows that you like the project, but doesn't update you on every detail.

You can sort issues by the following categories:

- Everyone's issues

- Issues assigned to you

- Issues created by you

- Issues in which you are mentioned

It's possible to create *milestones* as well. These are project-specific goals that you can create and customize. You can also create your own labels that help organize the issues for your project. Example labels are:

- Priority

- Defect

- Feature

- Enhancement

- Code review

- Bug

- Duplicate

- Won't fix

- Question

These project labels can be a quick way of prioritizing, because they visually identify the kinds of problems in the project.

Figure 2-23 shows the GitHub Issue Manager main page. In one view, you can get an idea of the "open" issues for a project. From here you can create new issues, and find issues that you have experienced. It also let's you search not just the "open" issues, but the "closed" issues as well.

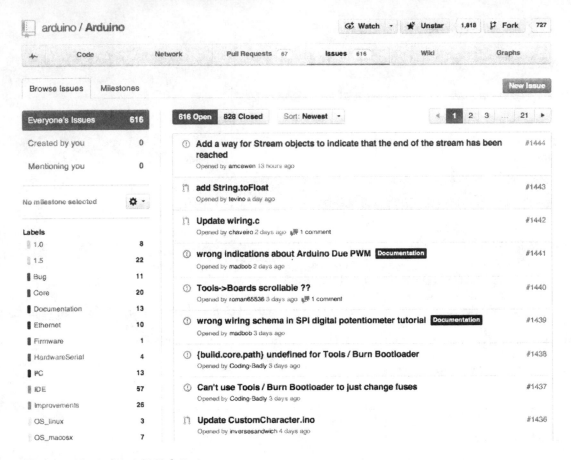

Figure 2-23. *Arduino GitHub Project*

Issue management with Github

For a quick way to think about issue tracking you can follow the following process:

1. Look for the issue in the issue list as shown in Figure 2-23.

2. If it does not exist, file a new issue and include a concise subject, a description that includes a way to reproduce the problem, and, if possible, a source code example or test that fails due to the noted issue. GitHub automatically e-mails the creation of new issues to maintainers.

3. Make your modification to the project files to fix the issue and submit a pull request from GitHub.

4. Confirm the issue is fixed by testing it.

5. Lastly, close the issue in the issue system, which will update its status.

Connecting Version Control with Issue Management

The ways you change your code and files to address an issue are collected in the message portion of a commit. These commits represent progress towards adding features or resolving issues. Connecting this progress to the issue tracking system is critical because you want to know what the code changes are for and you want to make it easy to track what code fixed which issue. GitHub has added some automatic linking features that automate part of this process. If you refer to issues by "#" pound issue number like "#1" in the commit message, or the issue comment GitHub will automatically link to the corresponding issue number. Every code commit should have the issue number and description of the code changes. When the issue number is used, GitHub automatically lists the commit in the issue history. In one issue discussion, you can follow the entire set of changes to code. issue management

Commit hashes are also automatically linked. Every commit has a Secure Hash Algorithm 1 (SHA-1). This hash is not a sequential number, but a 160 bit unique string, which looks like "f9bf52794286cd2acf664f8ffd7d7547c1b4dfea," and which is automatically linked to the commit by GitHub. This makes it easier to discuss multiple commits and peak at what was changed.

Documentation

Documentation is important. It is critical that you document what you do. When a project moves from one person who can control everything to a community of users and developers, it is important that people can find out how to use what you do, and the best way to help improve or enhance your work. It is possible to put all of your documentation into a readme file or into a documentation directory for the project, but it can be more convenient to use the GitHub wiki. Here is the quick and dirty way to use GitHub. Select the Wiki Tab on the project as shown in Figure 2-24.

Figure 2-24.

Github wiki

The default page is called Home and is automatically filled with the text "Welcome to the HelloGithub wiki!" From here, you can select Edit Page, and enter a main description and provide links to other important project pages.

Creating Pages

The Create and Edit buttons are located on the left side of the wiki page. To create pages, click the New Page button, and you'll be presented with the Create New Page dialog, as shown in Figure 2-25.

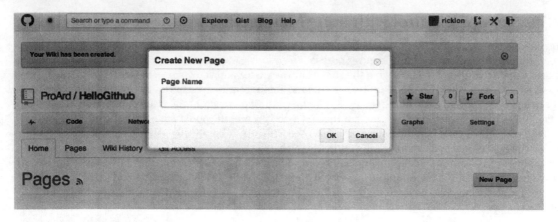

Figure 2-25. *The GitHub Create New Page dialog*

In the dialog in Figure 2-25, you give your page a title. After selecting "OK" the "Edit Page" screen appears and you can use the minimal web GUI or just write the new page using markdown syntax as shown in Figure 2-26.

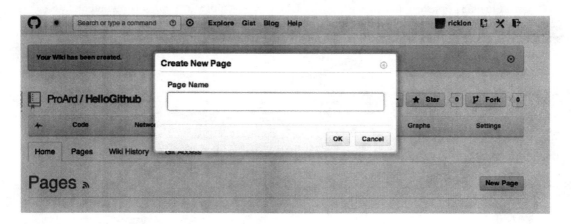

Figure 2-26. *Editing the page*

After entering the text in Figure 2-26, select the "save" option and the completed page appears. Figure 2-27 shows the published page you just saved.

Main

New Page   Edit Page   Page History

This is a sample Github repository that follows the pattern from repositories outline in Pro Arduino Chapter 2.

Last edited by ricklon, just now

Figure 2-27. *Reviewing the completed page*

Finally, you need to link the new page back to the home page by editing it and adding the line:

```
[Home](wiki/Home)
```

Anything between the brackets will be the hyperlink text. Then anything between the parentheses will be the link. In our case, we link the "wiki" and the page called "home." Anywhere this code appears will link back to the main "Home" page.

Using Markdown

Markdown is an efficient syntax for quickly generating wiki pages. GitHub-flavored markdown is very code friendly and easy to use. More details of GitHub markdown are found here: `https://help.github.com/articles/github-flavored-markdown`. Also, the HelloGitHub project has an interactive version of this file here: `https://github.com/ProArd/HelloGithub/wiki/Markdown`. The following are the basic code and page formatting options to get started quickly:

Code Blocks

We work with a lot of code in documentation, and showing examples quickly and easily is critical. To indicate a code section, we use three back ticks """" to start a code block and we use three more back ticks """" to close a code block. This makes it simple to add code into your documentation and examples. You can also specify the type of highlighting for your project. In the case of Arduino projects, you would be using C++ or C as the formatting and coloring options. You can choose not to show highlight with "no-highlght".

Markdown:

```
```C++
/*
* Code goes here.
*/
void setup() {
}
void loop() {
}
```
```

Display:

```
/*
* Code goes here.
*/
void setup() {
}
void loop() {
}
```

Linking to files.

The label for the hyperlink is placed between square brackets "[ ]", and then the link is placed between the parentheses "( )", as in the example. When linking external documents or images, the full link can go inside the parentheses. When linking to pages or files in the wiki, the the entry needs to begin "(wiki/", and everything after that is a page name or filename completed by the last ")".

Markdown:

```
[Link to remote site](http://github.com/proard)
[Link to remote file]( https://github.com/ProArd/attinysecretknock/blob/master/ATtinySecretKnock/
ATtinySecretKnock.ino)
[Link to wiki files](wiki/TestLink)
```

Output:

```
Link to remote site
Link to remote file
Link to wiki files
```

The results are hyperlinks with the link to labels.

Headings

Heading values are determined by the number of hash "#" symbols. A level 1 header would be one "#", level 2 "##", and level 3 "###".

Markdown:

```
# H1
## H2
### H3
#### H4
```

Output:

H1
H2
H3
H4

Lists

Lists can be ordered or unordered. It is possible to mix and match ordered and unordered lists. These shortcuts appear just like html ordered and unordered lists.

Ordered lists

Ordered lists just need to start with a number. GitHub wiki will substitute the correct sequence number.

```
Markdown:
10.  item 1
9.   item 2

Output:
    1.  item 1
    2.  item 2
```

Unordered lists

Unordered lists can use *, -, or, + as symbols. It doesn't matter which as long as there exists a space between the symbol and the start of the list value.

Markdown:

```
* item a
+ item b
- item c
```

Output:

- item a
- item b
- item c

Linking to Images

Linking to images is just another version of linking. Except the brackets "[]" denote the alt text for the image. The parentheses hold the link to the image. If the image is in your project you can hyperlink to the raw file. It is possible to add the image to your project wiki by checking out the project's GitHub wiki, adding an image, committing, and then pushing it back into your GitHub project wiki. The HelloGithub project wiki can be found here: https://github.com/ProArd/HelloGithub/wiki/_access

Here's the syntax of Markdown code to place an image, followed by a specific example:

```
![alt text](URL to image)
```

Markdown:

```
![ProArduino Image](ProArduino.jpeg)
```

Output:

Normal Text

For normal text you can type standard sentence structure. Paragraphs will automatically break at the new line. This combination of links, code formatting, and basic information structuring can get you started documenting your project. More importantly, effective documentation can help people understand why project is important, how they can help support it, and when to join in with you to document it.

Contributing to Arduino Development

Now that you're comfortable with the concepts and tools of social coding, I'll present an example workflow that sets up an Arduino social development environment, using the concepts and tools discussed in the preceding sections of this chapter.

The proper way to contribute code and fixes to the Arduino project is to fork the repository to your own area on GitHub. Then you can make changes to your repository and commit those changes to your repository. Next, you create a pull request on GitHub for those changes to be merged into the main project. This pull request can be reviewed, and then rejected or accepted into the project.

Forking Your Own Copy of Arduino

Here are the steps you would use to configure your own repository from Arduino's official repository on GitHub. Figure 2-28 shows Arduino GitHub project page.

1. Log into GitHub at `http://github.com`.

2. Go to the Arduino project:

    `http://github.com/arduino/Arduino`.

3. Select Fork for the Arduino project on the GitHub interface. This places a copy of the Arduino repository into your own GitHub area. Now that you have that in place, you need to clone your copy of Arduino to your local machine. This process is called cloning your fork of Arduino, and can be accomplished with the following command:

    ```
    $ git clone git@github.com:username/Arduino.git
    ```

4. If you don't need the entire project history, use this instead:

    ```
    $ git clone git@github.com:arduino/Arduino.git --depth 1
    ```

5. Set the official Arduino repository as the upstream repository. The upstream repository is needed so that you can pull down new code that other people add to the Arduino project. Here are the commands to do so:

    ```
    $ cd Arduino
    $ git remote add upstream git@github.com:arduino/Arduino.git
    ```

6. Now that you have this in place, you can start editing the code. After a while, you'll want to fetch and merge changes from Arduino every time new code is added. This is done with the following commands:

    ```
    $ git fetch upstream
    $ git merge upstream/master
    ```

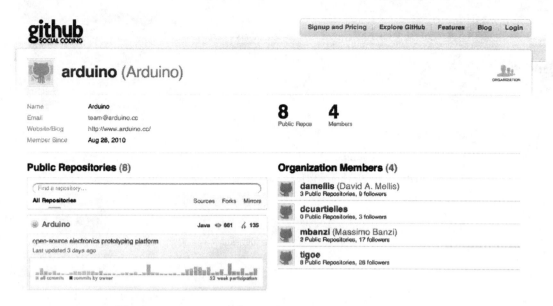

Figure 2-28. Arduino organization Arduino repository

Once you have the your own fork, and have cloned it locally you will want to compile and run the Arduino IDE from source code. Arduino has documented this process here: `https://code.google.com/p/arduino/wiki/BuildingArduino`. Once you are able to run the software using "ant run" you can now make changes to the source code. It is now possible to find issues in the Arduino project's issue list and fix them. Using the social coding techniques you will be able to make changes to the software, and submit your changes as pull requests back to the Arduino project. It's a big challenge to get this far with a large project, but it is really worthwhile to be able to make a great project even better with the power of the open source community.

The combination of tools allows for complete issue tracking and code management.

How to build the Arduino IDE from source

Now that you have the source code, you will want to run the code to identify the changes and test that everything is working. There is a straightforward process for doing this, but installing the toolkit is a little bit tricky. The process is different for the Windows, Mac OS X, and Linux platforms.

For Windows:

1. Install Cygwin:

2. Install JDK

3. Install ANT

4. Configure ANT home directory

5. Install GIT (you may have already installed it)

6. Clone your fork of Arduino or Clone Arduino

7. Go to project directory

8. Go to build directory

9. Type "ant clean"

10. Type "ant run"

For Mac OS X:

1. Install ANT

2. Configure ANT home directory

3. Install GIT (you may have already installed it)

4. Clone your fork of Arduino or Clone Arduino

5. Go to project directory

6. Go to build directory

7. Type "ant clean"

8. Type "ant run"

For Linux:

1. Install JDK:

2. Install ANT

3. Configure ANT home directory

4. Install GIT (you may have already installed it)

5. Clone your fork of Arduino or Clone Arduino

6. Go to project directory

7. Go to build directory

8. Type "ant clean"

9. Type "ant run"

Any Java compilation errors will stop the run. Any updates to the core files must be tested by compiling and uploading.

Community Resources

The Arduino community is a great source for both beginning and experienced developers. The community allows for users to share their experiences and help one another learn new skills and troubleshoot difficult problems. The following list provides some valuable resources offered by the Arduino community:

- The Arduino blog (http://arduino.cc/blog)

- The Twitter feed for the Arduino team (http://twitter.com/arduino)

- The Arduino forums (http://arduino.cc/forum/)

- The developer mailing list (https://groups.google.com/a/arduino.cc/forum/?fromgroups#!forum/developers)

- The Arduino Playground (`http://arduino.cc/playground/`)

- The Arduino Style Guide for Coding (`http://arduino.cc/en/Reference/StyleGuide`)

- The Arduino Style Guide for Writing Libraries (`http://arduino.cc/en/Reference/APIStyleGuide`)

Summary

Using the social-coding practices outlined in this chapter, you'll be able to create projects that can transition from personal projects, to group projects, to professional projects that use version control, issue tracking, and documentation. By using these processes, you can also join other open source projects and contribute feedback, documentation, issues, and code fixes. If you follow these procedures, your code and ideas can find there way into Arduino projects as features, fixes, and new libraries.

The patterns outlined in this chapter will be used throughout the book and code examples. All the code examples can be found at and forked from `http://github.com/proard`.

■ ■ ■

openFrameworks and Arduino

openFrameworks is a set of C++ libraries that provides an easy method of coding audio, video, and graphical components. openFrameworks provides mechanisms to easily connect serial devices and Arduinos to personal computers, making openFrameworks an invaluable tool for Arduino development and a useful next topic for discussion.

openFrameworks can be compared to interlocking plastic construction bricks in that using individual units does not require knowing how to make them. The libraries of openFrameworks are a lot like boxes of construction bricks, allowing creativity to flow without having to code from the ground up and always having a piece that will work. This is done by utilizing C++ object-oriented programming methods, which add abstraction and reusability. The advantage to openFrameworks in a development scene is that you can put together proofs of concept without having to do a lot of low-level coding. Working in openFrameworks also provides working code that can be used as a blueprint to migrate from when a final project goes into production and needs more optimizations.

Incorporating both openFrameworks and Arduino helps create a proof-of-concept environment for hardware and software interaction, which uses a development approach that "work fosters ideas"; an exploratory development style where ideas can be explored without waste. The key to this is reusability: not having to worry about permanently using a resource and having plenty components to play with. The combination of openFrameworks and Arduino is cross compatible on most systems.

The disadvantages to this setup are that it may not be production quality, optimized, reliable, or usable for the masses; things that are arguably less important than sharing and exploration in idea generation. The disadvantages are taken care of when moving away from the proof of concept to a prototype or putting the project into production. For developers, showing an idea is more impressive when that idea is something that can be fully manipulated. Physical models go a long way toward helping ideas to take life and can be easily created with clay, wood, 3D printing, or various other means. Adding openFrameworks and Arduinos to a physical model can, for example, help you create a new game controller design that can be used to play games.

Arduino and openFrameworks comprise a nice tool set to help breathe that extra life into an idea. With its simple code structure, designers, artists, it gives developers the ability to add buttons to make LEDs blink, create controllers to move virtual objects, and make systems that manipulate physical objects. Both Arduino and openFrameworks have vast online communities and a plethora of other documentation, making the knowledge to work and develop with these systems easily available. This chapter focuses on connecting the Arduino to computers via openFrameworks to expand the functionality of the Arduino.

Getting Started

To get started, make sure that the openFrameworks and Arduino software are set up and working, and also make sure there is a compatible Arduino board (e.g., an Uno, Leonardo or Nano) available. To download and install openFrameworks, go to www.openframeworks.cc and follow the setup instructions for your system. openFrameworks requires C++ and is built for integrated development environments (IDEs) such as Code::Blocks (www.codeblocks.org), Visual C++ (www.microsoft.com/express), and Xcode (http://developer.apple.com/xcode/).

The first four examples in this chapter (Listings 3-1 to 3-4) show how to set up serial communications. All the examples are written using Arduino 1.0.1 and openFrameworks version 0071 but have been tested with Arduino 1.5.1r2 and openFrameworks 0073.

Arduino Code

Listing 3-1 shows the code to set up the Arduino, connect to a push button on pin 8, and check if the button is pressed or released and report the change in this state to a serial connection using a character. The code also checks for an incoming character from the serial; a and s signify turning on and off an LED on pin 13, respectively. This passing of characters is important when developing code for openFrameworks to control the Arduino, thus making the Arduino a possible controller for a game, a sensor for a door, and so on.

Listing 3-1. Arduino Sketch That Sets Up the Arduino

```
int button = 8 , ledPin = 13; // pin assignments: button on pin 8,LED on pin 13
boolean oldState = 0 , newState = 0;     // state change variables
void setup() {
  pinMode(button, INPUT);     ////////////////////////////
  pinMode(ledPin,OUTPUT);     // set pin I/O types
  Serial.begin(9600);         // starts serial at baud rate 9600
} // end setup()
void loop() {
  newState = digitalRead(button); // save current button state
    if(newState != oldState){    // test for change in button state
      if (newState  == true)     // for button press, send the "h" to serial
        Serial.print('h');
      if (newState  == false)    // for button release, send the "l" to serial
        Serial.print('l');
    } // end if(state0 != state1)
  oldState = newState;          // save new state to old state for comparison
  delay(40);                    // delay for bounce control
} // end void loop()
void serialEvent() { // called upon incoming serial
  switch (Serial.read()){  // determine if serial is one of the required inputs
    case 'a': digitalWrite(ledPin, HIGH);
      break;                   // for input of "a", turn on LED
    case 's': digitalWrite(ledPin, LOW);
      break;                   // for input of "s", turn off LED
  }   // end switch (Serial.read())
}     // end serialEvent()
```

■ **Note**   The serialEvent() function does not work with the Leonardo board. To convert for the Leonardo board change void serialEvent() to if (Serial.available() > 0) and move the loop ending bracket to below the ex void serialEvent() function.

Verifying the Code

Load Listing 3-1 and hook up the Arduino with a momentary push-button switch and a pull-down resistor hooked to pin 8. The LED set up on pin 13 is optional because the Arduino has one on the board. With the board set up as per Figure 3-1 and plugged in, start the serial monitor in the Arduino IDE and match the baud rate of 9600. When the button is pressed, it causes an h or an l character to be displayed for a high or low state change. Sending the Arduino an a or an s will turn on or off the LED.

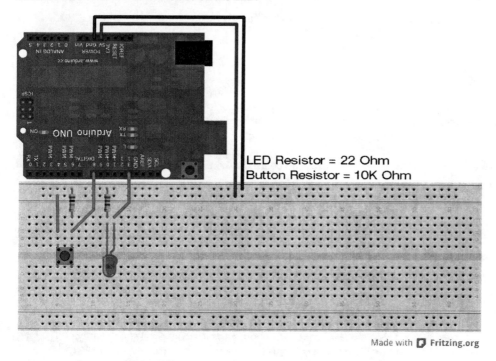

LED Resistor = 22 Ohm
Button Resistor = 10K Ohm

Made with ☐ Fritzing.org

Figure 3-1. *Arduino circuit for Listing 3-1*

Arduino Serial Functions

Listed following is a reference of Arduino serial functions and what they are used for. These functions reside in the predefined Serial object. To call any of the serial functions, use Serial. before the name, like so:

```
Serial.begin(9600);
```

- void begin(speed): Opens and sets a serial port at a baud speed equal to an unsigned long. Returns nothing.

- void end(): Closes the serial connection, releasing the TX and RX pins.

- int available(): Checks for data in the serial buffer and returns the number of bytes in the buffer.

- int read(): Returns the first incoming byte in the serial buffer as an int, and then removes the byte. Successive reads will move through the buffer, much like dealing a deck of cards.

- int peek(): Reads the incoming serial buffer's first byte, returns as an int, and leaves the data in the buffer. This function is like peeking at the top card of a deck of cards.

- void flush(): Clears the serial buffer's data. flush() will clear data after the buffer data is sent out.

- size_t print / println (value, format): Sends a human-readable translation of data. Digits are sent as ASCII-equivalent strings, and characters are sent as bytes. This function can have a format of DEC, HEX, BIN, or OCT. format can also be used to define the number of bytes to send. println is the same as print, except it sends a new line to the end of the value. Returns the number of bytes sent; reading is not required.

49

- `size_t write(value, size)`: Sends data in binary bytes instead of ASCII. `write()` can send a single byte value, in which case `size` is not needed. A string and buffer are sent as a series of bytes. `size` declares the buffer's number of bytes to send. Returns the number of bytes sent.

- `void serialEvent(){ }`: Can be added to a sketch that is called any time there is incoming serial activity.

openFrameworks Setup

With the Arduino code outputting and accepting input from the serial monitor, other programs can be developed using C, C++, Java, or any other computer language from scratch to connect the Arduino to the computer. Coding from scratch, however, can be a bit tedious for a proof-of-concept project. openFrameworks provides a nice prebuilt interface for programming serial with C++ and also adds many other useful tidbits for audio and graphics. The next set of examples will show how the openFrameworks libraries can be used to connect to the Arduino and the sketch from Listing 3-1.

To verify that openFrameworks is working properly and the library is compiled, make a copy of the empty example folder in the openFrameworks distribution; keep the folder in the same directory and rename it to ch3.

■ **Note**   The examples are located in the openFrameworks `examples` directory. An empty example to start with is located in the `apps/myApps` subdirectory of the openFrameworks main directory.

Open the workspace for Code::Blocks or the VC++ project file in the renamed folder, and then compile. Two things should compile: `emptyexample` and `libopenFrameworks`. After both parts are compiled successfully, openFrameworks is ready for new code. Coding the examples in this chapter for openFrameworks applications is done in the Code::Blocks project file or the Microsoft Visual Studio solution (*not* the one named `libopenFrameworks`, but the one named after the project—e.g., `emptyexample.workspace`). The files for the examples in this chapter are available for download from www.apress.com/9781430239390 and are contained in three files: `main.cpp`, `testapp.cpp`, and `testapp.h`. These three files can replace the files with the same name that are in the renamed folder `src` directory.

■ **Caution**   Moving and compiling projects outside of the openFrameworks `apps/examples` directory may cause dependencies issues. To solve this, point all the dependencies to the location of the openFrameworks main directory.

In 32-bit GNU/Linux, the workspace file for Code::Blocks may point to the 64-bit libraries. Solve this by opening the workspace file in a generic text editor and change linux64 to linux.

Connecting to the Arduino from openFrameworks

Listings 3-2 through 3-4 make up the three files to create and run a basic openFrameworks program to connect to an Arduino to send and receive data without having to use the serial monitor or console, while also providing extra computing power by allowing the Arduino to connect to a C++ program.

Listing 3-2. main.cpp

```cpp
#include "ofMain.h"              // include files
#include "testApp.h"             // declarations for the testapp class
#include "ofAppGlutWindow.h"  // for using OpenGL and creating windows
int main() {
    ofAppGlutWindow window;        // sets up an OpenGL window object
    ofSetupOpenGL(&window,200,100, OF_WINDOW);  //sets window size in pixels
    ofRunApp(new testApp());    // create testapp object & enter program loop
} // end int main()
```

openFrameworks code is set up to be event driven and window based, the same as other graphical-interface programs. The main.cpp file contains the main() function, which is the entry point to the openFrameworks programs. The main() function sets parameters for the window, including the window size and window mode. It is rare to make many changes in main.cpp; most of the time the only thing that will change is the window size.

Listing 3-3. testapp.h

```cpp
#include "ofMain.h"
class testApp : public ofBaseApp{
  public:
    void setup();            // for setting initial parameters
    void update();           // code in this function is constantly run, events will interrupt
    void draw();             // runs after update,this updates & creates the window objects
    void mousePressed(int x, int y, int button);  // on event function
    bool SendSerialMessage;        // signals that data needs to be sent
    char ledcommand ;              // hold what state the LED is in
    char Returned;                 // hold returned char from Arduino
    ofSerial serial;               // this is the object to handle serial
};// end class testApp : public ofBaseApp
```

The testApp class inherits common functionality from the ofBaseApp class. This is where the function prototypes are created. Variables that will be used in many functions can be declared here. There is a set of functions that are called when events occur, such as mouse movement or using the keyboard. Note the line where you need to change COM4 to match your Arduino setup.

Listing 3-4. testapp.cpp

```cpp
#include "testApp.h"
void testApp::setup(){
  ofSetVerticalSync(true);       // helps to smooth out object drawing
  ofBackground(255,255,255);     // set background color to an RGB value
  serial.setup("COM7", 9600);    // change "COM7" to match where the Arduino is
  ledcommand = 's';              // set initial state of the LED
  serial.writeByte(ledcommand);  // tell Arduino of the initial state
  SendSerialMessage = false;     // nothing to send yet
} // end void testApp::setup()
 void testApp::update(){
  if (SendSerialMessage)            // is there serial information that needs to be sent
    serial.writeByte(ledcommand);   // tell the Arduino to change LED state
  if (serial.available())           // check to see if there is incoming data
    Returned = serial.readByte(); // save the incoming data
```

```
  SendSerialMessage = false;        // reset the need to send data to the Arduino
}//end testApp::update
void testApp::draw(){     // defines placement and draws objects in the window
  ofFill();                         // fills geometry with a solid color
    if (Returned == 'h')    // is the button on the Arduino being pressed
      ofSetColor(0,0,255);    // set the first circle color to full blue
    else                            // the button is not pressed or the state is not known
      ofSetColor(0,0,127);    // set the first circle color to 1/2 blue
  ofCircle(50,50, 50);      // draw the first circle at last set color
    if (ledcommand == 'a')  // should the LED be on
      ofSetColor(0,255,0);    // set color to full green for the second circle
    else                            // LED should be off or not known
      ofSetColor(0,127,0);    // set color to 1/2 green for the second circle
  ofCircle(150,50, 50);     // draw the second circle at last set color
} //end void testApp::draw()
void testApp::mousePressed(int x, int y, int button){
  SendSerialMessage = true;  // inform update function that there is data to send
  if(ledcommand == 'a')     // if the LED is ON
    ledcommand = 's';       // change LED to be OFF
  else                      // if the LED is OFF
    ledcommand = 'a';       // change LED to be ON
} //end testApp::mousePressed
```

Verifying the Code

Make sure that the Arduino that was set up in Listing 3-1 is plugged into the computer and take note of the port that it is plugged into.

- COM* is for Windows

- /dev/tty* is used for Linux/Unix and Mac OS X

Change the serial.setup(COM4,9600) line in Listing 3-4 to match the Arduino's connecting point. Once the test app is set to know where the Arduino is, compile the examples. Running the program will open a window frame that looks like Figure 3-2, with the first circle representing the push button and the second circle showing the state of the LED. To change the LED state, click in the window with the mouse.

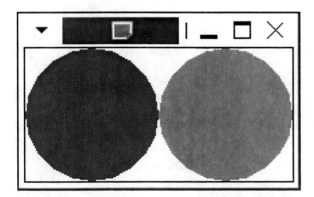

Figure 3-2. *Example of the running program*

openFrameworks Serial Functions

The following reference list is for the openFrameworks serial functions. Most of the functions work just like the Arduino's counterpart functions. The serial object must be declared before using and calling the openFrameworks serial functions. The serial object comes from the ofSerial class; just as a variable is declared, a serial object is created by using the following:

ofSerial serial;

To use any of the functions, use the name declared for the object—for example, serial.setup();. Here are the functions:

- void enumerateDevices(): Lists the available serial devices.

- void close(): Closes the serial connection.

- bool setup(int, int): Connects to the device number corresponding to the list outputted by enumerateDevices() at the desired baud speed.

- bool setup(): Opens a serial connection on the first available device at baud 9600 and returns a fail or succeed.

- bool setup(string, int): Uses a string to declare what serial device to connect to. The second parameter sets the baud speed and returns a fail or succeed.

- int readBytes(unsigned char, int): Takes a pointer to an array of characters, attempts to retrieve the number of bytes equal to the second parameter, and returns the number of actual bytes read (compare to the requested amount of bytes to error-check).

- int readByte(): Returns a single byte from the connected device.

- int writeBytes(unsigned char, int): Takes a character array or string and an amount of bytes to write, and returns the amount written for error checking.

- bool writeByte(unsigned char): Sends a single byte to the connected device and returns a fail or succeed.

- void flush(bool, bool): Clears one or both of the serial buffers (one buffer for send, one buffer for receive).

- int available(): Returns the number of available bytes in the receive buffer.

Coding Once Using Firmata and ofArduino

In keeping with the spirit of "work fosters ideas," working with two different pieces of code (one on the Arduino and one using openFrameworks) is a bit inefficient for exploring ideas, especially when changing things frequently. Luckily, there are items included with the Arduino IDE and openFrameworks (a program for the Arduino and a built-in class for openFrameworks) that make it possible to write single programs that take care of having to separately code the Arduino.

- Firmata is a communication protocol for the Arduino that allows for on-the-fly configurations without having to restart or reprogram the Arduino. Standard Firmata is included with the Arduino IDE.

- openFrameworks complements Firmata by including a class called ofArduino, which handles both communication and configuration of the Arduino.

Setting Up Firmata

Set up the Arduino board with the components connected as in the schematic in Figure 3-3, and then upload the Standard Firmata sketch. The sketch is located in the Arduino IDE under File ➤ Examples ➤ Firmata ➤ StandardFirmata.

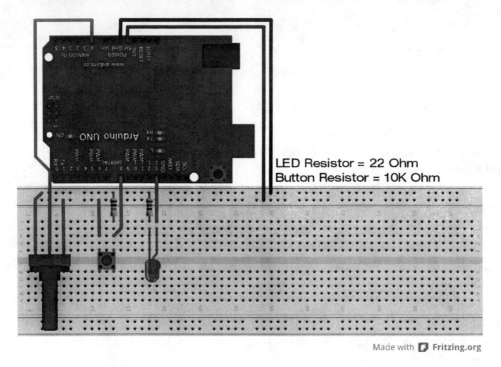

Figure 3-3. *Arduino circuit for Listing 3-5*

To verify that Firmata is working on the Arduino, download and run the test app from www.firmata.org/. Select the port to connect to from the drop-down menu, and the app will show all the pins, which have drop-down boxes for pin configuration and buttons for output values, as shown in Figure 3-4.

■ **Note** The Leonardo need the Firmata library updated. Instructions and updated library available at www.github.com/soundanalogous/Breakout/wiki/Updating-Firmata-in-Arduino

---

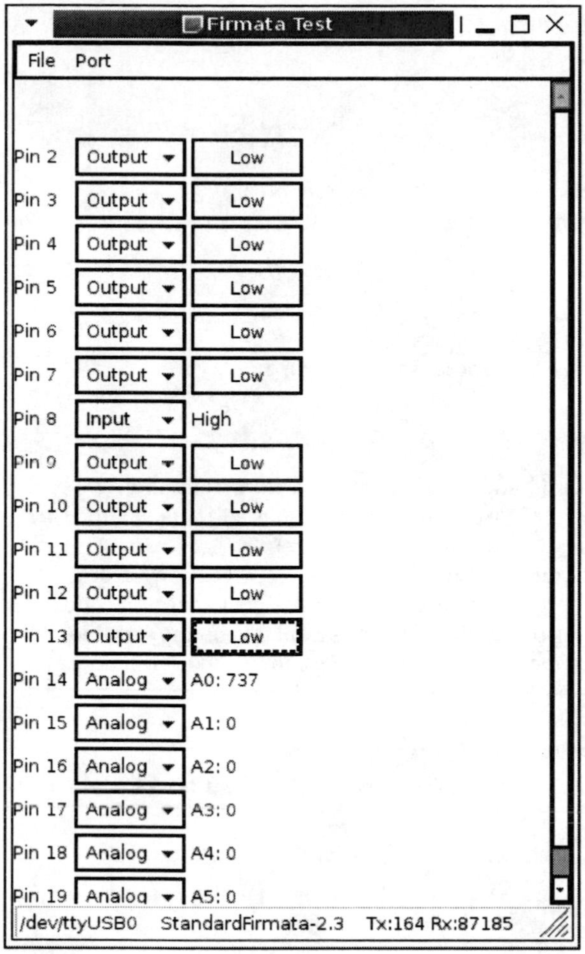

Figure 3-4. *Firmata testing application*

The Firmata test app is especially usefully for testing out component setups that use multiple pins, such as a three- to eight-line MUXs, seven-segment displays , keypads, and servomotors.

Controlling the Arduino with openFrameworks

The code in the next example uses the same main.cpp as Listing 3-2. The header file testapp.h in Listing 3-5 still declares the class function prototypes setup(), update(), draw(), and mousePressed(). The two new function prototypes are set up to mimic the Arduino's coding structure. The function arduinoSetup() is for initializing pin configurations, and the function arduinoLoop() is the equivalent to loop in Arduino sketches.

Listing 3-5. testapp.h for the Standard Firmata Sketch Communication

```
#include "ofMain.h"
#include "ofEvents.h"
```

```
class testApp : public ofBaseApp {
  public:
    void setup();
    void update();
    void draw();
    void mousePressed(int x, int y, int button);
    void arduinoSetup(const int & version); // Arduino equivalent setup function
    void arduinoLoop(); // Arduino-equivalent loop function
    bool ledcommand;
    bool pin13; // pin13 data container
    bool pin8; // pin8 data container
    float analogPin0; // pin8 data container
    bool isArduinoSet; // flag to know when Arduino is connected and configured
    ofArduino arduino; // the Arduino object
}; // end class testApp : public ofBaseApp
```

In `testapp.cpp` of Listing 3-6, the functions `arduinoSetup()` and `arduinoLoop()` perform the same functions of an Arduino sketch with openFrameworks on top of the Arduino-style functions. Firmata and the openFrameworks `ofArduino` class make the serial communication less apparent. By carefully mimicking the same structure as an Arduino sketch, the conversion to an actual Arduino sketch is made simpler if the conversion becomes necessary, as when moving to a more professional setup. Keep in mind it is possible to develop code in openFrameworks that may require more space and computing power than might be available on the Arduino. This is especially important to remember when using Firmata as a tool in making proofs of concept to eventually be used solely on the Arduino.

■ **Note**   Firmata is capable of using I2C and other communication functionality; however, openFrameworks does not currently support I2C functionality (as of version 0071).

Example 3-6. testapp.cpp for Standard Firmata Communication

```
#include "testApp.h"
void testApp::setup() {
  arduino.connect("COM7"); // remember! change this to the proper port
  ofAddListener(arduino.EInitialized, this, &testApp::arduinoSetup);
  /*the ofAddListener waits for the Arduino to perform a handshake telling the program that it is
ready to be configured and set up. This will call arduinoSetup*/
  isArduinoSet = false; // this flag is set false until the Arduino is set up
} // end void testApp::setup()
void testApp::update() {
  testApp::arduinoLoop();// perform the Arduino-style code
} // end void testApp::update()
void testApp::draw() { // objects are drawn to the screen in the order called
  if (isArduinoSet){ // do not run this code until Arduino is operating
    ofFill();
    if(pin8 == ARD_HIGH)
      ofSetColor(0,0,255);// if button on pin8 pressed, brighten the circle
    else
      ofSetColor(0,0,127);// blue is dim if button is released
```

```
      ofCircle(50,50,50); // draw circle at (x,y,radius) in pixels for button
      if(pin13 == ARD_HIGH)
        ofSetColor(0,255,0); // when LED is on, draw full green
      else
        ofSetColor(0,127,0);// green is dimmed when LED is off
      ofCircle(150,50, 50); // draw circle at (x,y,radius) in pixels for LED
      ofSetColor(255,0,0); // set color for analog potentiometer
                              // draw rectangle with corners at (x1,y1,x2,y2)
      ofRect(0, 45 ,(analogPin0*200) , 10); // rectangle is dynamic on the x-axis
              // analogPin0 is a percentage multiplied by window width
    } // end if (isArduinoSet)
}// end void testApp::draw()
void testApp::mousePressed(int x, int y, int button) {
    if(ledcommand == true) // if LED is ON
      ledcommand = false ;    // flag the LED to turn OFF
    else // the LED is OFF
      ledcommand = true; // flag the LED to turn ON
}// end testApp::mousePressed
void testApp::arduinoSetup(const int & version) {
  ofRemoveListener(arduino.EInitialized, this, &testApp::arduinoSetup);
  // there is no need to continue to listen for the Arduino, so clear memory
  arduino.sendAnalogPinReporting(0, ARD_ANALOG);// turn on analog pin0
  arduino.sendDigitalPinMode(8, ARD_INPUT);// set digital pin8 as input
  arduino.sendDigitalPinMode(13, ARD_OUTPUT);// set digital pin13 as output
  isArduinoSet = true;// inform the rest of the program that Arduino is ready
}//end void testApp::arduinoSetup(
void testApp::arduinoLoop() {
// do not run this code until Arduino is operating
    if (isArduinoSet){
     pin8 = arduino.getDigital(8);// digital read pin8
     pin13 = arduino.getDigital(13);// digital read pin13 verifying state
     analogPin0 = arduino.getAnalog(0)/1023.0; // analog read A0
     arduino.sendDigital(13, ledcommand);// digital write new state
     }// end if (isArduinoSet)
     arduino.update();// get any changes that the Arduino might have
}// end void testApp::arduinoLoop()
```

Verifying the Code

When done looking over and compiling the code, plug in the Arduino with the components set up in as Figure 3-3 and the standard Firmata sketch uploaded. When running, the program will open a window with the same size as the prior example. The program will also have the same two circles representing the button and LED, respectively performing the same functions. A red bar is added to the program that will go from side to side, representing the full sweep of the potentiometer.

■ **Note**   The Arduino may be required to reset, via the reset button, before the listener initializes and recognizes the Arduino. The listener is built into openFrameworks to listen for an Arduino on the connection.

Key Constants Used by ofArduino

ofArduino defines some useful constants for more readable code. The following list is a reference of names and values of the constants. The first part of the constants, ARD, is short for *Arduino*, and is a reminder that this is dealing with the hardware. The second part is the type—for example, the pin modes or state declarations.

- Pin modes:
  - ARD_INPUT = 0x00
  - ARD_OUTPUT = 0x01
  - ARD_ANALOG = 0x02
  - ARD_PWM = 0x03
  - ARD_SERVO = 0x04

- Pin states:
  - ARD_HIGH or ARD_ON = 1
  - ARD_LOW or ARD_OFF = 0

ofArduino Reference of Class Functions

The following list is a reference for the class functions that make up the ofArduino class. The functions that are included in the ofArduino class are used to control and connect to Arduinos that have the standard Firmata sketch loaded. Most of the functions are a direct counterpart of the functions used in the Arduino IDE and work the same way; for example, sendDigital() is the same as digitalWrite(). The functions require an ofArduino object declared before they can be used. You can connect multiple Arduinos to the same computer by declaring separate objects for each Arduino.

- bool Connect(port, speed): Opens an Arduino connection on a serial port and takes a string for the device connection, such as /dev/ttyUSB0, COM4 or /dev/tty.usbserial-A4001JEC. The second parameter is for nondefault baud speeds and can be omitted in standard configurations.

- void disconnect(): Releases the Arduino connection.

- bool isInitialized(): Returns true if a successful connection has been established and the Arduino has reported that firmware from the Firmata sketch has been uploaded.

- void update(): Used to update the current state of the Arduino's incoming information; this should be called regularly.

- void sendDigitalPinMode(pin, mode): Sets the pin mode of a digital pin (one of pins 2 through 13) and sets the pin as one of the digital modes of ARD_INPUT, ARD_OUTPUT, ARD_PWM, or ARD_SERVO. If the pin is an input, the reporting will be turned on.

- void sendAnalogPinReporting(pin, mode): For analog pins 0 through 5, turns the reporting to ARD_ON or ARD_OFF. Analog pins can be used as digital pins 16 through 21 or as PWM pins. The whole group is either analog or digital.

- void sendDigital(pin, state): Sets the state of the specified digital pin to either ARD_LOW or ARD_HIGH.

- `void sendPwm(pin, value)`: Sets the PWM value for pins set to ADR_PWM (chosen from pins 3, 5, 6, 9, 10, and 11); the value is between ON (255) and OFF (0).

- `void sendServo(pin, sweep)`: Uses pin 9 or 10 and sends servo signals between 0 and sweep-angle default 180.

- `void sendServoAttach(pin, min, max, sweep)`: Defines the following servo parameters:

  - The pin

  - Minimum pulse width (defaults to 544)

  - Maximum pulse width (defaults to 2400)

  - Angle of sweep (defaults to 180)

- `int getDigital(pin)`: Used on pins 2 through 13:

  - For pins set as ARD_INPUT returns the last state the pin reported

  - For pins set as ARD_OUTPUT returns the last value sent to the pin

- `int getPwm(pin)`: For pins set as ARD_PWM, returns the last set PWM value for the pin requested (usable pins are 3, 5, 6, 9, 10 and 11, or pins 16 through 21 if analog pins 0 through 5 are set as digital pins).

- `int getServo(pin)`: Returns the last value the servo was set to.

- `int getAnalog(pin)`: Used for analog pins 0 through 5 and returns a value between 0 and1023.

- `string getString()`: Returns the last string received.

- `int getDigitalPinMode(pin)`: Returns ARD_INPUT, ARD_OUTPUT, ARD_PWM, ARD_SERVO, or ARD_ANALOG.

- `int getAnalogPinReporting(pin)`. For analog pins 0 through 5, returns ARD_ON or ARD_OFF.

Expanding on the Idea

We now have openFrameworks controlling the Arduino, which is running the standard Firmata sketch. The next example illustrates the increase of efficiency that can be gained in development by having Arduino and openFrameworks integrated.

1. Start the next example by attaching a servo to pin 10 and another LED to pin 3, in addition to the other components from the last example. Use Figure 3-5 for reference.

2. After the two new components are in place, start the Firmata test app to check that all the components are working.

3. Set the pins to the following configuration:

   - `pin3 = PWM`

   - `pin8 = input`

   - `pin10 = servo`

   - `pin13 = output`

   - Analog pin 0

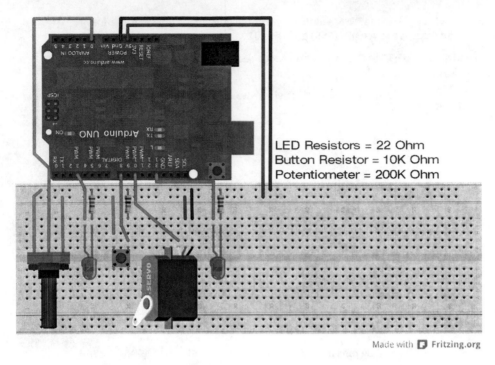

LED Resistors = 22 Ohm
Button Resistor = 10K Ohm
Potentiometer = 200K Ohm

Made with 🅑 Fritzing.org

Figure 3-5. *Arduino circuit for the "Expanding on the Idea" example*

For the rest of this example, the only changes are going to be to the code.

For the hardware, the potentiometer is going to control the servo, while the brightness of the LED on pin 3 will represent the position of the servo. When the button is pressed, the LED on pin 13 will turn on; at the same time, the servo and the other LED will pause and stop accepting new values from the potentiometer until the button is released.

Changing Code

While openFrameworks is controlling the Arduino, it will simultaneously be displaying a representation of what the hardware is doing. The program will have a window the same size as the two prior examples, with shapes representing the button, the LED, and the potentiometer's position. The only change to the graphics is that we will dynamically change the color of the bar to represent the new brightness value for the LED, with the color fading from black to full red with the servo and potentiometer's full swing.

Open the project from Listings 3-5 and 3-6. The same `main.cpp` will be used without alteration. Within `testapp.cpp`, the entire `mousePressed()` function can be removed or commented out, along with its prototype in `testapp.h`. You can omit the following line from the `arduinoLoop()` function:

```
arduino.sendDigital(13, ledcommand);
```

The last thing to comment out is the variable declaration `bool ledcommand;` from `testapp.h`. With the code that is no longer needed out of the way, change the line `ofSetColor(255,0,0);`, located in the `draw()` function, to

```
ofSetColor((analogPin0*255),0,0);
```

This change takes advantage of the analog percent value to evenly change the color in proportion to the bar.

Add the following code to the arduinoSetup() function below the code line arduino.sendDigitalPinMode(13, ARD_OUTPUT); defining the new componets. Note that the text following the comment delimiters (//) is optional.

```
arduino.sendDigitalPinMode(3, ARD_PWM); // set pin 3 for PWM
arduino.sendDigitalPinMode(10, ARD_SERVO);// set pin 10 to accept a servo
arduino.sendServoAttach(10);// define servo information as default
isArduinoSet = true;
```

Listing 3-7 shows the next portion of code to add, which is the last for this example. The code handles the button pause, the servo, and the PWM LED, and gets inserted into the arduinoLoop() function before the ending bracket of the if (isArduinoSet) statement and after analogPin0 = arduino.getAnalog(0)/1023.0;.

Listing 3 7. The End of "Expanding on the Idea" Example

```
if (pin8 == ARD_HIGH){ // check if button is being pressed
  pin13 = true; // flag the draw function to change
  arduino.sendDigital(13, ARD_HIGH);// turn on LED
} // end if pin8 == ARD_HIGH)
else {
  arduino.sendDigital(13, ARD_LOW);
  arduino.sendPwm(3,analogPin0*255);
  arduino.sendServo(10, analogPin0*180);
} // end else
```

Verifying the Code

With all the code changed and compiled, start the program with the Arduino plugged in. The program should look like Figure 3-6. When the screen is fully drawn, the pause button will have to be pressed to get the servo and the LED to activate.

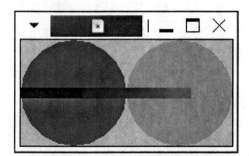

Figure 3-6. *The look of the final example*

The changes that were made make the Arduino act differently without your having to upload a new sketch. Note that the changes now allow the potentiometer to control the sweep of the servo and the brightness of the LED when the potentiometer is swept from maximum to minimum. Also take note of the behavior when the pause is held while the potentiometer is being moved.

More Ideas to Work With

openFrameworks has a lot more functionality than described in this chapter. openFrameworks can manipulate sound images or even 3D objects, and the connection to serial devices or Arduinos allows controllers to be built that can control the computer. You can create programs to control the Arduino as well. With all the possible projects that you can create using Arduinos, the extra features that openFrameworks provides may make it hard to decide where to go and what to do. Try out some of the ideas listed below; they came up during a few brainstorming sessions. These ideas should help further your exploration of openFrameworks while providing more experience with the platform.

- Use a keypad to select a song from a playlist (i.e., make a jukebox).

- Make a small game using an old hard drive motor for the input controls.

- Create a logging system that records data to a database such as MySQL using Arduino and openFrameworks.

- Build a dynamic scrolling LED marquee that also displays the characters being typed on the computer screen.

- Create an RGB LED array to build a mood light that changes in response to audio or visual cues.

Summary

This chapter discussed the fundamental steps to integrate openFrameworks with Arduino. As a development tool, openFrameworks may provide the catalyst that can take a good idea to the next step. Its versatility is only increased by providing two great ways to develop: using serial or Firmata. With time and use, most developers will find a preference for one method over the other.

openFrameworks has a lot more functionality than can be covered here, but this chapter should provide you the knowledge and confidence to delve deeper into openFrameworks. Also check out other resources available; the forums at www.arduino.cc/ and www.openframeworks.cc/ are great places to find more information. The examples included with openFrameworks can also provide excellent insight.

CHAPTER 4

■ ■ ■

Android ADK

Since the introduction of the Android operating system in 2007, Android has become one of the more popular embedded Linux distributions available to consumers and hobbyist for development purposes. Google provides a vast knowledge base to help with getting started in developing Android-specific applications; the Google documentation, reference material, and SDK are available at http://developer.android.com.

The popularity of Android development for the hobbyist can be attributed to the ease and cost of the available information. The draw for vendors to use Android as an operating system for many types of consumer electronics is that Android provides a great starting point by having much of the development for an operating system completed, and by providing the capacity for many different hardware configurations. As an operating system, Android provides a framework for vendors to add their own unique functionality, while having a support structure and standards of compatibility for third-party content developers. The market environment for Android mimics that of Linux—each system has variations within its individual distributions. The differences between Android versions and the modifications by vendors have led to a fragmentation in support for development. This became more apparent when Google announced the Accessory Development Kit (ADK) in 2011.

The ADK was announced to provide a toolkit to developers so that third-party devices could be made to expand the hardware functionality of systems running Android. The ADK was first released for version 3.1 and then ported back to version 2.3.4. The fragmentation of Android devices has made it difficult to develop commercial devices that could be supported on a majority of systems running Android. The amount of off-the-shelf device support that can support the ADK protocols could change as more devices adopt the Ice Cream Sandwich version of Android. The ADK is comprised of two parts: a protocol for the device and hardware for the actual accessory.

When Google released the ADK software and libraries for the operating system, it also released a hardware kit that resembles an Arduino Mega with a shield attachment, and since then, many open source hardware developers have made boards compatible with the original ADK device. Seeed Studio and Arduino both make an ADK board that uses the ATMega 2560 chip. Both boards work the same and can be programmed in the Arduino development environment. SparkFun Electronics makes an ADK-compatible board named IOIO (pronounced *Yo-Yo*), but is based on a PIC microcontroller and has a different programming environment.

At the heart of ADK methodology having a device that can act as a USB host give the impression that the Android device is plugged into a computer to initiate communications. On the Arduino Mega ADK board, this is done by adding an SPI-based USB host processor. The chip used in creating the host connection uses the SPI bus for data transmission and is connected to the appropriate MOSI (master out slave in), MISO (master in slave out), SS (slave select), and SCLK (serial clock) pins. The USB functionality also uses pin 7, making it unavailable for other uses. Arduino shields are available to add the ADK functionality to other Arduino boards, such as the UNO and the basic Mega. Theses ADK shields are created by third-party vendors, including SparkFun for the USB host (www.sparkfun.com/products/9947). A variety of different host shields are also available from Circuits@Home (www.circuitsathome.com).

Devices that use the USB host chip are not limited to working with Android; they are also capable of working with other client devices, such as USB keyboards. But the focus in this chapter is Android-specific functionality with the Arduino Mega ADK. Before the ADK was available, hobbyists and makers were using a method that involved the Android Debugging Bridge (ADB) to add the functionality that is available with the ADK. The ADK can be used to add controls for robotics, read from nonstandard sensors, and interface with machines such as the MakerBot.

Android Devices

Before getting a board that is capable of USB hosting, you must locate a suitable Android target. As mentioned before, not all Android devices are currently capable of handling the ADK protocol. Devices that were made before the release of the ADK are the ones most likely not able to support ADK protocol without modification. Devices that use versions of Android as old as or older than 2.3.3 are not capable of handling the ADK methods at all. The older devices are still capable of using the ADB to create data connections.

What to Check For

For a device running Android to be nativity capable of using the ADK, the version must be 2.3.4 or later, but this not conclusive. The conclusive check is in the Google Play app market: search for "ADK demo kit." If it's not available, the device does not have the required libraries installed. It has been found that some devices are capable of installing the demo kit, but lack an option that needs to be compiled into the operating systems kernel. This will show up when the demo kit is installed and run. The ADK hardware does not have to be connected; if the demo kit app shows a screen that asks for an ADK board to be connected the device is ready for ADK development.

Known Working Devices

Following is a list of Android devices that have been found to nativity work with ADK. (There are possibly more, with new Android devices coming out almost daily.) The devices that have native support are prime targets for commercial applications for developing accessories.

- *Acer Iconia A100*: This is a 7-inch tablet running Android version 3.2, running a dual-core 1 GHz Cortex-A9 with 1 GB of RAM.

- *Acer Iconia A500*: This is a 10.1-inch tablet with the same processor and RAM as the Iconia A100, running Android version 3.2. Both of the Acer tablets are planned to be upgraded to Ice Cream Sandwich at some point.

- *ASUS Eee Pad Transformer TF101*: This is 10.1-inch tablet with the same processor and RAM as the Acer tablets; it runs Android version 3.2 and is upgradable to Ice Cream Sandwich.

- *Google Nexus S*: This is a phone made by Samsung for Google. This device runs a single-core 1 GHz Arm Cortex-A8 with 512 MB of RAM, running Android version 2.3 and upgradable to Ice Cream Sandwich. This device is a Google development phone providing great support for new APIs and developments.

- *Google Galaxy Nexus*: This is also a Google development phone made by Samsung. It uses a dual-core 1 GHz Cortex-A9 with 1 GB of RAM and the Ice Cream Sandwich version of Android.

- *LG Optimus Pad*: This is an 8.9-inch tablet with a dual-core 1 GHz Cortex-A9 with 1 GB of RAM running Android version 3.0.

- *Motorola Xoom*: This is a 10.1-inch tablet with a dual-core 1 GHz NVIDIA Tegra 2 with 1 GB of RAM running Android version 3.0.

- *Samsung Galaxy Tab 10.1*: This is a 10.1-inch tablet with a dual-core 1 GHz NVIDIA Tegra 2 with 1 GB of RAM running Android version 3.1.

- *Samsung Galaxy S*: This is a phone with a single-core 1 GHz Arm Cortex-A8 with 512 MB of RAM. This device can be factory-upgraded to Android 2.3 to work with the ADK.

- *Samsung Galaxy Ace*: This is a phone with an 800 MHz ARM 11 and 278 MB of RAM running Android version 2.3.

Modding

The devices branded by Google are the better choice for heavy development. There are many devices that can be made to work with the ADK, but may require modding, also known as *rooting*. Modding is a great way to achieve extra functionality in an Android device. Modding is not without risks—for example, so-called *bricking*, voiding of warranties, and the possibility of devices becoming unstable are the biggest problems.

If you decide to modify a device, do a sufficient amount of research and weigh the risks and cost before proceeding. If you're unsure about mods, either don't do them or consult someone who has.

This chapter was developed with a Barnes and Noble NOOK Color running both CyanogenMod 7 (Android 2.3) and CyanogenMod 9 (Android 4.0), dual-boot from the SD card. *CyanogenMod* is an aftermarket Android distribution providing custom ROM for a variety of devices. You can find more information about it at the CyanogenMod web site (`www.cyanogenmod.com`). CyanogenMod is developed by the community and has a lot of support, and is one of the more popular aftermarket Android distributions. You can find great resources for modding and development of Android systems at the XDA Developers forums (`www.xda-developers.com`).

I chose the NOOK Color as a development platform because of the cost, ease of modification, and decent hardware specifications. CyanogenMod 7 for this device had to have a custom kernel compiled with the configure flag `CONFIG_USB_ANDROID_ACCESSORY` set during the compile, and the `usb.jar` libraries added to the system. CyanogenMod 9 for the NOOK Color can be installed on an 8 GB microSD card and booted—just like having multiple bootable devices on a normal PC. You don't need a NOOK Color for the examples in this chapter, although you will need an Android device capable of using the ADK protocols.

Arduino IDE Setup

This chapter will provide an introduction to building a classic Hello World hardware example with an Android twist. An Android device and an Arduino Mega ADK are needed for the rest of this chapter. Before any programming can be done, the Android and Arduino environments need to be set up. The Arduino 1.0 IDE (or later) should already be available, but a library is needed to work with the ADK protocol. The appropriate library is available from the Arduino labs web site (`http://labs.arduino.cc/uploads/ADK/GettingStarted/ArduinoADK-beta-001.zip`).

Contained in the ZIP file are files for Processing and Arduino; you can ignore the `Processing` folder. In the Arduino folder are two versions of the library. Extract the folder named `UsbHost` and the files located in the `libraries` folder to the `libraries` folder for the Arduino IDE. Start or restart the Arduino IDE, finishing the installation of the new library. Under File ➤ Examples ➤ UsbHost, examples should now be available. Open the first example and verify that it can compile. Once finished, the Arduino IDE will be ready to program ADK applications.

You need to set up a development environment to write the Android code and make the installation packages. Both Processing (`http://processing.org`) and Eclipse (`http://eclipse.org`) can create Android applications. Programming in Processing is similar to programming Arduino code, but lacks some finesse and control. This chapter focuses on the Eclipse IDE, which provides greater functionality but is a bit cumbersome. When using Eclipse for Android development, you need to understand two different styles of code: the main Java-related portion and XML. The Java-styled code is the grunt of any Android application and is the main programming language; XML is the fluff that defines the layout, objects, and text that gets displayed. I'll describe the programming methodologies for application development a bit later in the chapter. If this is your first introduction to Android development, check out Wallace Jackson's *Android Apps for Absolute Beginners* (Apress, 2011).

Installing the Eclipse IDE is fairly straightforward. For best results, follow the instructions on the Android Developers web site for your specific system (`http://developer.android.com/sdk/installing.html`). The complicated part of the setup is making sure that the ADB functions properly; this may actuality require that you have root access and that you turn on USB debugging in the device settings. To check if the ADB is working, in a command prompt change to the `platform-tools` directory and run the command adb, and the command's help should be printed to the screen. If the command does not run from any other directory, check to see if the SDK's installation directory has been added to the environment variables.

Once the help is displayed plug the intended device for development into the computer, and run the command adb devices to print a list of connected devices. If no device shows up, USB debugging might be turned off or root accesses might be needed. The ADB is not necessary for loading applications on the device, but it is helpful to be able to have the application automatically uploaded to the device from Eclipse when in development stages. If the ADB is not available, the application's APK file has to be manually installed on the system. For each change, a file manager will have to be installed from the market, and the system has to allow for untrusted sources. You can set this in the Manage Applications section in the systems settings. Eclipse has the ability to run emulators and use actual hardware for debugging. It is helpful if the ADB is available to run an application called ADB Wireless, available from the apps market. Note that this app requires root access. Running the ADB over a wireless network allows for the Arduino Mega ADK to be constantly attached to the Android device and the computer during developments.

Android Application Creation

After the Eclipse IDE is set up, you'll create a new Android project from the New Project wizard in Eclipse.

1. Choose File ➤ New ➤ Project, and then select Android Application Project in the Android folder within the wizard selector, as shown in Figure 4-1.

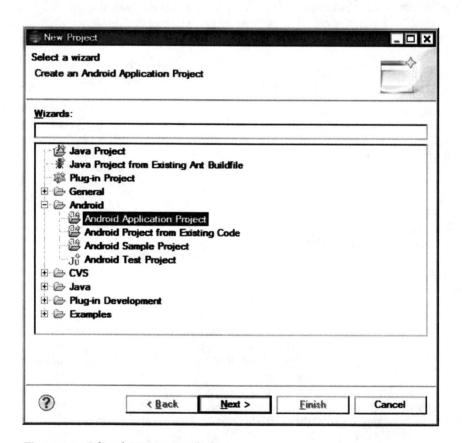

Figure 4-1. *Eclipse's New Project dialog*

The next prompt (see Figure 4-2) requires an application name, project name, package name, and declaration of the Android SDK version.

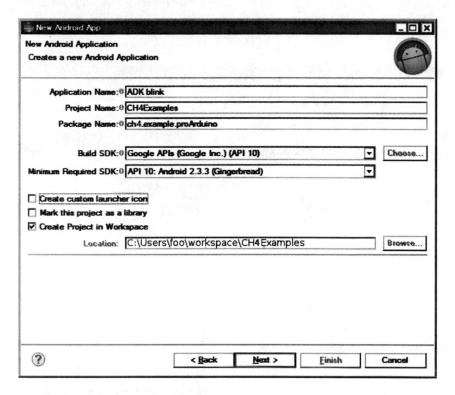

Figure 4-2. *The New Android App dialog*

2. Enter ADK blink as the application name for this chapter.

3. Name the project CH4Examples.

4. Name the package CH4.example.proarduino. The package name is a triplet descriptor that defines a base Java package that will be the program's entry point. The application name, project name, and package name can be set to anything for later projects and should be set in the wizard when creating projects; note that once you've created these names for a project, it is difficult to change them later on.

5. Next, you'll set which API level to use. Select Google APIs for the 2.3.3 platform, API version 10. The API sets the minimum version of Android that the application will work on, API version 10 will work on future Android releases. Do not use Android *X.X.X*, where *X.X.X* is the target version of Android, when developing ADK applications. Only the Google APIs have the required support for the ADK.

6. You can also choose to create a custom logo for the application. For now, though, deselect the "Create custom launcher icon" option. If the option is selected, you will be given an additional set of prompts for setting the application logo.

7. Finally, leave the "Mark this project as a library" and "Create Project in Workspace" options at their defaults, and then click Next.

8. On the next page of the wizard, you'll select options for the type of activity to create (see Figure 4-3). The activity is the main form of user interaction. Not all Android apps need an activity to run, and different API levels give different options. The only one that can be used for the project's current API is BlankActivity, so choose that, and then click Next.

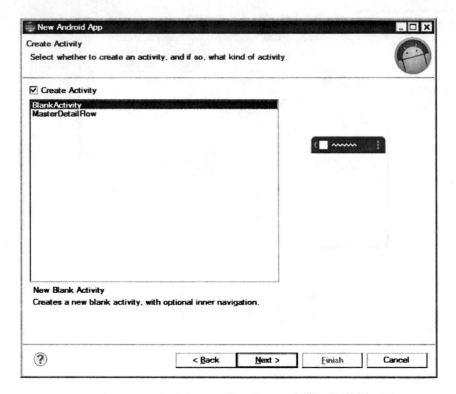

Figure 4-3. *Activity-creation options*

9. Finally, you'll set some of the names for some of the project's internal files (see Figure 4-4). Make sure that the names in the Activity Name and Title fields match those of the project's name, followed by Activity (e.g., CH4ExamplesActivity). For this exercise, change the layout name to main. The layout name describes the first user interface that the program will use by default. You can leave Navigation Type at the default of "None," since this is going to be a stand-alone application and does not require a parent program. For more advanced applications, you can change this to accommodate different user interactions, such as tabbed navigation.

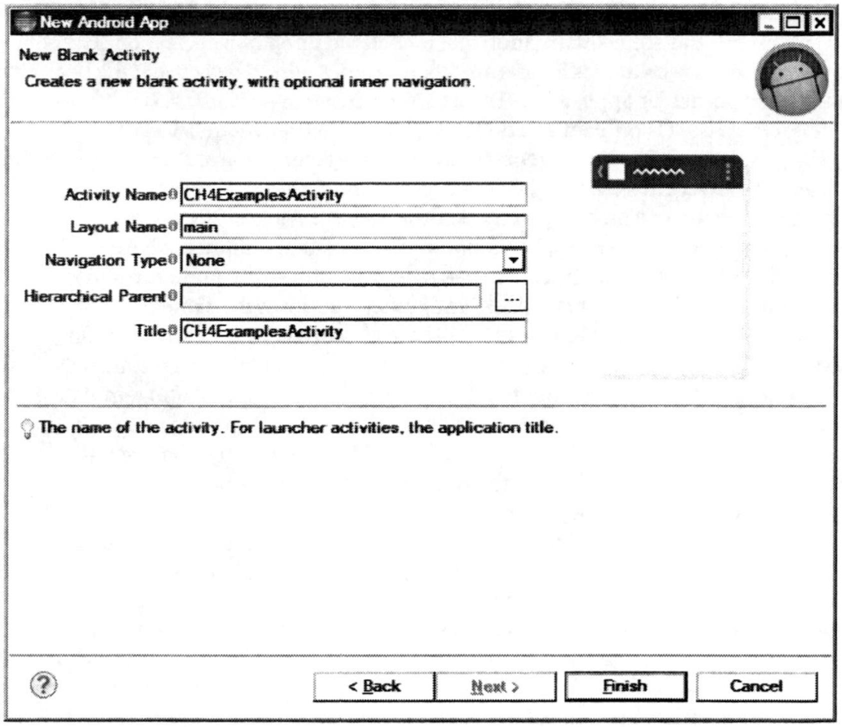

Figure 4-4. *Activity name and layout options*

When you click Finish, the wizard creates an autogenerated Hello World project and a `*.apk` file; these form the framework for the rest of the examples in this chapter. If this is the first time an Android application is being set up, there may be a need for the wizard to automatically download some extra software components.

If the ADB is set up and the device is available, you can load the basic app and start it on an Android device by clicking on the Play button on the toolbar, selecting Run from the Run menu, or pressing Ctrl+F11. When the project is initiated for the first time, Eclipse will ask how to run the application. Make sure to select "Android application" from the options. After you have selected the Run As options, you need to select the device to run; if the ADB is working and the device is connected an option will be shown to choose a running Android device. You can create an Android Virtual Device (AVD) to test running an application if a physical device is not plugged in or one is simply not available. Note that the AVD is not capable of testing ADK functionality, because of a USB host conflict.

The next section focuses on the Arduino and preparing to communicate with the ADK before building the actual Android app.

■ **Note**   If you're not running the ADB, you can copy the `.apk` file to an Android device from the workspace *project name*/bin folder and install it by running `.apk` from the Android device.

The Arduino Sketch

Working with the ADK with the Arduino is similar to working with software serial, in that a header needs to be included, an object declared, and that object started. The library that was added to the Arduino's IDE provides a clean method of declaring and initializing the host connection when compared to other libraries that are available, and is based on the Circuits@Home libraries. The header that needs to be included is `AndroidAccessory.h`. The object is of type `AndroidAccessory` and can be named anything; it has some information that is declared upon object creation. The data that is declared when the `AndroidAccessory` object is created is for identification to any Android device that the board is connected to, thus registering the Arduino to a particular application. The data is enclosed in parentheses and separated by commas after the object's name. The declared data is ordered and defined as manufacturer, model, description, version, Uniform Resource Identifier (URI), and serial. The data is represented as a character string and can be any reasonable number of printable characters. It's always available to the connected Android device. The manufacturer, model, and version are used to identify the accessory to a program on the Android device. The rest of declaration information can be used for tracking and debugging reports in applications for widespread or commercial use.

The accessory is started the same way as software serial: by calling `name.begin` in the `setup` function of the Arduino sketch. The object's public functions—`available`, `write`, `peek`, and `flush`—perform the same work as their serial or software-serial counterparts, along with `print` and `println`. There are two other functions to note when working with the `AndroidAccessory` library. One is `isConnected`, which returns a Boolean for the status of the connection between Arduino and Android. The last added function is `refresh`; it's used to reset and reinitialize the connection between the two devices after the devices have been reconnected. If the Arduino code checks for a connection from the `isConnected` function, it will also call `refresh` to try to reestablish the connection every time `isConnected` called. The use of `refresh` or an `isConnected` check in the Arduino code's main loop creates the ability to connect devices without having to power-cycle or rest the Arduino.

The first example sets up an LED to change state on the Arduino when a virtual button on the Android device is pressed. The Arduino is set up as per Figure 4-5, with an optional LED connected to Arduino pin 13. The code accomplishes the state change by receiving a 1 to turn on the LED and any other byte value from the Android device to turn it off. The code also implements the `refresh` function to allow for reconnecting the two devices without resetting the Arduino.

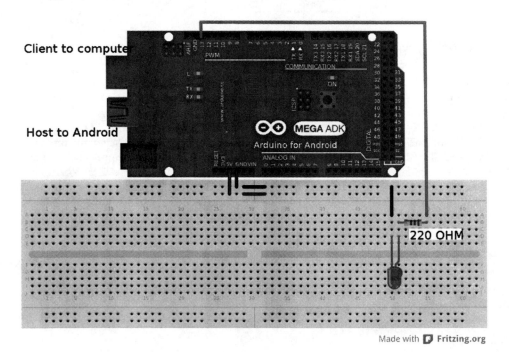

Figure 4-5. Arduino-to-Android configuration

■ **Note**   The host port on the Arduino Mega ADK provides some power to signify a live connection to the Android device; however, it is not capable of providing a charge. As such, extra circuitry is needed to introduce enough power to charge a connected device.

Connect the Arduino as in the preceding figure; it needs to be connected to the computer for programming, and then later to the Android via a micro USB-to-USB A cable after the Android application has been completed. Step through Listing 4-1 and upload the code to the Mega ADK board, remembering to switch the board type. To select the board type in the Arduino IDE, choose Tools ➤ Board ➤ Arduino Mega 2560 or Mega ADK. In conjunction with the connection between Android and the Arduino, the code also sets up a serial connection to the computer for debugging purposes at a baud rate of 115200. The code will print ready to the serial port when the setup function has finished, and other debugging information will be printed when the code is connected to a working application later.

Listing 4-1. Arduino Code for Connecting to an Android Application

```
#include <AndroidAccessory.h>   // needed library to work with ADK connections
// initialize the accessory object with identifying data
AndroidAccessory ADK("Manufacturer", "Model", "Description",
                     "1.0", "Pro Arduino", "0000000012345678");
void setup() {
   Serial.begin(115200);
   ADK.begin();                 // start the connection to the Android
   pinMode(13, OUTPUT);
   Serial.print("ready");                }   // end setup
void loop() {
   if (ADK .isConnected()) {             // check for live connection
      if (ADK.available() > 0){          // check for incoming data
         Serial.println(ADK .peek());    // print incoming data for visible inspection
         if (ADK.read() == 1)            // pin HIGH for an incoming value of 1
                                         // everything else pin is low

            digitalWrite(13 , HIGH);
         else
            digitalWrite(13 , LOW);
      }   // end if (ADK .available() > 0)
   }      // end if (ADK .isConnected())
}         // end void loop()
```

The Android ADK Application

Programming apps for Android can be an involved process, especially for widespread or commercial programs. This section provides a crash course in the development of Android applications; some of the ADK code is based on work from AllAboutEE (http://allaboutee.com). The focus is getting Arduinos to communicate with the Android devices—note that some of the fundamentals of Java and some advanced features of Android application programming may be glossed over. The hardest part for some when deciding to start writing applications for Android is the change in languages—Arduinos are coded in C++ and Android is developed in Java. For others, the event-driven GUI development might be a new experience. Chapter 3 introduced some of the concepts of event-driven applications and working with two different code structures. Aside from Java, Android also introduces XML resources; XML is another code language that is necessary when developing Android applications. Four different XML files are used when working with Android code; three are automatically generated during project generation: `main.xml`, `strings.xml`, and `AndroidManifest.xml`; the fourth, `accessory_filter.xml`, is not. The following list describes these four files:

- `main.xml` contains the layout for an application's first screen. The file contains descriptors for onscreen object layout, type, and identification. Eclipse has a built-in graphical tool for choosing and placing objects, and gives you the ability to view the XML. The `main.xml` file is located in the workspace of the project, in the `res/layout/main.xml` folder.

- `strings.xml` is used to define static information in the form of character strings. This file can be used to define information from many different attributes, such as object names, information for text fields, and file locations. This file is not absolutely necessary for small applications being developed, but note that Eclipse will throw a warning when strings are hard coded. Using `strings.xml` is good programming practice and is useful for when multiple instances of data are used throughout an application, providing a single place to update instead of requiring that every occurrence in the code be changed. The `strings.xml` file is located in the workspace of the project, in the `res/values/strings.xml` folder.

- `AndroidManifest.xml` defines what package and activity need to start when the application is launched, the type of the application, what system events are responded to, and some miscellaneous information for the Android device, along with the icons to be used. `AndroidManifest.xml` is similar to a `main` function in C or C++; this is where the application enters and starts. Android uses intent filters that are checked when a system event occurs, and if the filter in the file matches the event, the application can be started (e.g., when a call is received, an application is run for the user). The `AndroidManifest.xml` file is located in the workspace root.

- The `accessory_filter.xml` file needs to be created by the programmer and is used when `AndroidManifest.xml` responds when accessories are attached. The data in this file is compared to the created data in the Arduino sketch when a connection is getting established. To create this file, you need to create a folder in the workspace's `res` folder named `xml` and add a new file to this folder, named `accessory_filter.xml`.

■ **Note**   Before you insert the code from the listings in this chapter, you need to delete the `styles.xml` file and the `menus` folder from the `res` folder and the project's workspace.

The application framework and workspace were already created for this example when the Hello World application was created to test the functionality of the development environment. Step through the code in the examples following and compare to the code generated to get a feel for how everything is structured, and then replace the code in the workspace project with the appropriate example code.

■ **Note**   Eclipse with the Android SDK is sometimes a bit temperamental; errors that report that `R.*` is not capable of resolving are caused by the `R.java` not being generated. Try a clean and rebuild the project after checking for errors in the XML files. Try ctrl + shift + o to organize imports and select the activity if clean and rebuild doesn't work.

AndroidManifest.xml

The manifest file is the best place to start when developing applications, because it is the entry point for every Android application. The manifest is fairly consistent between applications and can be reused with minor changes across many different applications. The first line defines the XML version and the encoding, and will be the same in all the XML files. The tags following define the systems resources, package name, versions, main icon, application name, and activity to be used in the application. The package name has to match that of the first Java container that contains the code for the project to tell the operating system where to look, and the activity name has to match that of the first activity that will be run. Also, the entry point to an app is the constructor for the main activity class. The rest of the manifest file defines what needs to be done when the application is started either by the user or a system event, as well as any extra libraries on the system that the application needs.

This application is an activity-based program and has a user interface when started (alternatively, applications can be started as a process to run in the background and can have no user interface). Replace the original AndroidManifest.xml file with Listing 4-2; to make things easier, make sure that the package attribute and <activity> tag match those of the original code generated.

Listing 4-2. AndroidManifest.xml Replacing the Autogenerated Original

```xml
<?xml version="1.0" encoding="utf-8"?>
<!-- define entry package name, name space and code version -->
<manifest xmlns:android="http://schemas.android.com/apk/res/android"
  package="CH4.example.proArduino" android:versionCode="1"
  android:versionName="1.0">
  <!-- define minimum usable android version-->
  <uses-sdk android:minSdkVersion="10"/>
  <!-- application's definitions icons, name and entry activity -->
  <application android:icon="@drawable/ic_launcher" android:label="@string/app_name">
 <!-- activity to be launched when program starts -->
 <activity android:name=".CH4ExamplesActivity" android:label="@string/app_name">
      <!-- define events that this app responds to -->
      <intent-filter>
        <action android:name="android.intent.action.MAIN" />
        <category android:name="android.intent.category.LAUNCHER" />
      </intent-filter>
      <!-- respond when attaching accessories  -->
      <intent-filter>
        <action android:name="android.hardware.usb.action.USB_ACCESSORY_ATTACHED" />
      </intent-filter>
      <!-- use listed file to determine if accessory is for this application -->
      <meta-data android:name="android.hardware.usb.action.USB_ACCESSORY_ATTACHED"
      android:resource="@xml/accessory_filter" />
    </activity>
    <!-- ADK programs need this library -->
    <uses-library android:name="com.android.future.usb.accessory"></uses-library>
  </application>
</manifest>
<!-- end of AndroidManifest.xml -->
```

res/xml/accessory_filter.xml

The `accessory_filter.xml` file is created in a folder that is added after program creation in the workspace location `res/xml`. The information contained in this file is used by the manifest to load values for comparison into variables used by the main program when an accessory is detected and determines if the accessory belongs to the program. The code uses the manufacturer, model number, and version to detect a match. The description, URI, and serial number can be accessible to the program, but are not needed here. This file changes the accessory that the code will respond to upon a system event. The manifest and this file remain fairly consistent, although there are minor changes between programs that have user interaction and utilize ADK accessories. Listing 4-3 shows this file for our app.

Listing 4-3. accessory_filter.xml

```
<?xml version="1.0" encoding="UTF-8"?>
<resources>
    <!-- match to Arduino sketch's accessory declaration object -->
    <usb-accessory manufacturer="Manufacturer" model="Model" version="1.0" />
</resources>
<!-- end of accessory-filter.xml -->
```

res/layout/main.xml

This is the first file of the Android application that is different from one program to another, because this file defines the user interface. There can be multiple layout files in an Android application containing different objects to display information or receive interaction from the user. This file's initial section creates the layout area with specifications on how much of the device's screen is used. Following the layout area definition are tags for defining an object's ID, placement, and size, and the function to use when a user interface object is manipulated, either from the user or code.

There is a plethora of defining parameters for each object, such as the ability to define what function to run in the Java code when a button is pressed. The tag for the toggle button used in this example demonstrates implementing a called function; when the toggle button is pressed, a `blinkLED` function is called in the Java code. Eclipse has the ability to graphically lay out objects for the application and generates the required XML needed. Look over and compare the Listing 4-4 to the generated XML for `main.xml` and replace it.

Listing 4-4. main.xml Replacing the Autogenerated Original

```
<?xml version="1.0" encoding="utf-8"?>
<RelativeLayout xmlns:android="http://schemas.android.com/apk/res/android"
    android:id="@+id/relativeLayout1"
    android:layout_width="fill_parent"
    android:layout_height="fill_parent"
    android:layout_weight="0.72" >
    <ToggleButton
        android:id="@+id/toggleButtonLED"
        android:layout_width="200dp"
        android:layout_height="100dp"
        android:layout_centerInParent="true"
        android:layout_marginTop="89dp"
        android:onClick="blinkLED"
        android:text="@string/ToggleButton"
        android:textSize="50dp" />
</RelativeLayout>
<!-- end of main.xml -->
```

res/values/strings.xml

The `strings.xml` file is a container for reusable data such as button and application names. The strings are static, but could be uses throughout the program. It is good programming practice to define the strings in this file instead of hard-coding them into other locations. In the manifest `@string/app_name` and `@string/ToggleButton` are used as static variable containers, as shown in Listing 4-5. It is possible to replace the variable with the actual string value to save on code length, but it is not recommended.

Listing 4-5. strings.xml Replacing the Autogenerated Original

```xml
<?xml version="1.0" encoding="utf-8"?>
<resources>
    <string name="app_name">Mega ADK</string>
    <string name="ToggleButton">ToggleButton</string>
</resources>
<!-- end of strings.xml -->
```

src/CH4.example.proArduino/CH4ExamplesActivity.java

Here is the heart and soul of an Android app. Listing 4-6 is broken up in to seven parts to help explain everything that goes into the Java portion of Android applications. Listing 4-6 code appears in order of placement in the `CH4ExamplesActivity.java` file and makes up the complete file located in the workspace under `src/ch4.example.proArduino`. Most of the code for this example starts the basic framework to send data to the accessory board. Parts 3 through 6 are set up to be reusable. After we've finished this example, we'll set up a framework to perform two-way communications that you can use in any project by changing the activity class and the package name. Aside from the project name, package name, activity name, and accessory definition, `manifest.xml`, `accessory_filter.xml`, and Listing 4-6 remain relatively unchanged for new projects. Part 7 of Listing 4-6 is where you will change the code between projects.

Part 1, line 1 of Listing 4-6 describes the package that the Java file belongs to. This is also the entry package that was defined in the manifest file. The rest of the file imports needed functions and classes for the rest of the program. Imports are mostly equivalent to C/C++ `#include` statements and inform the code what classes are needed. USB communication is handled through a file, so the Java I/O file handlers need to be imported, but not all of the I/O library classes are needed and only a subset of the classes are imported. The same is true for the `android.*` libraries—only the ones that are actually needed are imported. It is possible to import every class in a library at once with a wildcard character (*), as is done with the `com.android.future.usb.*` libraries. When adding objects to the user interface, each object type will need to be imported from widgets in the same fashion as the toggle button.

Listing 4-6. CH4ExamplesActivity.java, Part 1 of 7

```java
package ch4.example.proArduino;
  import java.io.FileDescriptor;
  import java.io.FileInputStream;
  import java.io.FileOutputStream;
  import java.io.IOException;

  // Android components
  import android.app.Activity;
  import android.app.PendingIntent;
  import android.content.BroadcastReceiver;
  import android.content.Context;
  import android.content.Intent;
```

```
import android.content.IntentFilter;
import android.os.Bundle;
import android.os.ParcelFileDescriptor;
import android.util.Log;
import com.android.future.usb.*;

// UI components
import android.view.View;
import android.widget.ToggleButton;
```

Part 2 of the code starts the new class activity and inherits functionality from the parent class of the activity by extending the original class's functionality. This part also creates the object variable needed by the rest of the code to set up the ADK functionality, and create containers to hold user interface object registrations and debugging tags. Debugging tags are used to show what program sent a flag to the ADB. A function named Log sends the flag to the ADB as a string and can be read by issuing the command adb logcat in a command terminal on computer connected to the Android device when the ADB is available.

Listing 4-6. CH4ExamplesActivity.java, Part 2 of 7

```
public class CH4ExamplesActivity  extends Activity   {
    // ADK input and output declaration
    UsbAccessory ARDUINO_ADK; // the Accessory object
    ParcelFileDescriptor ADKstreamObj;
    FileInputStream ReciveFromADK;
    FileOutputStream SendtoADK;

    // setup and logging
    private static final String ACTION_USB_PERMISSION = "MEGA_ADK.USB_PERMISSION";
    private static final String TAG = "MEGA ADK";    // debug tag sent Log
    private UsbManager UsbManagerOBJ;
    private PendingIntent Needed_Permission;
    private boolean IsPermissionNeeded;

    // UI components
    private ToggleButton buttonLED;
```

Part 3 is a collection of functions used for program handling. The constructor and destructor are defined in this section along with definitions of how to handle the program when paused and resumed. These functions are overridden from the originals contained in the original activity class so that the extra functionality of the ADK protocol can be added.

The @Override lines tell the program that the function below is different from the function that is defined in the parent class; however, by using super.*functionName* we make sure that the parent's function is also called in the new code. In the onCreate function, the accessory is set up, the main view is registered to the program, and the user interface objects are linked. Because of the differences in the user interface layout between different projects, a registerUIobjects function has been created to contain and handle these differences.

Listing 4-6. CH4ExamplesActivity.java, Part 3 of 7

```
@Override
public void onCreate(Bundle savedInstanceState) {
    super.onCreate(savedInstanceState);
    setupAccessory();
```

```
    setContentView(R.layout.main);
    registerUIobjects();
}       // end onCreate

@Override
public void onDestroy() {
    unregisterReceiver(ADKReceiver);
    super.onDestroy();
}       // end onDestroy

@Override
public void onPause() {
    super.onPause();
    closeAccessory();
}       // end onPause()

@Override
public void onResume() {
    super.onResume();
    if (ReciveFromADK != null && SendtoADK != null) {
        return;
    }       // end  if (ReciveFromADK != ...
    UsbAccessory[] accessories = UsbManagerOBJ.getAccessoryList();
    UsbAccessory accessory = (accessories == null ? null : accessories[0]);
    if (accessory != null) {
      if (UsbManagerOBJ.hasPermission(accessory)) {
        openAccessory(accessory);
      }       // end if (UsbManagerOBJ.hasPermission(accessory))
      else {
       synchronized (ADKReceiver) {
        if (IsPermissionNeeded == true) {
          UsbManagerOBJ.requestPermission(accessory, Needed_Permission);
          IsPermissionNeeded = false;
        }       // end  if (IsPermissionNeeded == true)
       }       // end synchronized ADKReceiverr)
      }       // end else for  if (UsbManagerOBJ...
    }       // end if (accessory != null)
    else {
      Log.d(TAG, "mAccessory is null");
    }       // end else if (accessory != null)
}       // end onResume()
```

Part 4 handles the programs auto-start functionality and the request of permissions when the application is started. When a device is plugged in, this code receives information from the operating system's event broadcast and will ask the user to grant permission to use the application with the accessory. If the program is started by the user and not by a system event, the permission is assumed.

Listing 4-6. CH4ExamplesActivity.java, Part 4 of 7

```java
private BroadcastReceiver ADKReceiver = new BroadcastReceiver() {
 @Override
 public void onReceive(Context context, Intent intent) {
    String action = intent.getAction();
     if (ACTION_USB_PERMISSION.equals(action) == true) {
       synchronized (this) {
         UsbAccessory accessory = UsbManager.getAccessory(intent);
          if (intent.getBooleanExtra(UsbManager.EXTRA_PERMISSION_GRANTED, false)) {
            openAccessory(accessory);
          }
          else {
            Log.d(TAG, "permission denied for accessory "+ accessory);
          }
          IsPermissionNeeded = true;
       }    // end synchronized (this)
     }       // end if (ACTION_USB_PERMISSION.equals...
    else if (UsbManager.ACTION_USB_ACCESSORY_DETACHED.equals(action)) {
       UsbAccessory accessory = UsbManager.getAccessory(intent);
        if (accessory != null && accessory.equals(ARDUINO_ADK)) {
          closeAccessory();
        }
    } // end else if (UsbManager...
 }     // end void onReceive(Context contex ...
};     // end private BroadcastReceiver..

@Override
public Object onRetainNonConfigurationInstance() {
    if (ARDUINO_ADK != null) {
      return ARDUINO_ADK;
    }
    else {
       return super.onRetainNonConfigurationInstance();
    }
}    // end public Object  onRetainNon*...
```

Part 5 sets up the accessory to be used and handled by the program with the registration of the accessory object and the I/O streams. This section defines what needs to be done when opening and closing the accessory.

Listing 4-6. CH4ExamplesActivity.java, Part 5 of 7

```java
private void openAccessory(UsbAccessory accessory) {
    ADKstreamObj = UsbManagerOBJ.openAccessory(accessory);
    if (ADKstreamObj != null) {
      ARDUINO_ADK = accessory;
      FileDescriptor fd = ADKstreamObj.getFileDescriptor();
      ReciveFromADK = new FileInputStream(fd);
      SendtoADK = new FileOutputStream(fd);
      Log.d(TAG, "accessory opened");
    } // end if (ADKstreamObj
```

```
    else {
      Log.d(TAG, "accessory open fail");
    }
} // end void openAccessory...
private void setupAccessory() {
    UsbManagerOBJ = UsbManager.getInstance(this);
    Needed_Permission = PendingIntent.getBroadcast(this, 0, new Intent(ACTION_USB_PERMISSION), 0);
    IntentFilter filter = new IntentFilter(ACTION_USB_PERMISSION);
    filter.addAction(UsbManager.ACTION_USB_ACCESSORY_DETACHED);
    registerReceiver(ADKReceiver, filter);
     if (getLastNonConfigurationInstance() != null) {
        ARDUINO_ADK = (UsbAccessory) getLastNonConfigurationInstance();
       openAccessory(ARDUINO_ADK);
    }
} // end private void setupAccessory()
private void closeAccessory() {
    try {
     if (ADKstreamObj != null) {
       ADKstreamObj.close();
     }
    }// end try
    catch (IOException e) {
          Log.e(TAG, "IO Exception", e);
    }
    finally {
      ADKstreamObj = null;
      ARDUINO_ADK = null;
    }    // end of all try catch finally
}        // end private void closeAccessory()
```

Part 6 contains a function that writes data to the output file stream that can be read by the Mega ADK board's programming. For this example, only the output direction has been created. The write function accepts an array of bytes of any size and will send all the bytes contained in the array; there is no need to define an amount—the whole array is sent.

Listing 4-6. CH4ExamplesActivity.java, Part 6 of 7

```
private void write(byte[] send){
    if (SendtoADK != null) {
       try {
         SendtoADK.write(send);
       }
       catch (IOException e){
         Log.e(TAG, "write failed", e);
       }
    }// end if (SendtoADK != null)
}// end private void write...
```

Part 7 is where the code performs functions based upon user interaction and later actions performed by the Mega ADK. For the program to be able to interact with user interface objects (such as showing dynamic information or reading object information), the objects need to be registered. The registerUIobjects function is responsible for the registration; it finds the ID of the desired object and sets it to the variable created in the beginning of the class. The variable is not defined in the function because other functions will need to use the objects.

The blinkLED function is run every time the toggle button is pressed. This function creates an array of 1 byte that is set based upon what state the toggle button is in. The toggle button's state is handled by the widget class, so code does not need to be added. Once the array value is set, the write function is called to send the byte to the Arduino. Any number of buttons can be created to send any amount of data (for example, to create a directional pad to use an Android device as a robot controller).

Listing 4-6. CH4ExamplesActivity.java, Part 7 of 7

```java
private void registerUIobjects(){
    buttonLED = (ToggleButton) findViewById(R.id.toggleButtonLED);
}

public void blinkLED(View v) {
    byte[] BytestoSend = new byte[1];
    if (buttonLED.isChecked())
      BytestoSend[0] = (byte) 1; // button shows current LED State "ON"
    else
      BytestoSend[0] = (byte) 0; // button shows current LED State "OFF"
    write(BytestoSend); // sends the byte to the ADK
} // end void blinkLED(View v)
} // end public class CH4ExamplesActivity
```

Verifying the Code

Now that both parts of the example are complete, the Mega ADK board should already have the sketch from Listing 4-1 installed. The code for the Android needs to be installed on a supporting device. You can accomplish this by running the application from the Eclipse IDE with the Android device connected via the ADB or by manually installing it from the .apk file located in the bin folder of the workspace/*project name* folder. When the application is installed on the Android device, make sure that it can run; it will automatically start if the program was installed by Eclipse. The program will have a single button centered on the screen; the button will be in the off state.

Close the program for now and plug the Mega ADK into the computer to power the board. For debugging on the Arduino side, start the serial monitor at 115200 baud. After the Arduino is powered on, plug the Android device into the host side with the appropriate USB cable (in most circumstances, the cable used to charge the device will work). If all is working, a pop-up should appear on the Android screen asking for permission to start the application shortly after the board is plugged in. If the pop-up does not appear, try pressing the reset button on the Arduino or reconnecting the USB cable to the Android device.

Once the program is running, the toggle button should now be able to turn the LED off and on over the USB connection. The serial monitor should have printed the connection initiation and should echo a 1 or 0 every time the toggle button is pressed. If the ADB is available over wireless, type adb logcat into a terminal and check the printing log for mentions of the MEGA_ADK program.

■ **Note** If using completed Android project from Apress check that the Build target is GoogleAPIs API level 10 located in Project ➤ Properties ➤ Android ➤ Build target.

Completing the Framework

Now that Arduino and Android have been introduced to each other, the next example expands on the code from last example. The next example uses the same project and introduces the handling of two-way communication by creating an ADK monitor with similar functionality to the serial monitor included with the Arduino IDE.

The ability to send data is already complete and handled by the write function. The ability to receive data is not as straightforward. Because the code is event driven and normally responds to user interaction, a type of continuous loop needs to be created that does not interfere with the rest of the program. This is accomplished by implementing a thread that will listen to the incoming file stream for new data and call a function so that the data can be worked with. To implement a thread, we need to create and start a Runnable class, so add implements Runnable to the end of the activity declaration just before the starting curly brace and after extends Activity making the class declaration read as.

```
public class CH4ExamplesActivity extends Activity implements Runnable {
```

The thread needs to be created and started. This is done in the openAccessory function located in part 5 Listing 4-6. The two lines of code in Listing 4-7 are placed between the following existing lines:

```
SendtoADK = new FileOutputStream(fd);
Log.d(TAG, "accessory opened");
```

The new lines of code will start a function named run in the current class every time the openAccessory function is executed.

Listing 4-7. New Lines for the openAccessory Function

```
Thread ADKreadthread = new Thread(null, this, "ADK_Read_Thread");
ADKreadthread.start();
```

The run function needs to be defined within the class and can be added below the write function of part 6 Listing 4-6. The functions must be named run because of the abstraction from the runnable class. The new function is as described in Listing 4-8. The function normally would execute once and end as a separate thread from the original program. In this case, it needs to run in a continuous loop, so we create a while (true) loop. Under normal circumstances, once a loop of this nature is encountered, the rest of the program cannot continue to function until the loop is finished. However, this loop is in a separate place and acts as a different program from the main program, and allows for the rest of the code to execute as normal. This function constantly monitors the ReceiveFromADK data stream for new information, places the data in a new data class, and informs a function that there is new data ready to be handled by the main program.

Listing 4-8. New Function to Constantly Check for New Incoming Data

```
public void run() {
int RevivedBytes  = 0;
 while (true) { // run constantly
  byte[] buffer = new byte[80]; // max size capable is 16384 but slows the program down
  try {
     RevivedBytes = ReciveFromADK.read(buffer);
  }
  catch (IOException e) {
     Log.e(TAG, "Read failed", e);
     break;
  }
  if  (RevivedBytes >= 1 ) {
     Message MakeBufferTransferable = Message.obtain(IncomingDataHandler);
     MakeBufferTransferable.obj = new BufferData( buffer ,RevivedBytes);
     IncomingDataHandler.sendMessage(MakeBufferTransferable);
  }
 }// end while
}// end public void run()
```

A new data class has to be created to efficiently pass information from the thread to a receiving function. The class is created outside of the current Java file but still within the same package. Right-click the package name ch4.example.proArduino and select a new file to bring up a wizard, and enter the name BufferData.java for the newly created file. This new file will contain the BufferData class called by run and used for a data handler. The class declares two variables and has three functions; the variables are for the buffer and the amount of revived bytes. The first function takes both values in at once and stores them in the appropriate variable. The next two functions will return one of the two variables depending on the functions called. The class is outlined in Listing 4-9 because this file is part of the same package—the class does not need to be imported.

Listing 4-9. Buffer Data Container Class

```
package ch4.example.proArduino;
 public class BufferData {
     private byte[] Buffer;
     private int length;
     public BufferData ( byte[] Buffer , int length) {
         this.Buffer = Buffer;    // set data to variables
         this.length = length;
     }
     public byte[] getBuffer() {
         return Buffer;    // set data out
     }
     public int getLength(){
         return length; // set data out
     }
 }// end BufferData
```

The last thing needed to complete the framework for use in this application or other applications is a handler. This mechanism allows the rest of the program to work with the incoming data. The handler is included via an Android class and needs to be imported along with a message class so that run can notify the main program of changes. The Listing 4-10 shows the two import lines that need to be added to the import section at the beginning of the file.

Listing 4-10. Two New Lines for the Import Section

```
import android.os.Handler;
import android.os.Message;
```

For convenience, the function to be created in Listing 4-11 that uses the two new classes will be placed toward the end of the main file, or what was part 7 in Listing 4-6, just after the registerUIobjects function. The placement is important because the handler function is heavily modified between different projects. This function is wrapped inside of a class of type Handler and overrides the original class function of handleMessage. The original functionality of handleMessage is not needed and not included with a call to super.<functions name>. The function handleMessage links the data sent from run to a new BufferData object. At this point, the framework is complete and ready for the development of the rest of the program. To prep the data for the user, the code converts the BufferData to a string and appends the string to an editText widget for display.

Listing 4-11. The Last Part of the Framework

```
Handler IncomingDataHandler = new Handler() {
 @Override
 public void handleMessage(Message msg) {
 BufferData IncomingBuffer = (BufferData) msg.obj;
 // after this point the data is available for manipulation
   String str = new String(IncomingBuffer.getBuffer());
```

```
   DataFromArduino.append(str);
 }// end handleMessage(Message msg)
}; // end Handler IncomingDataHandler = new Handler()
```

Completing the Application

Now that the framework is complete, the rest of this section focuses on the creation of a serial monitor replica for use with the ADK protocol. The best place to start is with the user interface to get a feel for how the interaction will work, and at the same time prepare the resources to link to the Java portion of the application. The Arduino IDE has a serial monitor for ease of development; it is capable of printing any information at specified points in the code, and it is also capable of sending data to the Arduino. The application for the ADK side has to mimic the same functionality as the serial monitor. Two different text boxes are used: one for incoming data and one for outgoing; a single button is used to send the data from the outgoing text box. At bare minimum, three objects are needed to create the same user interface experience: two Android EditText boxes for the data and a regular button to send. To add a little extra flair, the program includes a second button for clearing the data in the user interface.

Figure 4-6 shows what user interface layout was chosen for this application. The send and clear buttons are at the bottom right, the input box it placed next to them at the bottom left, and the rest of the screen is filled with the data-revived box. For simplicity, the autoscroll is not implemented along with the line-ending options or the baud select. The TextEdit boxes automatically wrap the characters to a new line when used in a multiple-line configuration, as is need for the incoming data box, and will scroll automatically when the end of the box is reached. There is no speed setting because the ADK protocol's speed is set globally for all accessory devices. Listing 4-12 shows the main.xml file that produces the user interface shown in Figure 4-6. There are a few settings for each object. To better describe each of the objects, the example is divided it to three parts, ordered as they appear in the XML file. The XML file for Listing 4-12 replaces that used for the prior examples.

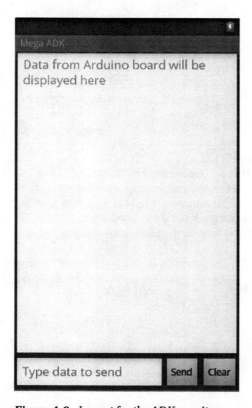

Figure 4-6. *Layout for the ADK monitor*

Part 1 of the XML file describes the overall layout style and the first EditText box along with the associated information, such as IDs, fill, location, and relative layout type. The ID for the first EditText box is incomingData. Because there is no need for the incoming-data box to be edited, the flags after the ID and positional definitions for this EditText box are set to turn off this functionality. The options for focus, cursor viability, and click ability of the box are turned off by setting the associated Android flags to false. The next two options set a scroll bar to show when the text has gone past the box's bottom edge. The gravity is set to the top so the incoming text does not sit centered. The flag android:inputType sets two options, telling the code that this box is a multiline box and that the spell check needs to be turned off and not show any spelling suggestions. The last flag sets the hint to a string located in the strings.xml file.

Listing 4-12. main.xml, Part 1 of 3

```xml
<?xml version="1.0" encoding="utf-8"?>
<RelativeLayout xmlns:android="http://schemas.android.com/apk/res/android"
    android:id="@+id/relativeLayout1"
    android:layout_width="fill_parent"
    android:layout_height="fill_parent"
    android:layout_weight="0.72" >
<EditText
    android:id="@+id/incomingData"
    android:layout_width="wrap_content"
    android:layout_height="wrap_content"
    android:layout_above="@+id/outgoingData"
    android:layout_alignParentLeft="true"
    android:layout_alignParentRight="true"
    android:layout_alignParentTop="true"
    android:clickable="false"
    android:cursorVisible="false"
    android:focusable="false"
    android:focusableInTouchMode="false"
    android:scrollbars="vertical"
    android:gravity="top"
    android:inputType="textMultiLine|textNoSuggestions"
    android:hint="@string/hint" >
</EditText>
```

Part 2 describes the EditText box, which is to be used as the output box to send data to the Arduino. The box will be identifiable to the code as outgoingData. The size is not described as absolute, as in the blink example, but as dynamic compared to the other objects—this user interface will always use the available screen no matter the size. The hint for this box is also set in the strings.xml file. Finally the input type is defined as text. This is a single-line input box with the overflow continuing to scroll horizontally. This box also turns off the spell check.

Listing 4-12. main.xml, Part 2 of 3

```xml
<EditText
    android:id="@+id/outgoingData"
    android:layout_width="wrap_content"
    android:layout_height="wrap_content"
    android:layout_alignParentBottom="true"
    android:layout_alignParentLeft="true"
    android:layout_toLeftOf="@+id/sendbutton"
    android:hint="@string/sendhint"
    android:inputType="text|textNoSuggestions" >
</EditText>
```

Part 3 describes the last two objects of the user interface: the buttons. These two buttons take up the reaming space at the bottom right of the screen, with the send button located closer to the input box. Both buttons are set up as the toggle button was in the blink example; the text of the button is linked to a string and the button is set up to call a function when it is pressed. As compared to the toggle button, these buttons are momentary and do not hold a changed state when released.

Listing 4-12. main.xml, Part 3 of 3

```
<Button
    android:id="@+id/clear"
    android:layout_width="wrap_content"
    android:layout_height="wrap_content"
    android:layout_alignParentBottom="true"
    android:layout_alignParentRight="true"
    android:onClick="clearScreen"
    android:text="@string/clear" >
</Button>
<Button
    android:id="@+id/sendbutton"
    android:layout_width="wrap_content"
    android:layout_height="wrap_content"
    android:layout_alignParentBottom="true"
    android:layout_toLeftOf="@+id/clear"
    android:onClick="SendData"
    android:text="@string/send"
</Button>
</RelativeLayout>
```

The `strings.xml` file needs to be modified to contain the resources for the buttons and the `EditText` boxes; Listing 4-13 shows the required changes. The new `strings.xml` file contains five tags: the app name, two hints, and two button names. `strings.xml` is the only other XML file that needs to be modified for this example. `AndroidManifest.xml` and `accessory_filter.xml` are needed, but require no modification.

Listing 4-13. New strings.xml File

```
<?xml version="1.0" encoding="utf-8"?>
<resources>
    <string name="app_name">Mega ADK</string>
    <string name="hint">Data from Arduino board will be displayed here</string>
    <string name="sendhint">Type data to send</string>
    <string name="send">Send</string>
    <string name="clear">Clear</string>
</resources>
```

With the user interface finished, the code can be added to the main Java file to complete the functionality of the serial monitor clone. Two different objects are used and therefore need to be imported. The following lines of code need to replace the `import android.widget.ToggleButton;` line in the import section of `CH4ExamplesActivity.java`:

```
import android.widget.Button;
import android.widget.EditText;
```

The toggle button is no longer needed for this example, and the variable declaration can be replaced by the following four lines of code in the variable section inside the class:

```
private Button buttonSend;
private Button ScreenClear;
private EditText DataFromArduino;
private EditText outgoingData ;
```

Listing 4-14 describes the last three functions needed to complete the application. The data-handling function was described in Listing 4-11 and should already be located below the registerUIobjects function. The IncomingDataHandler is already to go and includes the code to print the data to the EditText box. The EditText box, along with the three other user interface objects, needs to be linked to the program by type casting the return value of the findViewById method; the type cast follows this format:

```
(<object type>) findViewById(R.id.<object ID>);
```

The clearScreen and SendData functions are called when the user instates the event that is associated with the button in main.xml. When the clearScreen function is called, it sets the EditText box identified as incomingData back to the original sate by setting the text to null. The last function, SendData, grabs the text in outgoingData as a string and then converts that data to a byte array before calling the write function.

Listing 4-14. New and Edited Functions for CH4ExamplesActivity.java

```
private void registerUIobjects(){
   buttonSend = (Button) findViewById(R.id.sendbutton); // called in for other use, not
                                                         // implemented
   ScreenClear = (Button) findViewById(R.id.clear);        // in this program
   DataFromArduino = (EditText)findViewById(R.id.incomingData);
   outgoingData =  (EditText)findViewById(R.id.outgoingData);
}     // end registerUIobjects

//////////////////////////////////////////////
// Listing 4-11 code is inserted inplace of this block
//////////////////////////////////////////////

public void clearScreen (View v) {
    DataFromArduino.setText(null);
}     // end clearScreen (View v)
public void SendData(View v) {
   String convert = outgoingData.getText().toString();
   byte[] BytestoSend = convert .getBytes();
   write(BytestoSend); // sends buffer to the ADK
   outgoingData.setText(null);
}     // end void SendData(View v)
}     // end class CH4ExamplesActivity
```

The Android application is ready to be installed after any possible errors are fixed. The Eclipse IDE throws two warnings for this code because the buttons are declared and initialized but not referenced elsewhere in the code. It is good practice to declare the buttons even if the attributes or functions of the object are not going to be used; having the objects all set up and ready helps keep track of the objects available. This program will respond to any accessory that has the proper identifiable information, and will take the incoming bytes and print the value as related to

ASCII—a value of 0x61 sent will print an *a*. The Android app is ready to accept incoming messages from any Arduino sketch that is using the AndroidAccessory.h library, giving the same feeling as the serial functions.

■ **Note** The AndroidAccessory.h functions replicate the serial functions and inherit the functionality of print and println, and offer formatting options such as BIN, DEC, and HEX.

Arduino

The Arduino could be left up to the imagination at this point, but the next example sets up a quick echo from the serial monitor to the ADK application and vice versa. This is handled by two while loops that will write the incoming data when available from one side to the other. This example does not require any extra hardware connected to the pins on the Arduino.

Load the sketch in Listing 4-15 to the Arduino Mega ADK.

Listing 4-15. Modified Software Serial Sketch to Link the Echo Serial to the ADK and Vice Versa

```
#include <AndroidAccessory.h>
AndroidAccessory ADK("Manufacturer", "Model", "Description",
                "1.0", "Pro Arduino", "0000000012345678");
void setup() {
   Serial.begin(115200);
   ADK.begin();
}

void loop() {
   if (ADK.isConnected()) {
    while ( Serial.available() > 0){
         ADK.write (Serial.read());
     }
     while ( ADK.available() > 0){
       Serial.write(ADK.read());
     }
   }   // end if (ADK.isConnected)
}      // end loop
```

Verifying the Code

With the application on the Android device and the sketch installed on the Arduino, plug the USB from the computer into the Arduino and start a serial monitor at baud 115200. Once the monitor is ready, make sure that the application is not currently open on the Android device and plug the Mega ADK host side into the Android USB. The application should automatically ask for permission to start with the attached accessory. If after a few second the pop-up does not appear, try reconnecting the USB on the Android side or pressing the reset button on the Arduino. Once the program starts, the serial monitor should have printed some connection information, and data can be entered into either side's input boxes and sent, and should appear on the output box on the other device.

SPI and ADK

On the Mega ADK, as with other shields, the functionality to allow for the communication happens through a USB host processor that uses the SPI protocol to communicate with the microcontroller. To demonstrate that other SPI-capable devices still work with the ADK quite effectively, this last example reads a file from an SD card connected to the Mega ADK board and prints the contents to the ADK monitor installed on the Android device. Listing 4-16 requires an SD card and an SD breakout board. The SD board that was used in the development of this example was the microSD breakout made by Adafruit Industries (www.adafruit.com/products/254) and was chosen for its level-conversion feature, which converts from 5V to 3.3V logic and has the form factor of a breakout instead of a shield. A microSD card will also be needed for the Adafruit board. If a different SD board is currently available, there is no need to get the Adafruit board, provided your board has the capability to directly connect to the correct SPI pins. Shields for Atmel 328–based Arduino boards, such as the UNO, will not work because of the different SPI pin location.

Listing 4-16 is an Arduino sketch and uses the same Android application developed in the first example in this chapter. The Mega ADK needs to be connected to the SD breakout board as described in Figure 4-7. The pins marked DO (data out), DI (data in) and Clk (clock) on the SD breakout are connected to the MISO, MOSI, and SCK pins on the Arduino Mega ADK board. Also on the SD breakout, the pin marked CS (chip select) is connected to pin 10 on the Arduino. The power pins complete the setup, with 5V to 5V and ground to ground.

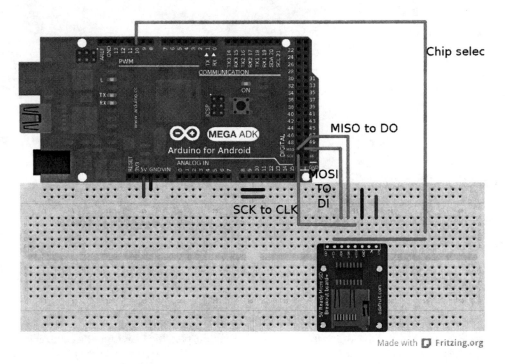

Figure 4-7. *Layout for the ADK monitor*

The sketch created in Listing 4-16 uses two libraries, SD.h and AndroidAccessory.h; to solve any pin definition conflicts the SD.h library need to be included first. A byte array of 80 elements is created to buffer the data gathered from the SD file before sending to the Android device. This is done to speed up the transfer, accommodating for both devices on the SPI bus. The accessory object is defined in the same way as in the other examples. Once the code enters the setup function, the ADK object is started and waits for the connection to be ready before proceeding to start the SD reader. Waiting for the connection to be fully operational allows for the information about the setup of the SD reader to be caught and printed to the Android application. The loop function checks for the connection and will try to reestablish the connection if disconnected. The code waits for a defined incoming character from the Android before opening and reading the test file on the SD card to the buffer. If the file is not available, an error is printed in the Android application. Step through Listing 4-16 and upload it to the Mega ADK board.

Listing 4-16. Arduino SD Reader and ADK Sketch

```
#include <SD.h> // must be included before AndroidAccessory.h
#include <AndroidAccessory.h> // needed library to work with ADK connections
  byte buffer[80];
  // initialize the accessory object with identifying data
  AndroidAccessory ADK("Manufacturer", "Model", "Description",
                       "1.0", "Pro Arduino", "0000000012345678");
void setup() {
  ADK.begin();      // start the connection to the Android
  while(!ADK.isConnected());   // wait till the ADK is connected to finish setup
  pinMode(10, OUTPUT);   // SD chip select
  if (!SD.begin(10)) {    // start the SD and check for failure
    ADK.println("SD initialization failed!");
  }
  else
    ADK.println("SD initialization done.");
}  // end setup
void loop() {
  if (ADK.isConnected()) {            // check for connection
    if (ADK.available() > 0){        //check for incoming data
      if (ADK.read() == 'a') {      // look for an incoming 'a' to start file transfer
          File TestFile = SD.open("test.txt");     // open the test.txt
        if (TestFile) { // if file did not open, throw an error
            while (TestFile.available()) { // read till the file end has been reached
                for (int i = 0 ; i < 80 ; i ++ ){ // read 80 bytes into buffer before sending
                buffer[i] = TestFile.read();
                }
              ADK.write (buffer , 80); // send buffer to the Android
            } // end while (TestFile.available())
          TestFile.close(); // close the file no longer needed
        }  // end if (TestFile)
        else{
            ADK.println ("File Error");
        }
      }  // end if (ADK.read() == 'a')
    }  // end if (ADK .available() > 0)
  }   // end if (ADK .isConnected())...
}        // end void loop()
```

Once the Arduino is configured with the SD reader and programmed with the sketch, a test.txt file must be created and located in the root directory of a FAT-formatted SD card. Copy any text readme file to the SD card from a computer and rename it test.txt on the SD card. Plug the Arduino into the Android device, insert the SD card into the reader, and power it on.

When the ADK application starts, the status of the SD initialization should be printed to the screen. You should see that the SD card has been found and is ready to use. If it fails, recheck the connections or reinsert the card. When the initialization is done, type a into the input box and press send. The text.txt file should start printing; the whole file will be printed 80 bytes at a time. If the file size does not divide evenly by 80 bytes, the last transmission will contain and print garbage characters in the bytes the file does not fill. This sketch's methods can be useful for pulling logs from a sensor network or interfacing with other SPI devices, such as the Ethernet shield, with modifications to work with the Mega-style pin out.

Summary

The world of Android-to-Arduino accessory development is now available to be further explored. Any Arduino code that outputs through a serial connection can output to the ADK by including the AndroidAccessory.h library and making a few changes to the serial references in any existing code.

This chapter demonstrated some of the basic workings of the Arduino Mega ADK. For further reading and more in-depth information, check out the Android Developers web site (http://developer.android.com) and *Beginning Android ADK with Arduino*, by Mario Böhmer (Apress, 2012).

This chapter described how to create a framework that can be used as a starting point for any Android application that connects to an accessory device, along with a tool that is helpful for debugging. With the ADK, you can build smarter robots, cooler blinking devices, and more dynamic art installations without having to lug around a bulky laptop. It is even possible to develop an IDE to program other Arduinos from an Android device connected through the Mega ADK. Aside from hardware constraints, imagination is the limit.

The software used in this chapter is sometimes a bit buggy and isn't supported on all devices because of their relative ages. As newer Android devices become available, support will increase, making it easier to develop accessories for a broader market. The open hardware community has done a wonderful job of adopting this new technology, with an ever-increasing number of development boards available—from the IOIO to the Mega ADK. The community of developers has also kept up on the software; for example, when version 1.0 of the Arduino IDE was released, the accessory library was difficult to work with and required some changes; now the Accessory library is as simple to work with as serial and is continually improved upon.

## CHAPTER 5

XBees

Radio communication is a fundamental method of communicating over varying distances without having an encumbrance of wires. Arduino developers take advantage of radio communication in robotics, home automation, and remote-sensing applications. To avoid the headaches of developing radio communications systems from scratch, a lot of developers use XBee radio modules to add wireless functionality to projects. The XBee is a full-featured radio transceiver module made by Digi International (www.digi.com) and is compliant with FCC regulations as long as you use the module without modification and adhere to a few other restrictions.

The restrictions that apply to the use of the XBee by the FCC and by other countries are listed in the data sheet provided by Digi. Most XBee modules are also compliant with the *ZigBee communication protocol*, a standard based on the IEEE 802.15.4 standard. XBees have the ability to communicate with other ZigBee-compliant devices.

The minimum hardware to get started exploring the world of XBees is a USB adapter, a serial adapter, an Arduino-compatible board, and two XBee modules. You can use the USB XBee adapter sold by Adafruit Industries (www.adafruit.com/products/247) or the one sold by SparkFun Electronics (www.sparkfun.com/products/8687). The USB adapter is needed to interface with the computer for initialization and setup, and can provide a connection from the computer to other XBee modules.

The XBee has a small pin pitch that's not breadboard compatible, and it's a 3.3V device, so to use the XBee with an Arduino, you need a serial adapter to make the connections more easily and to convert the voltage levels. There are a few different styles of serial adapters that can be used for connecting the Arduino to the XBee: the two most notable are shields and breakout boards. They come with and without voltage conversion. Shields provide a method of simplified packaging—excellent for semipermanent setups. Shields limit the number of devices that can be easily used and are usually restricted to boards with the standard Arduino pin out. For greater development flexibility, it is recommended to use breakout boards instead of shields. XBee breakout boards, such as the adapter available from Adafruit (www.adafruit.com/products/126) or SparkFun (www.sparkfun.com/products/9132), will work for the examples in this chapter and Chapter 6.

The examples in this chapter are built using one ATmega328 Arduino-compatible board, two series 2 XBee modules, one USB adapter, and a serial breakout board. The focus of this chapter is on the series 2 XBee modules, but they are not the only modules available from Digi. The first section describes the various models of the XBee modules and the differences in functionality.

Buying XBees

It can be a bit difficult to discern the differences between XBee modules and match them to your project requirements. There are currently nine different series, with multiple variations on antennas, functionality, and transmission power. The series number is not an indication of version revisions, but of functionality and features. Modules with the same series number are always compatible with one another. When deciding what XBee set to purchase, you need to take constraints and the type of project into consideration. For example, for remote-control robots, an XBee that uses a point-to-point communication protocol with an extended transmitting range would be sufficient, even though the data rate may not be as fast as other modules. XBees for large sensor networks, on the other hand, may need to use a mesh protocol to be more robust in getting the data to the endpoint, with the range not being as important. To avoid issues in debugging, and for best results when purchasing a first set of XBees, match modules according to the series number, transmission power, and antenna type.

There may be a need in some projects to mismatch the modules, such as when using two modules with greater range and having others in the network with lower transmitting power to more effectively cover an area. Keep in mind when mixing the ranges of the modules that they can usually receive data at a faster rate than they can transmit data. Another possible mismatch comes with pro versions of XBee modules. Pro modules are clearly labeled with the word *Pro* on the module itself; these modules provide an integrated programmable microcontroller that acts in the same way as attaching an Arduino to a standard XBee module. The pro modules are useful for stand-alone operations or removing overhead from the Arduino itself. The move to the pro module is not necessary, and can add more complexity because the microcontroller used is made by Freescale and has a programming methodology different from the Arduino.

Here are the different series (series 1 and 2 are the most commonly used in Arduino development):

- *Series 1*: This series has a network topology of spoke-and-hub or point-to-multipoint and uses the 2.4 GHz frequency band. Series 1 modules can be configured and used out of the box without extra software. This series works well for remote control applications and simple sensor networks. All communications go through a central node; outer nodes cannot communicate with one another. This series has a rage of 300 feet to 1 mile.

- *Series 2*: This series is a bit more complicated than series 1, but provides more functionality and flexibility. It's capable of *mesh networking*, which closely resembles the common wired networking topology of an ISP, router, and computer. There are three different internal firmware options that can be used for a mesh network.

    - There must be one controller in the network, which functions like a DHCP server or ISP. The controller assigns the address and determines if a new node can join the network.

    - Mesh networks also include router firmware and allow for multiple routers in the network.

    - Routers connect to the controller and to endpoints, which are the third firmware option.

    Both the controller and router have to be powered all the time and cannot take advantage of the power-saving feature of sleeping; this is due to the modules keeping track of routing information. The endpoint can be put into a sleep state. This series is usually marked on the board by an S2 below the XBee markings. There are two other variants in this series: S2B and S2C. S2B is the pro package and S2C is a surface-mount package. The regular S2 has the standard XBee through-hole configuration. This series has a range of 400 feet to 2 miles.

- *Series 3*: This series offers a 900 MHz point-to-multipoint module with about 6 miles of range.

- *Series 4*: Modules of this series can be used for proprietary Digi mesh and point-to-multipoint; they have an approximate range of 1.8 miles using 900 MHz.

- *Series 5*: This series is licensed for European point-to-multipoint in the 868 MHz band; it has about 25 miles of range.

- *Series 6*: This series offers a WiFi module packaged in the XBee format. It uses SPI or UART for connections and can work on B, G, and N networks.

- *Xtend*: Modules of this series have a range of 15 miles, the longest available for use in the United States. They communicate at 900MHz. The network topology is proprietary multipoint or proprietary mesh.

■ **Note** Creating a network bridge is possible by connecting two different series, which converts between network types.

Simple Setup

This section's example sets up a simple communication for a set of series 2 XBee modules. There is some software that needs to be set up before the XBees can start communicating. Unlike series 1 modules, which can be configured for communications via a serial terminal, series 2 modules need different firmware for different nodes on the XBee network. There are two different software packages that can perform the firmware configuration.:

- *X-CTU*: This is the Digi proprietary software package to program the XBee modules. The software is available from the Digi web site, as well as directly from http://ftp1.digi.com/ support/utilities/40003002_B.exe. The X-CTU is capable of running on other operating systems, such as Linux via WINE. You need to download the firmware ZIP file for series 2 devices if setting up the X-CTU on Linux. You can download it from www.digi.com/support/p roductdetail?pid=3430&type=drivers. You also need to define a link so the WINE software can use ttyUSB to create a link; to do so, type the following into a command shell:

  ln -s /dev/ttyUSB0 ~/.wine/dosdevices/com1

- *Moltosenso*: This software package is made by a third-party vendor and has the same functionality as the X-CTU. It natively works on the three common operating systems, Linux, Mac, and Windows, and is available at www.moltosenso.com. This software may be a bit buggy on some 64-bit Linux distributions. The ZIP files that contain the firmware have to be downloaded from Digi. Be aware that this software does not automatically determine the firmware that is compatible with the connected XBee module, but will work well for configuring the module's other settings.

When the XBee is loaded with the AT firmware, a serial terminal program such as minicom, PuTTY, or HyperTerminal can be used to set and read options.

There are two different communication modes that the XBee module can be set to via different firmware:

- *Transparent mode*: Also known as *AT command mode*, transparent mode acts as a direct serial connection, the same way hardwired connections work. Sensors like the Parallax RFID readers can be connected over XBees in transparent mode without any other microcontroller in between the sensor and the RF module. This mode provides a great method for direct XBee-to-XBee communications and is useful in instances where the user needs to change settings while a network is up and running. You can enter this mode by typing +++ without a carriage return into a serial program and waiting for an OK to return. All the commands are two characters prefixed by AT and followed by a carriage return. An example is the command ATSL, which will print the lower four bytes of the module's serial number.

- *API mode*: This is useful for lager dynamic network setups where the software or microcontroller can easily change configurations without having to convert the human-readable AT command mode. API has a predefined protocol and communicates via packets. The use of the API mode is discussed further on in this chapter.

Transparent (AT Command) Mode

When setting up the series 2 XBee modules, write down the serial numbers for all the modules in a convenient location. The serial numbers is also used as the hardware address and is located on the sticker just below the revision marking and to the right of the 2D bar code on the XBee module. The first eight numbers of the serial number are the higher 32 bits of the address—usually 0013A200. The second eight numbers is the lower 32 bits of the address.

Module Configuration

Now it's time to set up your modules:

1. Determine which module will be used as the coordinator and which will be used as the router, and mark them with a label to differentiate between them.

2. Plug the XBee module to be used as the router into the USB adapter, making sure to line up the pins to the connector properly. The flat end usually points toward the USB connector.

3. Start the X-CTU software and plug the USB adapter into the computer. On the PC Settings tab, select or enter the COM port that the adapter is connected to and click the Test/ Query button. The test should come up with the module type, firmware number, and serial number. If there is an error, check the connections and the COM port number in the device manager and retry. If this is the first time that the XBee module is being configured, the standard serial configuration is 9600 8N1.

4. After the test is complete, click the Modem Configuration tab and click the Read button in the Modem Parameter and Firmware box. If the module cannot be read at this point, click the "Download new versions..." button. If you're using Windows, choose "Web source," and for WINE setups, select file that was downloaded. Then retry reading the configuration.

5. Once you have read the module, select ZIGBEE ROUTER AT from the Function Set drop-down menu, and set the version of the firmware to the highest hex number available.

6. Check the "Always update firmware" box and click the Write button. This sets the firmware but not any of the networking options; once this operation completes, reread the module settings.

7. In the following list, the firmware drop-down shows the options available for change. Options highlighted in green are at their default setting, and options highlighted in blue are set to a different setting. The options that need to be changed are

    *   The pan ID (ID)

    *   Destination address high (DH)

    *   Destination address low (DL)

    In transparent mode, the address is where the data will be sent. This can be changed by entering the command mode. The pan ID is like the ESSID for WiFi networks, and can be set from 0 to FFFF. The pan ID chosen for this example is 3300. click "pan ID" and set to the chosen ID. The next two options are the serial numbers written down earlier: the destination's addresses. Both the high and low should be set to the serial number of the module chosen for the coordinator. These three settings prepare the module for communications in a network.

8. One last setting needs to be set before writing the options to the module, and it's specific to this example: the baud rate. There is a single number to identify the baud rate; the default is 3 for 9600 baud. Change this setting to 6 for a baud rate of 57600. When the options are highlighted in a yellow-green, they have been changed but not written to the module. Uncheck the "Always update firmware" box and click the Write button in the Modem Parameters and Firmware box, which will confirm and update the settings to the module.

9. Once the router is configured, unplug the adapter from the computer and remove the module. Plug in the module to be used as the coordinator and repeat the steps used to configure the router, but select ZIGBEE COORDINATOR AT for the firmware options and set the destination address as the router's serial number. Use the same baud and pan ID as for the router module.

Arduino Setup

The modules are now ready for communications, and it is time to set up the rest of the example.

1. Leave the coordinator plugged into the USB adapter and plug the router into the serial adapter.

2. Prepare an Arduino board by uploading the standard Firmata sketch as described in Chapter 3. Make sure that the Arduino can communicate to the Firmata test application before plunging the router into the Arduino, as shown in Figure 5-1.

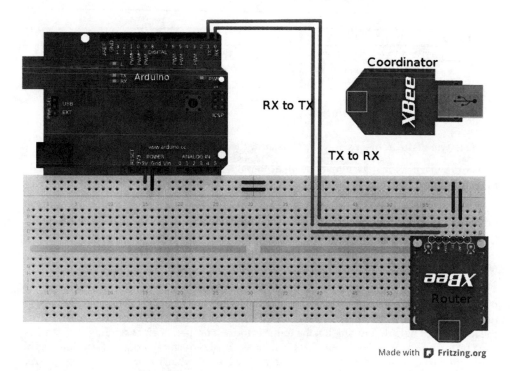

Figure 5-1. Arduino/XBee module configuration

95

Verifying the Code

The Firmata sketch is uploaded to the Arduino and the XBees are both plugged into the computer and Arduino. This configuration of the modules is in transparent mode, and the Firmata test app can now communicate with the Arduino. It is optional to add a few buttons, servos, or LEDs to explore the application's potential, or use the examples created in Chapter 3. If the modules are not communicating, check the connections, settings, and selected COM port.

■ **Note** You can make computer-to-computer chat possible with the XBee's transparent mode and serial terminals by connecting the XBee serial adapter to pins 2 and 3 of the Arduino and loading the software serial sketch onto the Arduino, changing the baud rates in the sketch to match the XBee module.

API Mode

API mode is the alternative to AT command mode. The API that is implemented with the XBee module allows programs to change internal settings, create direct routing, discover new nodes, and push remote AT commands or firmware updates, along with other advanced control options. This mode uses packets that are referred to as frames in the XBee data sheet.

There are currently 18 different frame types for series 2 modules; the first 4 bytes of the frame are always the same type of information, as described in Figure 5-2.

Byte number	1	2	3	4	n-4	n+1
name	Start Byte	Packet length		Frame type	Frame data	Checksum
value	0X7E	Byte 4 to Checksum			Frame specific structure	0xFF - (sum of Bytes from 4 to n)

Figure 5-2. *API packet structure*

- The first byte of the frame is always 0x7E to show that a frame is starting,

- The next two bytes are the length of the data contained in the frame; this number is the total bytes from the fourth byte to the checksum.

- Byte 4 is the frame type; this describes the data that makes up the data section of the frame, notifying a program how to interpret the data. The frame data is specific to the frame type. The structure is outlined for the various frames in the "API Operation" section of the XBee data sheet; the series 2 data sheet is available at http://ftp1.digi.com/support/documentation/90000976_K.pdf.

- The last byte of the frame is the checksum and is calculated by subtracting the total value of bytes from the frame type to the last byte of the frame data from 0xFF. This calculation is done within a single byte, and any value above 255 is truncated. The checksum is used by the modules to help determine that the frame is formed properly before sending and can be used by the program to determine that the data received is the proper data. The frame may be malformed when a verification frame is not returned or the when frame ID byte is set to zero. The frame ID is usually the first byte of the frame data section of the frame; this is to determine what frame is being talked about when information frames are returned. The frame ID is also useful for sequential frames to determine the order when receiving frames.

■ **Note**   Frames are what Digi's data sheet calls the series of data that is used for API mode; the term *frame* is interchangeable with *packet*.

Module Configuration

Configuring the modules for API mode is similar to the setup for the AT command configuration:

1. A single coordinator is needed. Change the firmware settings to ZIGBEE COORDINATOR API and ZIGBEE ROUTER API for the router.

2. Set the PANID along with the baud rate; you can use the same settings as before for this setup.

3. The destination address is not necessary for this mode to communicate; packets determine where the information is going.

4. Choose a name for the node identification (NI) setting when configuring the module; ROUTER and COORDINATOR will suffice. The NI setting is helpful for identifying the node. This is independent of the addresses and equivalent to a computers host name.

5. Upload the software serial sketch to an Arduino with both baud rates set to the XBee modules' rate of 57600, and connect the serial adapter to pins 2 and 3 of the Arduino, as shown in Figure 5-3.

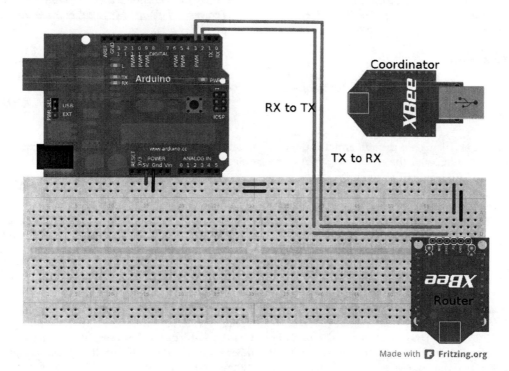

Figure 5-3. Setup for API examples. The XBee is connected to pins 2 and 3 for software serial

6. Once the Arduino is configured, connect via a serial terminal such as PuTTY, minicom, or HyperTerminal, with the setting 57600 8N1.

API Packet Construction

Before delving into writing code, I'll describe the X-CTU software, which provides a utility on the Terminal tab to manually build packets. With the Arduino set up and the serial program running, "Goodnight moon!" should be printed the Arduino's serial monitor, indicating everything is working. Plug the coordinator into the USB adapter, start the X-CTU software, double-check that the module can be accessed, and click the Terminal tab. On the Terminal tab is information on the line status and a few options. Click the Show Hex button to get a side-by-side ASCII-and-hex display, which will be a bit easier to read. Click the Assemble Packet button to bring up a window with an input box to place packet information; by default the input box is in ASCII mode, so make sure to select the Hex option so that the raw data can be entered.

The first packet you're going to assemble is an AT command; this is equivalent to entering +++ ATND (followed by a carriage return) in transparent mode. The **ND** command is for network discovery and will return information on all XBees that can be accessed in the network; for example, the network ID, the 64-bit address, and the plain-text name (if you set that option in the configuration). Packets are ordered from left to right or top to bottom. You can lay out the general structure of the packet on a piece of paper: the first four bytes are essentially the header that contains the start, the length, and the frame type.

Two of the bytes are known and can be filled in: 0x7E for the start and 0x08 for the frame type of the AT command to be sent. The packet is not complete, so the length cannot be determined yet. The first byte after the header is the frame ID that identifies the packet and enables the response to the packet: this is going to be set to 0x01 because only this packet is going to be sent for this example.

The AT command comes after the frame ID and is the hex value of the two characters that describe the command; in this case N (0x4E) and D (0x44) for the node-discovery command. Following the AT command characters is the setting value used when changing the setting for this packet, No setting change is needed, so no more bytes are added to this packet. The last byte of the packet is the checksum, which is calculated using the bytes that make up the frame packet with the frame type byte, so add the following value:

0x08 +0x01+0x4E+0x44 = 0x9B

Then subtract this value from 0xFF to get the checksum value:

0xFF - 0x9B = 0x64

The last byte to calculate is the size, which is done by counting the bytes between the size and the checksum (or the bytes used to calculate the checksum); in this case the size is 4 bytes. The final packet looks like this:

0x7E 0x00 0x04 0x08 0x01 0x4E 0x44 0x64

With the packet manually calculated, enter the bytes into the packet-assembly window in the X-CTU software and send the data to the module connected to the computer. The node-discovery command sent will discover the other modules that can receive data from the coordinator. After the command was sent, a reply packet will be received that contains information on the nodes seen. The header of this packet will be 0x7E followed by the size and the frame type 0x88, indicating that it is a response to the AT command sent. Any received frame will be identified by the frame type, and can be compared to the packet type lists later on to help determine how to interpret the frame.

In the frame data, the first byte is the frame ID, which should match the frame ID originally sent, followed by the command being responded to (which should be ND) and the command status of 0x00, indicating that the command was successful. The rest of the data contained in packet includes the 16-bit network address, the 64-bit serial number, a space, the node identifier, the parent network address, the device type, the status, the profile ID, the manufacture ID, and the checksum. If the node-identifier variable was set on all the modules, their plain-text ID should be readable; in this example, the string ROUTER should be clear on the ASCII side of the terminal window.

Sending Commands

There are two frame types that affect the local module:

- The AT command frame (0x08), which will immediately change values.

- The AT command queue (0x09), which holds changes until the apply-changes (AC) command has been issued or a subsequent AT command (0x08) is sent.

The ability to send AT commands to a remote module is a unique function that is not available in AT command mode. Sending remote AT commands uses a frame type of 0x17 and is constructed in a similar fashion as the local AT frame (0x08). There is extra data contained in the frame data section after the frame ID byte:

- First is the 64-bit destination address followed by the 16-bit network address. For the example following, (0x00 00 00 00 00 00 FF FF) will be used for the 64-bit and (0xFF FE) for 16-bit.

- The next byte is a command option; it has the same effect if set to 0x00 as the AT command queue and needs the AC command to finalize the changes. The other options for the command option byte are 0x02 to apply the changes immediately, 0x20 to use encryption if globally set in the EE register, and 0x40 to use a longer transmission timeout. Settings 0x00 and 0x02 are the only two of interest for this example.

- The AT command is after the command option byte; the node-discovery command will be used for this packet to see what the ROUTER module can transmit to.

The example packet is the following:

0x7E 0x00 0x0F 0x17 0x01 0x00 0x00 0x00 0x00 0x00 0x00 0xFF 0xFF 0xFF 0xFE 0x00 0x4E 0x44 0x5A

The example packet sends a request to all devices on the network, asking for those modules to perform a node discovery and send back their findings to the originating device. The return packet follows the same structure as any other packet, with the header, frame data, and checksum being in the same order. The returned packet's frame data has the 64- and 16-bit network address of the remote module added between the frame ID and the command bytes. The frame data is identical in structure to the local command, excluding the added address bytes. The value for this frame type is 0x97.

The example remote AT command packet will execute on all the modules that can hear the coordinator. On large networks this can cause talk-over communication packet corruptions and is not advisable. In some situations broadcasting a change-setting packet is needed, as when changing the pan ID of the whole network or changing encryption settings. When changing settings across an entire network, change and apply the settings to the remote modules before changing the local module.

Sending Data

Up to this point, configuration packets have been constructed and sent, but no data has been sent through to the Arduino that is connected to the serial program. The packets for sending data are constructed in the same order as the AT command packets, with the frame IDs being 0x10 and 0x11.

- The 0x10 data packets are general-purpose data containers that leave the network routing up to the modules.

- In contrast, 0x11 packets have more options on how the packet should reach its destination.

Digi provides a web-based utility that makes the manual assembly of packets easy; it's available at http://ftp1.digi.com/support/utilities/digi_apiframes.htm. The utility calculates the errorsum and the size bytes for any of the frame types, with a convenient layout of the byte field. To use this utility, select the frame ID to be constructed.

1. For this example, select the request transmit (0x10), and use the broadcast address of 0x00 00 00 00 00 00 FF FF for the 64-bit address and 0xFF FE for the 16-bit address.

2. Leave the other options as they are and add the hexadecimal equivalent of "HELLO" to the RF packet field (0x48 45 4C 4C 4F).

3. The button next to the packet field will build the packet that needs to be entered into the packet assembly window of the X-CTU. The packet should appear as follows:

   7E 00 13 10 01 00 00 00 00 00 00 FF FF FF FE 00 00 48 45 4C 4C 4F 7F

On the local module's side, the return packet is of frame type 0x8B and contains the 16-bit destination address, the number of transmit retries, the delivery status, and the discovery status. If both broadcast addresses are used, the 16-bit network address will be 0xFF FE if the 64-bit address of the module was used in transmitting with the 0xFF FE network address. The returned packet will have discovered the actual network address of the remote module. The three bytes after the network address indicate status—if the values come back as zeros, then the transition succeeded for the example packet.

The Arduino that has the receiving XBee connected should have echoed the packet to the screen. The packet shows up in the serial program as the printable characters, making most of the packet unreadable, but the data section should be a clearly readable "HELLO." The packet received that is echoed is the reply packet with frame type 0x90. This packet has no frame ID, the bytes after the frame type are the 64-bit and 16-bit addresses. The byte after the network address and before the data is a *status byte*; this byte provides the program with information that can be valuable when dealing with this packet. The status byte is a sum of four possible options:

- 0x01: Packet was acknowledged
- 0x02: Packet was acknowledged and is a broadcast
- 0x20: Packet is encrypted
- 0x40: Packet was sent from an end device

So, for example, if the byte is sent from an end device with a broadcast, the byte will have a value of 0x22. The remaining bytes that complete the packet are the data and checksum.

Request Packets

Table 5-1 is a reference for the various packets that can be used to control the XBee modules. The frame name, the frame type, a general description, and the frame data are provided. Remember that the frame type is the last byte of the header, and following the frame data is the checksum.

Table 5-1. *Packet Reference*

Frame Name	Frame Type	Description	Frame Data
AT command	0x08	Changes or reads local AT commands.	Frame ID: 1 byte AT command: 2 bytes Command parameter: Variable
AT command queue	0x09	Prepares a change that is placed in a queue.	Frame ID: 1 byte AT command: 2 bytes Command parameter: Variable
Transmit request	0x10	Sends data without a specified route.	Frame ID: 1 byte Destination address: 8 bytes Network address: 2 bytes Broadcast radius: 1 byte Options: 1 byte Data payload: Variable
Remote command request	0x17	Sends an AT command to a module over the air.	Frame ID: 1 byte Destination address: 8 bytes Network address: 2 bytes Command options: 1 byte AT Command: 2 bytes Command parameter: Variable
Explicit addressing transmit command	0x11	Directly controls the route a data packet will take.	Frame ID: 1 byte Destination address: 8 bytes Network address: 2 bytes Source endpoint: 1 byte Destination endpoint: 1 byte Cluster ID: 2 bytes Profile ID: 2 bytes Broadcast radius: 1 byte Options: 1 byte Data payload: Variable
Create source route	0x21	Creates a source route for the local module to a destination module. All transmitted packets will take the specified route from point A to B.	Frame ID: 1 byte set to 0x00 Destination address: 8 bytes Network address: 2 bytes Options reserved: 1 byte set to 0x00 Number of addresses or hops: 1 byte Network address of hop along route: 2 byte variable sets

Reply Packets

Table 5-2 shows the packets that are usually formed in a response to another packet. They are created outside of the program that creates the packet. These packets contain information that needs to be phrased so that the program can use the information. These packets still follow the same general structure as the request packets.

Table 5-2.

Frame Name	Frame Type	Description	Frame Data
AT command response	0x88	Notification of AT command status and data contained within the register when read.	Frame ID: 1 byte AT command: 2 bytes Command status: 1 byte Register data: Variable
Remote command response	0x97	Same function as AT command response for a remote module.	Frame ID: 1 byte Source address: 8 bytes Source network address: 2 bytes AT command: 2 bytes Command status: 1 byte Register data: Variable
Transmit status	0x8B	The acknowledgment packet of data transmission.	Frame ID: 1 byte Destination network address: 2 bytes Number of retries 1 byte Delivery status: 1 byte Discovery status: 1 byte
Receive packet	0x90	The transformation of the transmit request when received.	Source address: 8 bytes Source network address: 2 bytes Options: 1 byte Data payload: Variable
Explicit Rx indicator	0x91	The transformation of route transmit request.	Source address: 8 bytes Source network address: 2 bytes Source endpoint: 1 byte Destination endpoint: 1 byte Cluster ID: 2 bytes Profile ID: 2 bytes Options: 1 byte Data payload: Variable
IO sample indicator	0x92	The packet used to signify I/O activity revived when configured to do such.	Source address: 8 bytes Source network address: 2 bytes Options: 1 byte Number of samples: 1 byte Digital channel mask: 1 byte Analog channel mask: 1 byte Digital sample sets: 2-byte variable sets Analog sample sets: 2-byte variable sets
Sensor read indicator	0x94	Packet received from Digi 1-wire adapter.	Source address: 8 bytes Source network address: 2 bytes Options: 1 byte 1-wire sensor: 1 byte A/D values: 8 bytes Temperature read: 1 byte

(continued)

Table 5-2. (*continued*)

Frame Name	Frame Type	Description	Frame Data
Node identification	0x95	Packet used when replying to a ND command not always seen through the serial.	Source address: 8 bytes Source network address: 2 bytes Options: 1 byte 1-wire sensor: 1 byte A/D values: 8 bytes Temperature read: 1 byte
Modem status	0x8A	Module status packet.	Status message: 1 byte
Route record indicator	0xA1	Used when requesting route records command not always seen through the serial.	Source address: 8 bytes Source network address: 2 bytes Options: 1 byte Number of addresses: 1 byte Address set: 2-byte variable sets
Many to one route request indicator	0xA3	Seen by modules when a many-to-one route has been received.	Source address: 8 bytes Source network address: 2 bytes Options: 1 byte Reserved: 1 byte
Over the air firmware update status	0xA0	Status of remote firmware update.	Source address: 8 bytes Source network address: 2 bytes Options: 1 byte Boot loader message: 1 byte Block number: 1 byte Target address: 8 bytes

Arduino Data Echo

With a bit of understanding of the formation and reading of packets, this example will demonstrate in code the phrasing, retransmission, and construction of packets the code receives. The code will run on the Arduino and take incoming data packets (0x90) from any module in the network and pull the data out to reassemble the packet and retransmit back to the original source.

While the packet gets transmitted to the source, the code will print relative data to a serial monitor, such as a notification when an incoming packet has been received, the raw packet itself, addresses of the originating source, and the raw reply packet for sending. The code currently identifies and displays two different packets types (0x90) and (0x8B). This is accomplished through a switch statement after the whole packet has been captured.

The switch statement is pretty effective and can be expanded to recognize and handle current packet types plus any future additions. The packets are received and constructed in a byte array of 80 bytes, which is done to buffer the packets and to help ensure they're complete before any phrasing is done or transmission starts. Although the XBee modules are capable of sending packets of greater sizes, this limit is to save on some space on the Arduino.

The setup is the same as in Figure 5-3, previously. The code uses software serial at 9600 baud and standard serial at 57600 baud; the XBee modules have to be reconfigured to 9600 baud. There are two ways to reconfigure the baud settings:

- Use the X-CTU software to set the baud back to setting 3.

- Construct and issue two AT command packets: one for the remote module and the other for the local module. The AT command is BD or 0x42 44, with the parameter being 3.

Both require you to change the X-CTU COM setting back to 9600 to accommodate the new setting. This example is one-sided, so packets sent to the Arduino will still have to be constructed in the terminal of the X-CTU; the HELLO packet will work for this example, although any properly formed transmit request will work with this code. To finish the setup for this example, step through the code and upload it to the Arduino.

Listing 5-1 is comprised of three parts. The first part sets up the variables and all the initialization of the Arduino's serial connections before entering the loop function. The loop functions waits for the software serial to be available and checks for the packet start byte of 0x7E. A loop captures the packet and counts the incoming bytes while the software serial is available. When the packet is received, the user is informed of the incoming packet along with the contents of the raw packet by printing the details to the serial monitor before processing the packet. The first part of packet processing is to calculate the checksum by calling a function. If the checksum is correct, the program continues with parsing the packet and constructing and sending a reply packet that contains the same data that the received packet contained.

Listing 5-1. Arduino Packet Echo Code, Part 1 of 3

```
#include <SoftwareSerial.h>
byte incomePacket[80];                          // buffer for incoming data
char incomeData [64];                           // phrased data holder
byte replyPacket[80];                           // packet construction buffer
byte sourceADR[10];                             // source addresses
int datalen;                                    // length of data received
int count;                                      // total length of incoming packet
int length;                                     // misc. length holder
byte calcsum ;                                  // checksum
SoftwareSerial softSerial(2, 3);         // the main software serial

void setup()  {
   Serial.begin(57600);        // serial to monitor
   softSerial.begin(9600);     // serial to XBee
   Serial.println("Ready");
} // end setup

void loop(){
  if (softSerial.available() && 0x7E == softSerial.read() ){ // check for start byte
    incomePacket[0] = 0x7E;
    count = 1;
    while (softSerial.available()){
      incomePacket[count] =  softSerial.read();  // receive the incoming packet
      count ++;  // keep track of incoming bytes
    }  // end while (softSerial.available())
    Serial.println ("Recived a new packet");
    Serial.print ("Incoming packet is: ");
    for (int i = 0 ; i < count-1 ; i++){    // print raw packet
      Serial.print (incomePacket[i],HEX);
      Serial.print (' ');
    }
    Serial.println (incomePacket[count-1],HEX);    // last byte of the raw packet
    calcChecksum ();
    if (calcsum == incomePacket[count-1]){  // throw error if the checksum does not match
      processPacket();
    } // end if calcsum
    else {
      Serial.println ("Error packet is not proper");  // the error when packets are malformed
```

```
        while (softSerial.available()){
        softSerial.read();  // on error flush software serial buffer
      }
    }
  }// end looking for start byte
}// end loop
```

Part 2 of the program contains the functions to calculate the checksum and parse the packets' data. The calcChecksum function pulls the length of the packet from the first two bytes after the packet start, and then the checksum is calculated before retuning back to the loop function. When the processPacket function is called, the user is informed that the packet has the correct checksum; the code then determines the packet type using the fourth position of the packet. The switch statement responds to a transmission-reply packet (0x8B) and a data-receive packet (0x90). The transmission-reply packet is handled by informing the user by printing to the serial monitor. The data packet is handled by parsing out the address of the sending XBee and pulling out the data to be used to construct a reply packet. During the whole process, the information is printed to the serial monitor.

Listing 5-1. Arduino Packet Echo Code, Part 2 of 3

```
void calcChecksum () {
  calcsum =0;       // begin calculating errorsum of incoming packet
  length = incomePacket[1] +incomePacket[2];
  for (int i = 3 ; i <= length+2 ; i++){
    calcsum = calcsum + incomePacket[i];
  }
  calcsum = 0xFF - calcsum;  // finish calculating errorsum
}     // end void calcChecksum ()

void processPacket(){
  Serial.println ("Packet has correct checksum ");
  switch (incomePacket[3]){  // check packet type and perform any responses
    case 0x90:
      Serial.println ("The packet is a data packet"); // announce packet type
      for (int i = 4 ; i <= 13 ; i++){  // get both addresses of the source device
        sourceADR[i-4]= incomePacket[i];
      }
      datalen = count - 16 ;  // reduce to just the data length to get the data
      for (int i = 15 ; i < datalen+15 ; i++){
        incomeData [i-15] = incomePacket[i]; // phrase out the data
      }
      Serial.print ("source addess is: ");  // begin printing 64 bit address
      for (int i =0 ; i < 7 ; i++){
        Serial.print (sourceADR[i],HEX);
        Serial.print (' ');
      }
      Serial.println (sourceADR[7],HEX); // finish 64-bit address
      Serial.print ("network addess is: "); // begin printing 16-bit address
      Serial.print(sourceADR[8] ,HEX);
      Serial.print (' ');
      Serial.println(sourceADR[9] ,HEX); // finish 64-bit address
      Serial.print ("the packet contains: ");  // start printing the data from packet
      for (int i =0 ; i < datalen ; i++){
        Serial.print (incomeData [i]);
```

```
    }
      Serial.println (" : For data");    // finish the data print
      constructReply();
      break; // done with the received packet
    case 0x8B: //start response to the return packet from sending data
      Serial.println ("Received reply ");
      break;
    default: // anouce unknown packet type
      Serial.println ("error: packet type not known");
  }// end switch
}    // end processPacket()
```

Part 3 of the code echoes the data received from another XBee. The reply packet is built one byte at a time in an array starting with the packet start frame, the type, and the frame ID. Portions of the packet that are a single-byte setting are set one at a time. The parts of the packet that are from the received packet are added to the outgoing packet via for loops (the parts added include the address to send the new packet to and a copy of the received data). When the packet is almost complete, the packet size is calculated and added. The final calculation to be added to the packet is for the checksum before the packet is sent, and the program continues waiting for new packets.

Listing 5-1. Arduino Packet Echo Code, Part 3 of 3

```
void constructReply(){
  Serial.println ("Constructing a reply packet"); // announce packet construction
  // start adding data to the reply packet buffer
  replyPacket[0] = 0x7E;     // start byte
  replyPacket[1] = 0; // 1st address byte will be zero with current limitations
  replyPacket[3] = 0x10;         // frame type
  replyPacket[4] =   1;          // frame ID
  for (int i =5 ; i <= 14 ; i++){     // add addresses
    replyPacket[i] = sourceADR[i-5] ;
  }
  replyPacket[15] = 0 ;           // set both options
  replyPacket[16] = 0 ;
  for (int i =17 ; i < datalen+17 ; i++){
    replyPacket[i] = incomeData [i-17];  // add data to packet
  }
  replyPacket[2] = 14 + datalen ;      // set the lower length byte
  calcsum = 0; // start calculating errorsum
  replyPacket[17 + datalen] = 0;
  for (int i = 3 ; i <= replyPacket[2]+3 ; i++){
    calcsum = calcsum + replyPacket[i];
  }
  replyPacket[17 + datalen]= 0xFF - calcsum; // finish packet by adding checksum
  Serial.print ("The packet is: ");  // start printing raw packet before sending
  for (int i = 0 ; i < replyPacket[2]+3 ; i++){
    Serial.print (replyPacket[i],HEX);
    Serial.print (' ');
  }
  Serial.println (replyPacket[17 + datalen],HEX); // finish printing packet
  Serial.println ("Sending Packet");    // start sending packet to original source
```

```
    for (int i =0 ; i <= 17 + datalen ; i++){
        softSerial.write ( replyPacket[i]);
    }
} // end void constructReply()
```

With everything compiled and hooked up, a prepared packet can be sent from the X-CTU's packet-assembly window. Watch the code's actions in a serial monitor that is connected to the Arduino. The serial monitor should start printing information when a packet is received and proceed through the programmed responses. This code is a demonstration of packet handling and sometimes messes up on receive and transmit packets, because of the lack of more robust error correction.

To make the error checking a bit more robust, you can the check the reply packet against the created checksum for the new packet and re-create it before the packet is sent. Other error checking can be performed with flow control, timeouts, resends, and packet-acknowledgement communication. The transmit status frame type (0x8B) that is returned when a packet is sent does not indicate that the packet was successfully received by anything other than XBee modules. A microcontroller should form a reply packet to the state of a received packet if the incoming packets are from serial out from an XBee module. This method of packet handling is demonstrated in greater depth in Chapter 8.

If the code in Listing 5-1 does not respond, resend the packet a few times before checking the configurations. You can also issue an ND command to check the XBee radio connection. If the radios can see one another, double-check the serial connections on the Arduino and, if necessary, revert to the software serial, and then double-check the code.

Endpoint Firmware

The last firmware option is that of endpoint for both AT and API modes. They act similarly to any other module firmware by issuing and receiving data. However, unlike the router and coordinator, end devices do not route packets to other devices. End devices also have the capability to enter sleep mode because they do not store routing information. Sleep mode makes end devices the preferred choice when making remote sensors or controllers that need low power consumption.

There are three types of sleep configuration that are set via the sleep mode (SM) register:

- Setting a value of 1 in the SM register will put the module in hibernate mode. When XBee pin 9 is high, the module will not respond to any transmissions or requests, but will return from sleep.

- Setting the SM register to 4 is for cyclic sleep. In this mode, the endpoint module will still respond to incoming transmissions. When using API mode, the extended timeout option (0x40) needs to be set in the packet's transmit options, giving the end device time to wake up and respond. The controlling program in this mode must wait till the Clear to Send (CTS) flow-control line is low.

- Setting the value to 5 works the same as 4, but allows a transition from low to high on XBee pin 9 to wake the module for transmission.

Endpoint modules have the capability to connect to either routers or coordinators. The code and setup for the last example will work for the end device.

1. For this setup, reconfigure the router module with ZIGBEE END DEVICE API.

2. Use the same settings to create a network, change the node identifier to ENDDEVICE, set the SM register to 4, and connect back to the Arduino.

3. Reconstruct the HELLO packet with 0x40 in the options byte, and send this packet to watch the code work. In this configuration, when the end device receives a packet, it will be awake for a period of time to allow the module to transmit the outgoing packet.

The next example (see Listing 5-2) Arduino sketch uses sleep mode 5, demonstrating a method of allowing other modules in the network to wake and send data to the end device, while allowing the code to wake up the module to send data. The code examples use the setup in Figure 5-4; the only change to the Arduino connections is that an extra connection is added between the serial adapter and the Arduino, connecting XBee pin 9 to Arduino pin 9. Both modules need to be set with AT command mode firmware—ZIGBEE COODINATOR AT for one and ZIGBEE END DEVICE AT for the other. The modules need the destination addressed set to be able to communicate. When configuring the end device, set the SM register to 5, allowing the code and other external events wake up the module.

Listing 5-2. Arduino Dual-Direction Communication with Sleep Mode Communications

```
#include <SoftwareSerial.h>
SoftwareSerial mySerial(2, 3); //rx,tx
void setup()  {
  pinMode (9 , OUTPUT);
  Serial.begin(9600);
  Serial.println("Ready");
  mySerial.begin(9600);
} // end setup

void loop() {
  digitalWrite (9 , LOW);
  if (mySerial.available())
    Serial.write(mySerial.read());
  if (Serial.available()){
    digitalWrite (9 , HIGH);  // transition from LOW to HIGH to wake up module
    delay (2);
    digitalWrite (9 , LOW);
    delay (2);                         // delay to give the chip time to recognize the transition
    mySerial.write(Serial.read());
  } // end if (Serial.available())

}   // end loop
```

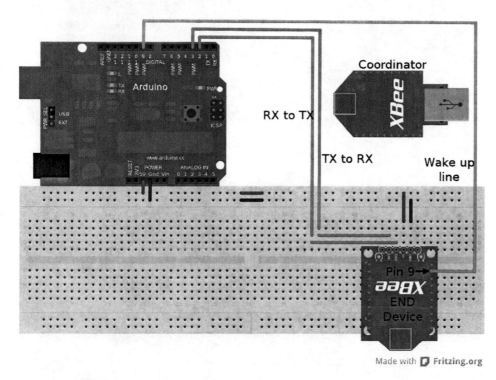

Coordinator

RX to TX

TX to RX

Wake up line

Pin 9→

XBee

END Device

Made with ⬛ Fritzing.org

Figure 5-4. *End-device configuration*

The code is a simple chat-style program that can receive data from another XBee and transmit data itself. With everything configured and plugged in, start a serial program to monitor and send data from the Arduino; use the terminal in the X-CTU's terminal for the coordinator. Any data typed into either terminal will show up on the other terminal. When typing in the terminal for the Arduino, the code does not echo the typed data back to the terminal; the local echo in the terminal would need to be set for you to see the typed characters. This setup is good when devices need to access or poll from the end device when power consumption is a concern.

Summary

This chapter demonstrated working with XBee modules in both AT command mode and API packet mode. There are a lot more configuration and communication options available, such as implementing encryption, working with other ZigBee-compatible devices, and using the other available pins for analog-to-digital sensors or controlling PWM. The XBee data sheet for the modules provides a wealth of information. This chapter did not discuss setting up a large network of XBees, but the concepts described are scalable.

■ ■ ■

## CHAPTER 6

Simulating Sensors

Arduinos can be used to simulate sensors for Arduinos or other platforms that use sensors. Simulating sensors allows you to produce repeatable and known data that can be used to test and debug systems, as well as explore sensors that may not be available. The concepts in this chapter focus on the connection types of various sensors instead of the data sent. Although the data is purposely skewed, it is being sent via the same methods used by the actual sensors. To better demonstrate that Arduinos can directly simulate the various sensors, reader code for each type of interface is included with the examples; this code is unmodified sensor reader code available from various sources.

These concepts are not designed to replace sensors, and may take more time to get working than using the actual sensor for small projects. The techniques of sensor simulation become useful for applications that require controlled data manipulation, such as robotic development, testing platforms, and studying how a sensor works. Ultimately, this chapter aims to help you get over some of the speed bumps you'll encounter when developing systems to simulate sensors or creating more complex sensor packages.

Sensors convert various physical changes to electrical data, which can then be read by computer systems. Temperature, position, and chemical concentrations are examples of physical elements that can be measured by sensors. When emulating sensors, it is not important to simulate the entire workings or the complete functionality; however, the data needs to be sent at the same time, in the same order, and with the same method as the sensor being simulated. Data sheets provide the necessary information for a sensor's important functions (e.g., data range, communication types, and data types). The hardware requirements for this chapter are two Arduino-compatible boards based on the ATmega 328P and a good assortment of general prototyping components. One Arduino is to be used as the sensor reader and the other is to simulate a sensor. Using two boards will accommodate a wide range of sensors and allows the sensor sketch to remain separate from the reader's sketch. This allows for the most accurate simulation in terms of program timing, and when the simulated sensor is replaced with a functional sensor, it requires no modification of the sketch on the reader side.

Analog Sensors

There are a variety of analog sensors that can measure temperature, movement, or position, for example. These types of sensors continuously control the output voltage, which is directly correlated with the state of the sensor. The output information can then be read by the Arduino when the analog pins are accessed. You could mimic the analog data with a potentiometer, but since a potentiometer is a sensor type itself, it is not effective for automated control.

The Arduino has analog inputs but no true analog out. There are methods to remedy the lack of analog output with a digital-to-analog converter (DAC) or a digital potentiometer, which are great for full production systems, but they are rarely found in the average collection of components. The examples in this section demonstrate how to make two different DACs using only resistors and capacitors to produce analog signals. The first example is focused on an Analog Devices TMP35 temperature sensor code for the Arduino.

Analog Sensor Reader

Listing 6-1 is the reader code for both analog sensor examples. This code should be loaded onto the Arduino that is to be used as the sensor reader; the other Arduino will be used as the sensor that provides the analog signal. The way the code works for Listing 6-1 has not been changed from the original online example from the LadyADA web site (located at www.ladyada.net/learn/sensors/tmp36.html), although the comments have been reworked. The example is for a temperature sensor, but the concept of reading the analog pin and then correlating the math with the sensor's output works for other analog-type sensors. Listing 6-1 reads analog pin 0 and prints the data converted to temperature to the serial monitor.

Listing 6-1. LadyADA Temperature Sensor Reader Code with Reworked Comments

```
int sensorPin = 0;

void setup() {
  Serial.begin(9600);
} // end void setup()

void loop() {
 int reading = analogRead(sensorPin);
 float voltage = reading * 5.0; // covert reading to voltage
 voltage /= 1024.0; // divide the income voltage by max resolution of the ADC
 Serial.print(voltage); Serial.println(" volts");
 float temperatureC = (voltage - 0.5) * 100 ; // reduce by 500mV and mutiply
                                              // 100 to get degrees Celcius
 Serial.print(temperatureC); Serial.println(" degrees C");
 float temperatureF = (temperatureC * 9.0 / 5.0) + 32.0; // convert C to F
 Serial.print(temperatureF); Serial.println(" degrees F");
 delay(1000);
} // end void loop()
```

RC Low-Pass Filter

The first method to achieve analog output is to use an RC low-pass filter. The filter is comprised of a capacitor and a resistor connected in serial. The capacitor is charged by a pulse-width modulation (PWM) signal from the Arduino and drains through the resistor to the analog input on the reading Arduino. This method of converting a digital signal to an analog signal works because a capacitor takes time to fully charge, and by controlling the time that the digital pin is high, the charge within the capacitor will achieve a percentage of the total voltage possible from the digital pin. A PWM at a duty cycle of 50 percent will charge to approximately 50 percent, making it half of the voltage available. For a digital pin capable of 5V, the total charge will be ~2.5V.

In this setup, if the capacitor is too small, it will drain faster than the pulses can charge it and not provide an adequate voltage to the analog pin; a large capacitor will increase the time the filter takes to drop from a full charge. As long as the capacitor value is not to small, a low capacitance can be used to simulate sensors that are very responsive and undergo rapid voltage changes. It may be advantageous on less responsive sensors to use not only a higher capacitance but a somewhat higher resistance to slow the voltage change. The resistor keeps the capacitor from draining back into the PWM pin: use a low resistance to avoid lowering the overall voltage. This method is an effective way to convert a digital signal to analog when precision is not as important because the PWM only has 256 steps (0 to 255) for a 5V system that is approximately 0.019 to 0.02V per step. There is also a small amount of jitter associated with the RC filter in this setup, which reduces the precision. This jitter is not entirely a bad thing, especially for a sensor setup such as a control loop that responds directly to the input. Simply, a sensor that sends an analog signal may experience some jitter, so a simulated sensor that jitters will in those cases better match the actual sensor.

To set up the hardware, refer to Figure 6-1; the 5V pins and one ground on each Arduino are hooked together so the sensor Arduino can get power and to ensure that the Arduinos can communicate by having a common ground (this is the same for all examples). The RC filter setup uses an electrolytic capacitor with the ground side hooked up to Arduino ground and the positive side to analog in on the reader. On the sensor Arduino, pin 9 is connected to one side of a resistor, and the other side is connected to the positive pin on the capacitor.

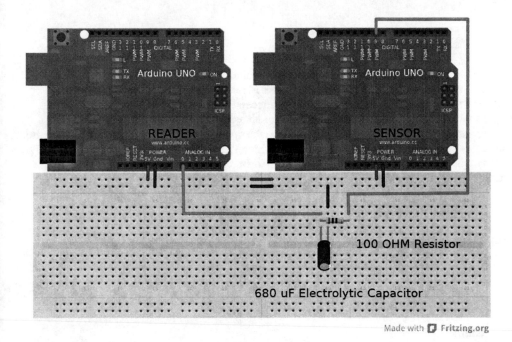

Figure 6-1. *RC low-pass filter setup*

Listing 6-2 demonstrates the output by manipulating a variable that is declared as type byte and then written to the PWM pin 9. Any type of manipulation can be performed on the sensorOut variable by receiving commands from the serial monitor to set the output value, or computing a range to better match the sensor type being simulated (such as one that sweeps from 0 to 100°C).

Listing 6-2. Code to Be Uploaded to the Sensor Arduino

```
byte sensorOut = 0x00;

void setup() {
 pinMode(9,OUTPUT); // serial can be set up here
}// end void setup()

void loop() {
  sensorOut++; // the manipulation of the output variable
  analogWrite (9,sensorOut); // the actual sensor simulation
  delay(1000); // delay is to match the update speed of the sensor
}// end void loop()
```

Verifying the Code

Once everything is uploaded and set up, plug in the USB from the computer to the reader Arduino and start the serial monitor. The reader will print what it receives off the analog pin and print the voltage, the degrees Celsius, and the Fahrenheit conversion. The sensor Arduino will output from 0V to ~5V at ~0.02V per step, or approximately –50°C to 450°C at 2C° per step.

Resistor Ladder

The resistor ladder, or R-R2 ladder, offers the other method to give an Arduino analog out. It uses 20 resistors, with 9 being one value and the other 11 being twice that value. An R-R2 ladder is essentially a network of voltage dividers. This method works by chaining many digital inputs to one output by successively changing voltage across different sets of resistors. This is a parallel binary method of controlling the output voltage. The lowest significant bit is the input closest to the ground resistor, and the highest significant bit is on the opposite end of the chain connected to the output. Figure 6-2 demonstrates a schematic of the resistor ladder, in which Vin 0 is the lowest significant bit and will have the smallest voltage change when it is in a high state. You can expand a resistor ladder to any bit resolution by adding extra Vin n+1 units to the end of the ladder.

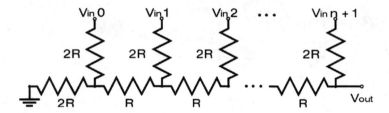

Figure 6-2. *R-R2 ladder schematic*

The resistor values used can be arbitrary, as long as one value is twice the value of the other and not so great as to affect the final output. Decent values to start with are 1kΩ and 470Ω. With a stack of 5% resistors and a good voltmeter, it is possible to get a good 2:1 ratio with these resistors. You can make an R-R2 ladder scalable to any bit precision by adding or removing two resistors from the chain.

For this example, a 10-bit converter will be made to match the resolution of the Arduino's ADC. Then the code will implement a 10-bit binary counter to control the constructed DAC. The resistor values will be referred to as 1R for the lower-value resistors and 2R for the ones of twice that value.

To get set up refer to Figure 6-3, start with one 2R and connect one end to ground and the other end to another terminal strip on the same side of the board. Then from that terminal strip in a continuing pattern down that side of the board place the nine 1R connecting, the last one to analog pin 0 on the reader Arduino. The remaining ten 2Rs have one end placed at all the junctions of the 1R and the other end connected to sensor Arduino pins starting from pin 2 to pin 11 in order from the resistor closest to the ground 2R. The other remaining connections are the 5V and ground pins between the Arduinos. The code for the reader is the same as loaded for the RC low-pass filter.

Figure 6-3. R-R2 ladder setup

The sensor code implements a basic binary counter and introduces the use of programming an Arduino using the AVR registers. The use of the registers in some cases can simplify the code and make it smaller, but it also increases the complexity of the program. Four registers will need to be manipulated for this code: DDRB, DDRD, PORTB, and PORTD. The first four letters of these names refer to the register's type, and the last letter designates which set of pins on the Arduino is being referenced. All the ports discussed are going to be 8 bits in size (or 2 nybbles).

- If the register descriptor is followed by a D, this refers to pins 0 through 7.

- If followed by a B, then it refers to pins 8 through 13, with the last two bits being unusable on anything being referenced to B.

Correlating the binary to the pin starts at the lowest significant bit as read, so to turn on pin 0 the Arduino PORTD will be equal to 0b00000001.

- The DDRx is the data direction register, which tells the pins whether to be input(0) or output(1). This is done by setting the DDRx equal to a byte of data, such as DDRD = 0b11100011, which will tell pins 7,6,5,1, and 0 to be outputs and pins 4, 3, and 2 to be inputs. Setting pins by this method is the same as calling the pinMode(pin, direction) function for each pin in the setup() function. If serial functions are still required, the two lower bits on *xxxx*D must be left alone, making the whole byte unavailable.

- Setting the PORTx register equal to a byte allows the groups of pins to be turned on or off within one line of code, depending on the bytes. In contrast, if a variable is set to equal a PORTx, then the contents of the register are read, and, depending on the mode that is set in the DDRx, will determine where the bits of data come from: internally for output(1) and externally for input(0).

You need to load the code from Listing 6-3 onto the Arduino to use it as the sensor. The code sets up pins 2 through 11 with the register to demonstrate the same function as pinMode(). The code then counts a variable of type unsigned int up to a value of 1024 so that the count will not continue to the maximum 16-bit value of 65535, truncating the count to 10 bits by an AND mask. The code then shifts the data to match the proper pins and masks out unneeded bits with the bitwise AND, placing the data in respective registers. Because the Arduino IDE is built on top of the AVR C compiler, nothing needs to be included or declared to use the register names; they can just be typed and work the same way as any variable.

■ **Caution**   Manipulating the registers directly is an advanced programming technique that may not work consistently on all Arduino-capable boards. Check the pin mapping for the specific board and the data sheet for the register. For example, the Arduino Mega PORTB controls pins 10 through 13 as the upper four bits and pins 50 through 53 for the lower four bits.

Listing 6-3. Sensor code

```
unsigned int manipVar=0; // the only variable needed to achieve output

void setup() {
DDRD = DDRD | 0b11111100; // set pins 2-7 as output  or leave pins 1,2
                          // alone for serial comunications
DDRB = DDRB | 0b00001111; // set 8-11 as output, leaving the rest alone
} // end void setup()

void loop() {
  manipVar++; // any manipulation can be performed on manipVar
  manipVar &= 0b0000001111111111; // mask that resets manipVar when 1024 is
                                  // reached
  PORTD = (manipVar << 2) & 0b11111100;// shift left by 2 bits then mask
                                       // to get pins 2-7 straight out of manipVar
                                       // then write value to pins on pins 2-7
  PORTB = (manipVar >> 6) & 0b00001111;// shift right by nibble+crumb
                                       // to set the value for pins 8-11
  delay (1000); // to match refresh of sensor type
} // end void loop()
```

Verifying the Code

With the code uploaded to both Arduinos and the breadboard populated, plug in the reader and start the serial monitor. The same information that was displayed in the last example will print to the screen this time, with approximately 0.0048V per step, or about 0.5°C and the same temperature range.

This method reduces the jitter that is associated with the RC filter and matches the maximum resolution of the ADC, making it a better choice to simulate an analog sensor. The disadvantages are the number of pins used, the number of parts, and the advanced programming method required to achieve a clean count. With the setup demonstrated in this section minus the delay, it takes around 4ms to count from 0 back to 0, making a ~250HZ sawtooth wave and about 4µs between output changes. If the code is kept small, it is feasible to make a lightweight function generator out of an Arduino by looping a byte array; it is also feasible to simulate piezoelectric knock sensors.

■ **Note** To explore this code a bit more, replace the R-2R ladder with an array of ten LEDs, hook up a potentiometer to analog 0, and then set manipVar equal to analogRead(0) and lower the delay to 100 ms. Power up and watch the conversion from the potentiometer to binary.

Digital Sensors

When working with sensors, it often feels like there are as many different ways to digitally work with them as there are sensor types. This section covers a common cross-section of communication styles. To simulate these sensors, it is important to match the specifications of the various protocols. Data can be sent or received, sent in any order, sent to multiple devices, or requested at any time, making some of these devices very difficult to implement. Both the devices and the Atmel data sheets are valuable resources for determining the best method needed to simulate a sensor.

PWM

PWM sensors are not as common as other types, but still deserve an honorable mention. PWM is commonly used to control servos; in a sense, PWM sensors replace the R/C receiver, which is arguably a type of sensor. Although the microcontrollers used in Arduino lack some elements to precisely match the specifications of a majority of the sensors that use PWM as a data mechanism, they are capable of reading them. The pulseIn() function can read the output PWM signal of another pin with enough consistency that a data correlation can be formed. The code that can be used to simulate a sensor of this type is similar to the code in Listing 6-2; couple that with a lack of sensors that implement PWM within the timing tolerances of the Arduino, and there is no need for an example in this section. The use of this style of passing digital information can be useful in the creation of other sensor packages.

Gray Code

Gray code is a digital method that uses two or more pins to produce a square wave that is out of phase from one sensor output pin to another. The method of phasing multiple signals allows the direction and position changes to be read at any time. The way in which the square waves are out of phase determines whether the bit shift is left or right. Gray code is also known as *reflected binary*, and is commonly used to make sensors that convert either linear or angular movement into countable pulses to determine position, direction, and speed. This is how scroll wheels on computer mice work. Gray code is also commonly used in robotics for rotary encoders. If one output is read as a reference signal on either a falling or rising logic, then the other outputs read at that time will denote the direction. If the second output is LOW before the first pin is read, it is moving one direction, and if HIGH, it is going the other direction.

The minimum amount of pins needed for this sensor is two for data and one for ground/voltage supply. The more logic pins a sensor has, the more accurate it can be, by providing the ability to error-check for missing pulses. Figure 6-4 shows the pulses of a dual-output encoder with one output read as rising and falling; the state of the second output depends on the shift direction of the first output at read time.

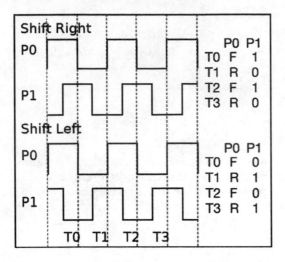

Figure 6-4. *Pulses of a dual-output encoder*

It is up to the reader/controller to keep track of the pulses to determine if a full rotation or swing has been achieved. The code for the reader also has to determine the direction the gray code is shifting. For the sensor reader, Dr. Ayars wrote an article on how to read a rotary encoder (SparkFun part number COM-09117). In this example, the code increments/decrements a variable depending on the direction the encoder was traveling when the detent was reached, but not the number of rotations preformed. More information on reading this type of sensor is available on Dr. Ayars' blog, at http://hacks.ayars.org/2009/12/using-quadrature-encoder-rotary-switch.html.

The technique used in Listing 6-4 is one method of reading gray code and is excellent for reading two output encoders. A more advanced method is needed for three or more pin encoders to achieve the error correction of positioning and count. The following code needs to be loaded on the Arduino to be used as the reader for the first half of this example.

Listing 6-4. Dr. Ayars' Code with Reworked Comments

```
byte Blinker = 13;
int Delay = 250;
byte A = 2;// 1st sensor Out pin
byte B = 3;// 2nd sensor Out pin
volatile int Rotor = 0; // sensor click count

void setup() {
   pinMode(Blinker, OUTPUT);
   pinMode(A, INPUT);
   pinMode(B, INPUT);
   digitalWrite(A, HIGH); // Turn on pull-up resistors
   digitalWrite(B, HIGH);
   attachInterrupt(0, UpdateRotation, FALLING);// use interrupt on pin A
   Serial.begin(9600);
}// end setup()

void loop() {
 digitalWrite(Blinker, HIGH); // Blink LED
  delay(Delay);                // any code can run here. the sensor will be
 digitalWrite(Blinker, LOW);  // updated upon interrupt on pin 2.
  delay(Delay);
} // end loop()
```

```
void UpdateRotation() {
  // update sensor's reading upon the falling edge of pin 2
  if (digitalRead(B)) {
    Rotor++;              // increment direction if second pin is HI
  }                       // at time of the interrupt
  else {
    Rotor--;              // decrement direction if second pin is LOW
  }                       // at time of the interrupt
  Serial.println(Rotor, DEC);
} // end UpdateRotation()
```

Outputting Gray Code

For the Arduino to mimic the gray code, it must produce multiple square waves that are evenly out of phase from one to another. Using a series of digitalWrite() function calls to control the output pins' states and a delay() to control the phase is a perfect way to control a series of digital signals that need a specific order. One digitalWrite() is used per output of the rotary encoder to be mimicked, with a delay() after each write to make an overlap of the digital cycle. An encoder that has two outputs needs two digitalWrite() calls in a loop, with a delay() after each write, flipping the state that is written to the pin each time the loop is run. A square wave will be produced, having a total cycle time equal to twice the total delay time. Each time the loop is run, one half of the gray code cycle is output. The order in which the pins are manipulated determines the direction of the encoder; the orders are opposite if the forward order goes from pin 1 to 3 and the reverse order goes from 3 to 1. The percentage of time that the cycle is out of phase is controlled by the delay() after the digitalWrite(). To calculate the phase difference, the individual delay() is divided by total delay(). For two outputs having a total delay of 6ms and individual delays of 3ms, the second output is out of phase by 50 percent.

Some rotary encoders have outputs that are out of phase by 100 percent, being in completely opposite states. To achieve a four-output encoder with the third output being the opposite of the first output and still having an even distribution of phase, the first output has to flip state at the same time as the third, and the fourth output needs no delay, creating a cycle of 6ms with a 1ms phase shift. The cycle time created is representative of how fast the sensor can be manipulated.

To calculate the maximum rate an encoder can simulate, divide 60 by the total cycle time multiplied the total steps over a specific distance. The distance for rotary style is one revolution and the linear distance can be inches, centimeters, or another unit. The encoder being emulated for the example has a cycle of 12 steps per revolution. The shortest cycle time implemented by the reader code is 8ms, making the calculation 60s / (0.008s / step * 12 steps / revolution) = 625rpm. The digitalWrite() is negligible in calculating maximum manipulation speed. The added time is about 6.75μs for this code, giving a 0.3% tolerance. If the delay is removed, the sensor can run at about 1.8 million rpm.

Calculating the maximum speed capable is not for determining the delay to use, but for information about the application of the simulated hardware in control feedback loops. The delay to use between the pin writes should be at least 1ms, and a separate delay should be used to control and vary the manipulation speed. If the sensor code is having problems accurately reading the sensor's output, increase the delay between the digitalWrite() function calls.

The setup for the hardware is as shown in Figure 6-5, with reader pins 2 and 3 connected to sensor pins 10 and 11, respectively. Two momentary switches used to control the direction of the output pulses are connected to ground and independently connected to sensor pin 2 for down and 3 for up. The code from Listing 6-5 needs to be loaded on the Arduino to be used as the sensor. The reader Arduino is loaded with the code from Listing 6-4. Simulating this rotary encoder requires one more pin than the actual sensor; the ground and 5V pins need to be connected between the two Arduinos.

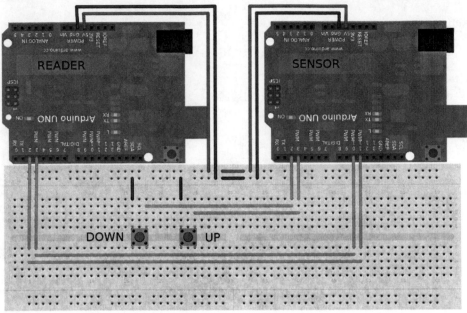

Figure 6-5. *Gray code simulation setup*

Listing 6-5. Arduino Sensor Code

```
byte first , second; // order of pin change
boolean click , stateChang;// send click and the state to change to variables

void setup() {
  pinMode(2 , INPUT); // encoder down button
  pinMode(3 , INPUT); // encoder up button
  pinMode(11 , OUTPUT); pinMode(10 , OUTPUT); // encoder outputs
  digitalWrite(2 , HIGH); digitalWrite(3 , HIGH);  // input pull-up resistors
  digitalWrite(10 , HIGH); // initial state
  digitalWrite(11 , LOW);
  stateChang = true;
}// end void setup()

void loop() {
  if (digitalRead(2) == 0 ){ // down
    first = 10; second = 11; // pin 10 writen befor pin 11 for down diretion
    click = true;
  }
  if (digitalRead(3) == 0 ){ // up
    first = 11; second = 10; // pin 11 written before pin 10 for up direction
    click  = true;
  }
  if (click == true ) {  // send 1/2 pulse when a button is pressed
  stateChang = !stateChang; // flip the state to be written
  digitalWrite(first, stateChang); // change 1st pin
  delay (2); // delay befor changinng next pin
```

```
    digitalWrite(second , stateChang); // change 2nd pin
    delay (2); // delay befor changning next pin at highest speed
    click = false ; // reset
    }
     delay (100); // slowing the code down = moving encoder slower
}// end void loop()
```

Verifying the Code

With everything set up, plug the reader Arduino into the computer and start the serial monitor. The reader prints the count when pin 2 transitions low, decrementing or incrementing the count depending on the incoming signal. The sensor Arduino will send one-half of the gray code per button press. If a button is held down, a continuous signal will be sent at a maximum rate of 208ms, as defined in the code. When the code is running and the buttons are not being pressed, the Arduino will be held in the last state. Using this sensor simulation is very helpful in debugging control code for robots CNC or any system using control loops.

▓ **Note**   If an oscilloscope is not available to visualize what happens in the sensor code, increase all the delays to about 200ms and replace the reader with two LEDs.

Serial Sensors

Serial communication is one of the cornerstone communication types in computer engineering, and many sensors communicate via this method. Serial sensors are capable of sending and receiving more information than analog sensors by sending data by the byte. Setting up a simulated serial sensor is simple on the Arduino using the built-in serial functions or with software serial. The trick is matching the baud rate and the actual data being sent; the specifications should be available on the sensor's data sheet. It is recommended that software serial be used so that the other serial connection is still available for control and monitoring.

Outputting Serial Data

The sensor for this section is the blue Parallax RFID reader that transmits serial at a baud of 2400. The RFID reader reads special tags that contain a 40-bit identifier that is transmitted as ten hexadecimal numbers converted to plain ASCII. A byte with a value of 10 is sent at the beginning of the tag code and is ended by a byte value of 13; there is also a pin to activate the RFID reader. The code for the Arduino to access the RFID information is available at http://arduino.cc/playground/Learning/PRFID, in the section modified by Worapoht K. using software serial. Upload Listing 6-6 to the Arduino that will be used for retrieving the RFID data.

Listing 6-6. Worapoht K. Code with Reworked Comments

```
#include <SoftwareSerial.h>
int  val = 0; // temporary holder
char code[10]; // the Tag ID
int bytesread = 0; // byte count
#define rxPin 8 // RFID reader SOUT pin
#define txPin 9 // no connection

void setup() {
  Serial.begin(2400);   // Hardware serial for Monitor 2400bps
```

```
  pinMode(2,OUTPUT); // RFID ENABLE pin
  digitalWrite(2, LOW);     // Activates RFID reader
} // end void setup()

void loop() {
  SoftwareSerial RFID = SoftwareSerial(rxPin,txPin);
  RFID.begin(2400);
  if((val = RFID.read()) == 10) {    // check for header
    bytesread = 0;
    while(bytesread<10) {  // read 10-digit code
      val = RFID.read();
      if((val == 10)||(val == 13)) {  // check for a value of 10 or 13
        break;                        // stop reading
      }
      code[bytesread] = val;          // add the digit
      bytesread++;                    // ready to read next digit
    }
    if(bytesread == 10)  {  // if 10-digit read is complete
      Serial.print("TAG code is: ");   // possibly a good TAG
      Serial.println(code);            // print the TAG code
    }
    bytesread = 0;    // reset byte count
    delay(500);
  }
} // end void loop()
```

As shown in Figure 6-6, this simulated sensor setup is very similar to the actual sensor: pin 2 on both Arduinos are connected together, and pin 8 on the reader is connected to pin 9 on the sensor Arduino. Also, the 5V and GND need to be connected.

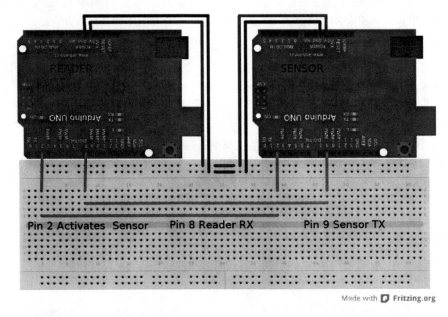

Figure 6-6. RFID serial setup

Listing 6-7 shows the code for simulating the RFID.

Listing 6-7. RFID Simulator

```
#include <SoftwareSerial.h>

void setup() {
  Serial.begin(2400);  // Hardware serial for Monitor 2400bps
  pinMode(2,INPUT);
} // end void setup()

void loop() {
  SoftwareSerial RFID = SoftwareSerial(8,9); // pin 8 noconnect, pin 9 transmit
  RFID.begin(2400);
  if(LOW == digitalRead(2)) {   // does the sensor need to be active
  RFID.write(10);  // transmit header
  RFID.write("HelloWorld"); // transmit Tag ID code
  RFID.write(13); // transmit end
  }
} // end void loop()
```

Verifying the Code

Get everything uploaded and connected, and start the serial monitor running at 2400 baud. The code for simulating the RFID sensor sets up software serial at 2400 baud, and then waits for pin 2 to be low before sending the data sequence. The data that is sent to the reader Arduino starts with a byte value of 10 and ends with a byte value of 13. HelloWorld will then be printed to the serial monitor TAG code is:. HelloWorld just happened to be ten characters and can be replaced with actual tag codes. Sometimes incoherent data will be printed. This is caused by the serial not being synchronous. More code is needed to verify the data, but for this application, it just needs to get at least one good RFID code to compare to the list of valid codes to perform an action.

I2C

The communication method I2C, also known as two-wire, is a synchronous serial communication method using one wire for a clock signal and another wire for data. I2C is a cousin to basic serial, with a few differences in what the hardware does during communications. Sensors that use this type of communication can handle a wide variety of data, devices, and commands. Sensors that communicate via I2C can have multiple functions measuring multiple activities on the same package. The sensor that will be simulated in this section is the SRF10 Ultrasonic Ranger Finder. Its code is included in the Arduino IDE by selecting File ➤ Examples ➤ Wire ➤ SFRRange_reader, and should be loaded on the Arduino to be used as the reader.

I2C data transfers happen on one wire, meaning that one only device can transmit at a time; however, more than two devices can be connected together with just two wires. In most common I2C setups, there is one master device that is the receiver of the data and the controller of what devices communicate. Arduino includes a library that implements this communication, and for most basic setups, it works well, especially when used on the master device. The library lacks a bit of finesse that is required when attempting to simulate the workings of an I2C sensors, however.

Getting the best control to simulate sensors using I2C requires manipulating the hardware registers; this method of setting up the I2C bus is a bit more complicated, but isn't difficult once you have a bit of understanding of the registers.

▓ **Note**   Refer to section 22.5 in the ATmega 328P data sheet (pages 223–247); this section gives an overview of the I2C module included in the Arduino's microcontroller.

I2C communications happen on analog pin 5 for the shared clock (SCL) and analog pin 4 for data (SDL). TWAR, TWCR, TWDR, and TWSR are the four registers that are used to set up I2C slave mode. TWBR is a fifth register in the I2C hardware and is unimportant for slave applications. TWBR is used in master mode to control the SCL speed. SREG is the one register outside the I2C module that will have to be modified for this section. Registers work the same way as variables in that all the manipulation methods for variables work the same way. The register names have already been defined by the main libraries used by the Arduino IDE; declarations to use them are not necessary. All the registers used in this section are 1 byte in size. Some of the registers are for data and others are for control.

The TWCR Register

The TWCR register is the two-wire control register; this is what defines the main working of the I2C communications. Each bit in the byte of the TWCR register controls a different function within the hardware; the name of the bit describes its location within the byte.

- To put the Arduino into slave mode, you must set the TWI Enable Acknowledge (TWEA) and TWI Enable (TWEN) bits to 1 in the TWCR. TWEN (bit 2) activates the I2C hardware, and TWEA (bit 6) tells the hardware to send acknowledgments when appropriate; if the TWEA is not set, this device will not respond to other devices trying to communicate.

- TWI Interrupt (TWINT) (bit 7) and TWI Interrupt Enable (TWIE) (bit 0) are the other two bits that are important in the TWCR and are used for software control. TWINT is a flag that gets set to 1 when there is something that needs attention from the software; the software then has to clear the flag by writing 1 to the TWINT bit when it's finished handling what needed attention. You can also set up TWINT in conjunction with TWIE as an internal interrupt.

Data being transferred on the I2C is time sensitive, so it is wise to set the communications to be handled using the internal interrupts on the Arduino. This is accomplished by setting the TWIE and the global interrupt enable in the SREG to on. SREG needs to be set with a bitwise OR (|) mask so that the other bits are not manipulated, and has to be reset every time an interrupt happens. When the TWINT flag gets set to 1 by the hardware, the interrupt is triggered. The interrupt service routine (ISR(vector)) is run when an interrupt is triggered; the ISR() works very similarly to a normal function such as Setup() or Loop(). ISR() can be written directly in the Arduino sketch with no preceding information, but a vector is required. A *vector* is a name that describes the interrupt that the ISR responds to for code execution.

▦ **Note** A reference of the vector names used in the AVR libraries that the Arduino is built upon is located at www.nongnu.org/avr-libc/user-manual/group__avr__interrupts.html. The vector name that is needed for I2C interrupt on the Arduinos with the 328P chips is TWI_vect.

The TWAR Register

The last register that has to be set to get the I2C slave to respond to information moving on the bus is an address. The address is set in the TWI Address Register (TWAR). The top seven bits (7-1) are the address; bit 0 tells the device that it is OK to respond to the general call address. The general call address is 0, and when the master sends this address, every device set to have a response will respond. When the address is set to the TWAR register, it has to shift to the left by 1, making 126 unique devices that can be on the I2C bus.

The TWDR Register

The TWI Data Register (TWDR) is where all the data bytes will go through. When this register is written (TWDR = FOO;), a data transfer will begin. To read the incoming data, read the data register into a variable (FOO = TWDR). I2C uses unique start and stop values to encapsulate the data; this leaves a full byte for data transmission. This is unlike plain serial, where a portion of a byte is used to denote the beginning and end of larger data amounts, as in the previous example. The TWI Status Register (TWSR) makes it easier to send larger variable types and keep them in proper order.

The TWSR Register

The TWSR register contains information about what is happening on the I2C bus, such as data direction, errors, and transmission requests. Reading the TWSR is important for controlling the software; there is a list of status codes in the TWI module section of the Atmel data sheet. 0X80 and 0XA8 are the codes of interest for simulating the sensor. 0X80 tells the code that there is incoming data that needs to be read, and 0XA8 tells the sensor to transmit its data. There are three bits in this register—located from 2 to 0—that are not important for the running of the slave and need to be masked out (0b11111000) by a bitwise AND (&); the status codes are calculated for this and do not need any shift.

Outputting I2C Data

Setting up the example as shown in Figure 6-7 involves using two pull-up resistors to make sure the SCL and SDA line are high in accordance with the requirements of I2C. The Arduinos are connected through analog pins 4 and 5, as well as ground and power. The code in Listing 6-8 is uploaded to the Arduino that is to be used as the sensor.

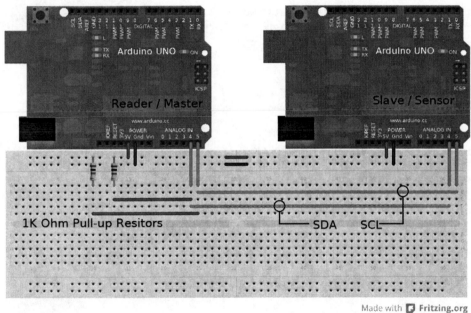

Made with 🟧 Fritzing.org

Figure 6-7. *I2C setup*

The code demonstrates how to implement I2C communications by directly manipulating hardware registers while combining direct AVR C and Arduino code. For clarity, the value that is set to the registers is in binary, matching the position of the bit in the register. The code increments manipVar each time the loop function is run. The LED on the board turns on or off depending on the command received from the master. All the communication happens in the ISR() function; the data manipulated in the interrupt has to be global; it is not possible to pass data to the ISR() function, because it is called from hardware, not code.

Listing 6-8. I2C Simulated Sensor Code

```
byte address = 112; // address of this sensor
unsigned int manipVar = 0; // variable to change data
byte bytessent = 2 ; // number of bytes to send
byte bytestosend[2] ; // prepare data to send
byte command = 0 ; // command storage

void setup() {
TWAR = (address << 1) | 0b00000001; // set address and general call response
TWCR = 0b01000101; // set TWEA TWEN and TWIE to 1
SREG |= 0b10000000; // enable global interrupt
pinMode(13 , OUTPUT);
} //end void setup()

void loop() {
    if (command == 0x50){  // turn ON LED to a command 0x50
      digitalWrite (13 , HIGH);
    }
    if (command == 0x02){ // turn OFF LED to a command 0x02
      digitalWrite (13 , LOW);
    }
     manipVar++; // main variable to manipulate outdata two bytes
      bytestosend [0] = manipVar;  // prepare manipVar in to HI and LOW bytes
      bytestosend [1] = manipVar >> 8 ; // manipVar HI
     delay (250); // something else to do while wating
} // end void loop()

ISR (TWI_vect){  // interrupt service routine set to vector
    if (TWCR & (1 << TWINT)) {  // double-check for proper interrupt
       if ((TWSR & 0b11111000) == 0x80){ // incoming data
         command = TWDR; // copy command data for future use
         TWCR = 0b11000100; // reset back to original config
       }
       if ((TWSR & 0b11111000) == 0xA8 ) { // request for outgoing data
         while (bytessent > 0 ){ // send bytes to master
           bytessent--;
           TWDR = bytestosend [bytessent]; // send data from HI to LOW byte
           TWCR = 0b11000101; // reset for each send
           delay (5); // pause a moment on send
         }
           if (bytessent == 0 ){ // reset byte count check to see if empty
           bytessent = 2;
           }
       } // end if ((TWSR & 0b11111000) == 0xA8 )
       TWCR = 0b11000101; // one last reset to make sure
       SREG |= 0b10000000; // reenable interrupt
    } // end if (TWCR & (1 << TWINT))
} // end ISR (TWI_vect)
```

Verifying the Code

With everything set up and loaded onto the respective Arduinos, plug the reader into the USB and start the serial monitor. Consecutive numbers should print to the screen, counting up, and the simulated sensor's LED should blink when the master sends specific commands. Using direct register manipulation to replicate sensors allows maximum control of the I2C interface that the library does not currently allow.

■ **Note** Chapter 10 on multi processing, covers methods of SPI communication that can be applied for sensor simulation.

Summary

The techniques described in this chapter are not limited to sensors, and can be applied to other systems that move data from one component to another. This chapter focused on the connection of the sensor to the Arduino, because that is the most difficult hurdle in simulating sensors.

When writing code to simulate sensors, work slowly and tackle one part of the sensor at a time to avoid complications. Also take the time to practice writing code to simulate sensors that are readily available for verification against the code you created.

CHAPTER 7

■ ■ ■

PID Controllers

Proportional-Integral-Derivative (PID) is a cornerstone algorithm in control theory. The PID algorithm smoothly and precisely controls a system, such as temperature in an oven or the position of a control surface on an airplane. A PID controller works by calculating an amount of error based upon the difference between a set value and a feedback value, and provides an adjustment to the output to correct that error. The control and decision of the adjustment is done in math instead of pure logic control such as `if...else` statements. PID controllers have many types of uses, including controlling robotics, temperature, speed, and positioning. The basics, coding setup, and tuning of PID controllers for the Arduino platform are discussed in this chapter.

The Mathematics

Setting up a PID controller involves constantly calculating an algorithm. The following equation is the sum of the three parts of PID: *proportional*, *integral*, and *derivative*. The equation for the PID algorithm attempts to lower the amount of difference between a setpoint (the value desired) and a measured value, also known as the *feedback*. The output is altered so that the setpoint is maintained. PID controllers can easily work with systems that have control over a variable output.

The variables of the equation are

- E: The calculated error determined by subtracting the input from the setpoint (Sp - Input)
- t: The change in time from the last time the equation has run
- Kp: The gain for the proportional component
- Ki: The gain for the integral component
- Kd: The gain for the derivative component

The Proportional Statement

The *P* in *PID* is a proportional statement of the error, or the difference between the input and the setpoint value. Kp is the gain value and determines how the P statement reacts to change in error; the lower the gain, the less the system reacts to an error. Kp is what tunes the proportional part of the equation. All gain values are set by the programmer or dynamically via a user input. The proportional statement aids in the steady-state error control by always trying to keep the error minimal. The *steady state* describes when a system has reached the desired setpoint. The first part of the proportional code will calculate the amount of error and will appear something like this:

```
error = setpoint - input ;
```

The second part of the code multiplies the error by the gain variable:

```
Pout = Kp * error;
```

The proportional statement attempts to lower the error by calculating the error to zero where input = setpoint. A pure proportional controller, with this equation and code, will not settle at the setpoint, but usually somewhere below the setpoint. The reason the proportional statement settles below the setpoint is because the proportional control always tries to reach a value of zero, and the settling is a balance between the input and the feedback. The integral statement is responsible for achieving the desired setpoint.

■ **Note** If Kp is set too high, the system will become unstable. The gain value when this happens is different for each system.

The Integral Statement

The *I* in *PID* is for an integral; this is a major concept in calculus, but integrals are not scary. Put simply, *integration* is the calculation of the area under a curve. This is accomplished by constantly adding a very small area to an accumulated total. For a refresher of some calculus, the area is calculated by length × width; to find the area under a curve, the length is determined by the function's value and a small difference that then is added to all other function values. For reference, the integral in this type of setup is similar to a Riemann sum.

The PID algorithm does not have a specific function; the length is determined by the error, and the width of the rectangle is the change in time. The program constantly adds this area up based on the error. The code for the integral is

```
errorsum = (errorsum + currenterror) * timechange;
Iout = Ki * errorsum ;
```

The integral reacts to the amount of error and duration of the error. The errorsum value increases when the input value is below the setpoint, and decreases when the input is above the setpoint. The integral will hold at the setpoint when the error becomes zero and there is nothing to subtract or add. When the integral is added to proportional statement, the integral corrects for the offset to the error caused by the proportional statement's settling. The integral will control how fast the algorithm attempts to reach the setpoint: lower gain values approach at a slower rate; higher values approach the setpoint quicker, but have the tendency to overshoot and can cause ringing by constantly overshooting above and below the setpoint and never settling. Some systems, like ovens, have problems returning from overshoots, where the controller does not have the ability to apply a negative power. It's perfectly fine to use just the *PI* part of a PID equation for control, and sometimes a PI controller is satisfactory.

■ **Note** The integral will constantly get larger or smaller depending on how long there is an error, and in some cases this can lead to windup. *Windup* occurs when the integral goes outside the feasible output range and induces a lag. This can be corrected by checking if Iout goes outside the output range. To correct for this, check Iout and reset it to the bound it exceeded.

The Derivative Statement

The *D* in *PID* is the derivative, another calculus concept, which is just a snapshot of the slope of an equation. The slope is calculated as *rise over run*—the *rise* comes from the change in the error, or the current error subtracted from the last error; the *run* is the change in time. When the rise is divided by the time change, the rate at which the input is changing is known. Code for the derivative component is

```
Derror = (Error - lasterror) / timechange ;
Dout = Kd * Derror ;
```

or

```
Derror = (Input - lastinput) / timechange ;
Dout = Kd * Derror ;
```

The derivative aids in the control of overshooting and controls the ringing that can occur from the integral. High gain values in the derivative can have a tendency to cause an unstable system that will never reach a stable state. The two versions of code both work, and mostly serve the same function. The code that uses the slope of the input reduces the derivative kick caused when the setpoint is changed; this is good for systems in which the setpoint changes regularly. By using the input instead of the calculated error, we get a better calculation on how the system is changing; the code that is based on the error will have a greater perceived change, and thus a higher slope will be added to the final output of the PID controller.

Adding It All Up

With the individual parts calculated, the proportion, integral, and the derivative have to be added together to achieve a usable output. One line of code is used to produce the output:

```
Output = Pout + Iout + Dout ;
```

The output might need to be normalized for the input when the output equates to power. Some systems need the output to be zero when the setpoint is achieved (e.g., ovens) so that no more heat will be added; and for motor controls, the output might have to go negative to reverse the motor.

Time

PID controllers use the change in time to work out the order that data is entered and relates to when the PID is calculated and how much time has passed since the last time the program calculated the PID. The individual system's implementation determines the required time necessary for calculation. Fast systems like radio-controlled aircraft may require time in milliseconds, ovens or refrigerators may have their time differences calculated in seconds, and chemical and HVAC systems may require minutes. This is all based on the system's ability to change; just as in physics, larger objects will move slower to a given force than a smaller ones at the same force.

There are two ways to set up time calculation. The first takes the current time and subtracts that from the last time and uses the resulting change in the PID calculation. The other waits for a set amount of time to pass before calculating the next iteration. The code to calculate based on time is as follows and would be in a loop:

```
// loop
now = millis() ;
timechage = (now - lasttime);
// pid caculations
lasttime = now;
```

This method is good for fast systems like servo controllers where the change in time is based on how fast the code runs through a loop. Sometimes it is necessary to sample at a greater time interval than that at which the code runs or have more consistency between the time the PID calculates. For these instances, the time change can be assumed to be 1 and can be dropped out of the calculation for the I and D components, saving the continual multiplication and division from the code. To speed up the PID calculation, the change in time can be calculated against the gains instead of being calculated within the PID. The transformation of the calculation is `Ki * settime` and `Kd / settime`. The code then looks like this, with gains of .5 picked as a general untuned starting point:

```
// setup
settime = 1000 ; // 1000 milliseconds is 1 second
Kp = .5;
Ki = .5 * settime;
Kd = .5 / settime;
// loop
now = millis() ;
timechage = (now - lasttime);
if (timechange >= time change){
    error = Setpoint - Input;
    errorsum = errorsum + error;
    Derror = (Input - lastinput);
    Pout = Kp * error;
    Iout = Ki * errorsum ;
    Dout = Kd * Derror ;
    Output = Pout + Iout + Dout ;
}
```

PID Controller Setup

Now that the math and the framework are out of the way, it is time to set up a basic PID system on an Arduino. This example uses an RC low-pass filter (from Chapter 6) with an added potentiometer to simulate external disturbance.

Wiring the Hardware

Set up an Arduino as per Figure 7-1. After the Arduino is set up with the components, upload the code in Listing 7-1.

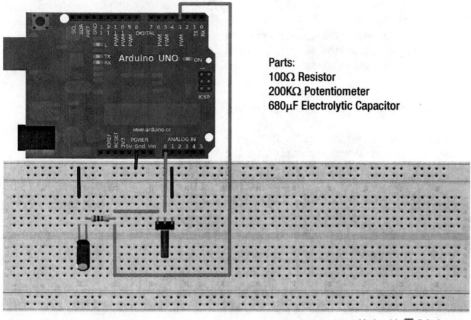

Parts:
100Ω Resistor
200KΩ Potentiometer
680µF Electrolytic Capacitor

Made with **Fritzing.org**

Figure 7-1. *PID example circuit setup*

Listing 7-1. Basic PID Arduino Sketch

```
float Kp = .5 , Ki = .5, Kd = .5 ; // PID gain values
float Pout , Iout , Dout , Output; // PID final ouput variables
float now , lasttime = 0 , timechange; // important time
float Input , lastinput , Setpoint = 127.0; // input-based variables
float error , errorsum = 0, Derror; // output of the PID components
int settime = 1000; // this = 1 second, so Ki and Kd do not need modification
void setup (){
   Serial.begin(9600); // serial setup for verification
} // end void setup (){

void loop (){
   now = millis() ; // get current milliseconds
   timechange = (now - lasttime); // calculate difference
   if (timechange >= settime) { // run PID when the time is at the set time
      Input = (analogRead(0)/4.0); // read Input and normalize to output range
      error = Setpoint - Input; // calculate error
      errorsum = errorsum + error; // add curent error to running total of error
      Derror = (Input - lastinput); // calculate slope of the input
      Pout = Kp * error;  // calculate PID gains
      Iout = Ki * errorsum ;
      Dout = Kd * Derror ;
      if (Iout > 255)         // check for integral windup and correct
         Iout = 255;
```

```
      if (Iout < 0)
         Iout = 0;
      Output = Pout + Iout + Dout ; // prep the output variable
      if (Output > 255)  // sanity check of the output, keeping it within the
            Output = 255; // available output range
      if (Output < 0)
            Output = 0;
      lastinput = Input; // save the input and time for the next loop
      lasttime = now;
      analogWrite (3, Output); // write the output to PWM pin 3
      Serial.print (Setpoint); // print some information to the serial monitor
      Serial.print (" : ");
      Serial.print (Input);
      Serial.print (" : ");
      Serial.println (Output);
   } // end if (timechange >= settime)
} // end void loop ()
```

Verifying the Code

Run the code uploaded to the Arduino and start the serial monitor. The code will print one line containing the Setpoint : Input : Output values, and print one line per iteration of the running PID about every second. The system will stabilize around a value of the setpoint—the first value of every printed line in the serial monitor. However, because of the inherent noise in the RC filter, it will never settle directly at the setpoint. Using an RC circuit is one of the easier ways to demonstrate a PID controller in action, along with the noise simulating a possible jitter in the system. The potentiometer is used to simulate a negative external disturbance; if the resistance on potentiometer is increased, the controller will increase the output to keep the input at the setpoint.

■ **Note**   If the Arduino were fast enough and had a higher precision on the PWM, it would be possible to eliminate the jitter in the RC filter with a PID controller.

PID Tuner

To graphically represent the different controllers in real time and on actual hardware, there is an app called PID tuner available at the books github repository (https://github.com/ProArd/Pidtuner). PID Tuner implements the P, I, and D types of controllers with the openFrameworks-and-Firmata combination (as in Chapter 3). Figures 7-2 through 7-4 were made from the PID Tuner app (see the next section, in which we'll start to examine different types of controllers in more detail). The PID Tuner application was developed to provide a functional graphical front end to the Arduino hardware and implement a few control algorithms for testing and tuning purposes. With PID Tuner, it is possible to test many different gain values without having to upload a new sketch to the Arduino each time.

After downloading the file, do the following:

1.   Unzip it to the openFrameworks apps /myapps folder.

2.   Change the serial port connection to connect to an Arduino configured as shown in Figure 7-1 and loaded with the standard Firmata sketch.

3.   Open the PID folder and compile the project.

Once the PID Tuner is compiled and running, and the Arduino is set up as per Figure 7-1, the program controls the PWM pin for the PID controller and simulates a linear rise and fall time for both an ON/OFF and a DEAD BAND controller; the application uses single key commands to set tuning.

- Keys o, y, and h turn on or off a single controller type:
    - o = PID
    - y = ON/OFF
- Keys c, r, and z clear, reset, and zero the graph:
    - c = clear
    - r= reset
    - z = zero
- Keys S and s increase and decrease the first setpoint, and A and a increase and decrease the second setpoint that is used for the DEAD BAND controller.
- Keys M and m increase and decrease the PWM output on the Arduino.
- Keys p, i, and d turn on and off the individual statements of the PID controller.
- Keys Q, W, and E increase the individual gain values for the PID controller in .01 increments. q, w, and e decreases the gains:
    - Q = Kp + .01
    - q = Kp − .01
    - W = Ki + .01
    - w = Ki − .01
    - E = Kd + .01
    - e = Kd − .01
- The spacebar starts and stops the reading of controllers and pauses the graph's output.

■ **Note**   As of the writing of this book, the PID Tuner app is in preliminary development; it may be a bit buggy, and it requires the connection to be manually changed in the code. The application also runs at the fastest running speed and assumes a nonadjustable time of 1.

Comparing PID, DEAD BAND, and ON/OFF Controllers

With a basic PID controller set up and running, it is time to discuss a couple of other common control methods and how they compare to PID. Both DEAD BAND and ON/OFF controllers are from the logic controller family, meaning they use logic controls such as if/else statements to determine how to change the output.

The DEAD BAND controller is common for thermostats, where a high and a low value are set. If the input is below the low value, the controller turns on the output, and vice versa for the high value, creating a range that output must be kept within.

The ON/OFF controller is much like the DEAD BAND controller, but uses only a single setpoint. When the input is below the value, the output is turned on, and then it is turned off when above the setpoint.

Figure 7-2 is the graph of a PID using the RC filter; the gains are equal to .5 for this particular tuning and setup. There is a slight overshoot produced, but the system quickly reaches a steady state, with an approximate steady-state error of +/−4. This is normal for the noise produced in the system.

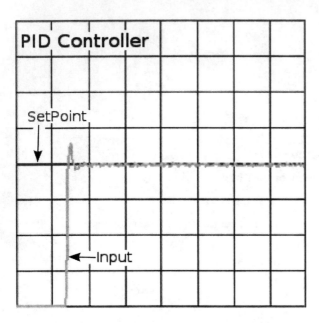

Figure 7-2. *A graph of a PID setup with an RC low-pass filter*

Figure 7-3 demonstrates an ON/OFF controller that has a higher rise and a slower fall per program step; this simulates how an thermostat might work. This controller is set up with the same components as Figure 7-2, just using different code. One of the biggest comparisons between the ON/OFF and the PID is the steady state contains much more disturbance and there is no direct control on how long the system will stay at the setpoint.

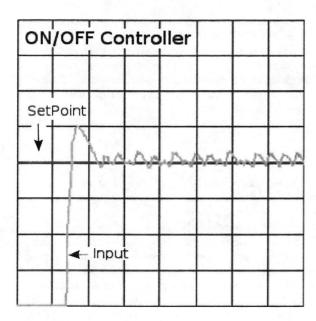

Figure 7-3. *An ON/OFF controller*

Figure 7-4 shows a DEAD BAND controller using the same setup as the preceding graphs. The DEAD BAND is formed by a high setpoint and a low setpoint. The advantage this provides over a basic ON/OFF is that the cycle frequency is decreased to lower the amount of switching of the state either on or off. This is the average controller style for HVAC systems, where turning on and off can lead to higher power consumption and increased mechanical fatigue.

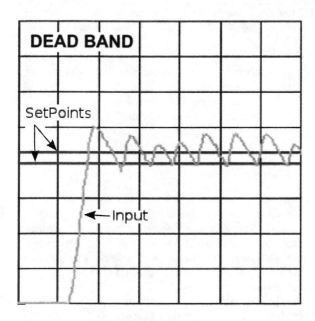

Figure 7-4. *A DEAD BAND controller*

The main disadvantages of the both of these logic controllers is in the control of the output being discrete. With the output control being just on or off, there is no prediction on the change of the output that will allow us to determine how far they are from the setpoints. However, logic controllers are usually easier to set up and implement than PID controllers, which is why it is more common to see these controllers in commercial products. PID controllers, though, have a distinct advantage over logic controllers: if they are implemented properly, PID controllers won't add more noise to a system and will have tighter control at a steady state. But after the math, it is the implementations that make PID controllers a bit more difficult to work with.

PID Can Control

There are many ways to implement a PID with a proper match to a sensor and an output method. The math will remain reliability constant. There may be a need for some added logic control to achieve a desired system, however. This next section provides a glimpse of other PID implementations and some possible ideas.

It is common for PID controllers to be used in positioning for flight controls, balancing robots, and some CNC systems. A common setup is to have a motor for the output and a potentiometer for the input, connected through a series of gears, much the same way a servo is set up. Another common implementation is to use a light-break sensor and a slotted disk as the input, as would be found in a printer. This implementation requires some extra logic to count, store, and manipulate steps of the input. The logic would be added to control the motor's forward or reverse motion when counts are changed. It is also possible to use rotary encoders or flex sensors for the input. Many types of physical-manipulation system can be created from electric-type motors and linear actuators—for example, air and hydraulic systems.

Systems that control speed need sensors that calculate speed to power output, such as in automotive cruise control, where the speed is controlled by the throttle position. In an automotive application, a logic controller would be impractical for smoothly controlling the throttle.

Controlling temperature systems may require other logic to control heating and cooling elements, with discrete output such as relays. PID controllers are fairly simple to plan when the output is variable, but in systems that provide only on-or-off output, this planning can be more complicated. This is accomplished in much the same way as PWM charges a compositor to produce a voltage output that an ADC can read. The PID controller needs a bit of logic to control the time at which the element is turned on. With temperature-based PID controllers, the gains may have to be negative to achieve a controller that cools to a setpoint.

With a proper type of sensor and a way to control output, a PID can be implemented for chemical systems, such as controlling the pH value of a pool or hot tub. When dealing with systems that work with chemicals, it is important that the reaction time is taken into account for how and when the reagents are added.

Other PID systems can control flow rates for fluids, such as using electric valves and moisture meters to control watering a garden or lawn. If there is a sensor that can measure and quantify, and a way to control, a PID can be implemented.

Tuning

The tuning of a PID can be where most of the setup time is spent; entire semesters can be spent in classes on how to tune and set up PID controllers. There are many methods and mathematical models for achieving a tune that will work. In short, there is no absolute correct tuning, and what works for one implementation may not work for another. How a particular setup works and reacts to changes will differ from one system to another, and the desired reactions of the controller changes how everything is tuned. Once the output is controllable with the loopback and the algorithm, there are three parameters that tune the controller: the gains of Kp, Ki, and Kd. Figures 7-5 through 7-7 show the differences between low gain and high gain using the same setup from earlier in the chapter.

The proportional control gains control how aggressively the system reacts to error and the distance from the setpoint at which the proportional component will settle. On the left of Figure 7-5, using a gain of 1, the system stabilizes at about 50 percent of the setpoint value. At a gain of 7 (the right side of Figure 7-5), the system becomes unstable. To tune a decent gain for a fast-reacting system, start with the proportion, set the integral and the derivative to zero, and increase the Kp value until the system becomes unstable; then back off a bit until it becomes stable again. This particular system becomes stable around a Kp value of 2.27. For a slower system or one that needs a slower reaction to error, a lower gain will be required. After the proportional component is set, move on to the integral.

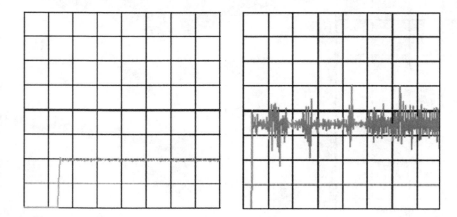

Figure 7-5. *Proportional control: Kp = 1 (left) and Kp = 7 (right)*

Figure 7-6 demonstrates the addition of the integral component, making a PI controller. The left side of the figure shows that a lower Ki gain produces a slower controller that approaches the setpoint without overshoot. The right side of the figure, with a gain of 2, shows a graph with a faster rise, followed by overshoot and a ringing before settling at the setpoint. Setting a proper gain for this part is dependent on the needs of the system and the ability to react to overshoot. A temperature system may need a lower gain than a system that controls positing; it is about finding a good balance.

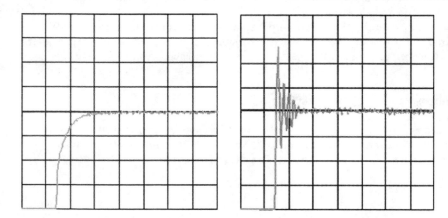

Figure 7-6. *Proportional integral control: Kp = .5; Ki = .1 (left) and Ki = 2 (right)*

The derivative value is a bit more difficult to tune because of the interaction of the other two components. The derivative is similar to a damper attempting to limit the overshoot. It is perfectly fine omit the derivate portion and simply use a PI controller. To tune the derivative, the balance of the PI portions should be as close as possible to the reaction required for the setup. Once you've achieved this, then you can slowly change the gain in the derivative to provide some extra dampening. Figure 7-7 demonstrates a fully functional PID with the PID Tuner program. In this graph, there is a small amount of overshoot, but the derivate function corrects and allows the setpoint to be reached quickly.

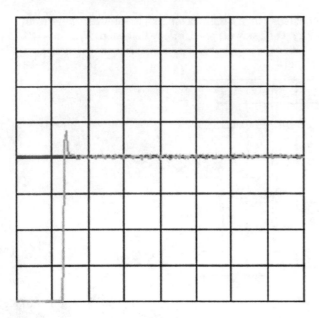

Figure 7-7. *A full PID controller using an Arduino and an RC low-pass filter, with the following gains: Kp = 1.5, Ki =.8, and Kd = .25*

PID Library

There is a user-made library available from Arduino Playground that implements all the math and control for setting up a PID controller on an Arduino (see `www.arduino.cc/playground/Code/PIDLibrary/`). The library makes it simple to have multiple PID controllers running on a single Arduino.

After downloading the library, set it up by unzipping the file into the Arduino `libraries` folder. To use a PID controller in Arduino code, add `#include <PID_v1.h>` before declaring variables `Setpoint`, `Input`, and `Output`. After the library and variables are set up, you need to create a `PID` object, which is accomplished by the following line of code:

```
PID myPID(&Input, &Output, &Setpoint, Kp, Ki, Kd, DIRECT);
```

This informs the new `PID` object about the variables used for `Setpoint`, `Input`, and `Output`, as well as the gains `Kp`, `Ki`, and `Kd`. The final parameter is the direction: use `DIRECT` unless the system needs to drop to a setpoint.

After all of this is coded, read the input before calling the `myPID.Compute()` function.

PID Library Functions

Following is a list of the important basic functions for the PID library:

- `PID(&Input, &Output, &Setpoint, Kp, Ki, Kd, Direction)`: This is the constructer function, which takes the address of the `Input`, `Output`, and `Setpoint` variables, and the gain values.

- `Compute()`: Calling `Compute()` after the input is read will perform the math required to produce an output value.

- `SetOutputLimits(min ,max)`: This sets the values that the output should not exceed.

- `SetTunings(Kp,Ki,Kd)`: This is used to change the gains dynamically after the PID has been initialized.

- `SetSampleTime(milliseconds)`: This sets the amount of time that must pass before the `Compute()` function will execute the PID calculation again. If the set time has not passed when `Compute()` is called, the function returns back to the calling code without calculating the PID.

- `SetControllerDirection(direction)`: This sets the controller direction. Use `DIRECT` for positive movements, such as in motor control or ovens; use `REVERSE` for systems like refrigerators.

Listing 7-2 is a modified version of the basic PID example using the PID library given at the library's Arduino Playground web page (`www.arduino.cc/playground/Code/PIDLibrary/`). The modifications to the sketch include a serial output to display what is going on. There is a loss in performance when using the library compared to the direct implementation of Listing 7-1, and the gains had to be turned down in comparison while using the same hardware configuration as in Figure 7-1. The library can easily handle slower-reacting systems; to simulate this. a lager capacitor can be used in the RC circuit.

Listing 7-2. PID Impemented with the PID Library

```
#include <PID_v1.h>

double Setpoint, Input, Output;
float Kp = .09;
float Ki = .1;
float Kd = .07;

// set up the PID's gains and link to variables
PID myPID(&Input, &Output, &Setpoint,Kp,Ki,Kd, DIRECT);

void setup(){

  Serial.begin(9600);
  // variable setup
  Input = analogRead(0) / 4; // calculate input to match output values
  Setpoint = 100   ;
  // turn the PID on
  myPID.SetMode(AUTOMATIC);
  // myPID.SetSampleTime(100);
}

void loop(){

  // read input and calculate PID
  Input = analogRead(0) / 4;
  myPID.Compute();
  analogWrite(3,Output);

 // print value to serial monitor
  Serial.print(Setpoint);
  Serial.print(" : ");
```

```
  Serial.print(Output);
  Serial.print(" : ");
  Serial.println(Input);
}
```

Other Resources

For reference, here is a list of some online resources that will help expand your knowledge of the topics covered in this chapter:

- http://wikipedia.org/wiki/PID_controller

- www.siam.org/books/dc14/DC14Sample.pdf

- www.arduino.cc/playground/Code/PIDLibrary/

- http://brettbeauregard.com/blog/2011/04/improving-the-beginners-pid-introduction/

- http://sourceforge.net/projects/pidtuner/

Summary

This chapter provided the basic information for setting up a PID controller on an Arduino and listed some possible applications. There are a lot of different setups that a PID can fulfill, and some can be difficult to achieve. However, with some experimentation and exploration, you can learn to use PID controllers to your advantage.

■ ■ ■

## CHAPTER 8

Android Sensor Networks

A sensor network is a series of stand-alone distributed sensor nodes that communicate information to a gateway for retrieval. Sensor networks are used to monitor a wide range of conditions over a greater area than is possible with a single sensor package. There is no typical setup for a sensor network; networks can range from just a few nodes to hundreds, collecting any kind of imaginable data. Sensor networks are commonly used for industrial, security, and scientific applications and can be set up as passive data collectors or active controllers. Sensor networks are not made upon any single technology; they are made by integrating a variety of other technologies.

Arduino provides a great development platform for sensor packages for data logging and system control. A sensor node is created when a sensor package is integrated with a communication method such as Bluetooth, Ethernet, XBees, Cellular/GSM, or light to create a network. Arduino has been used to make sensor networks to monitor environmental changes. For example, a distributed sensor network was created for the Fukushima nuclear disaster to keep track of radiation levels. The network for Fukushima used a combination of GSM and Ethernet to pass information from a Geiger sensor to a web service. Sebastian Alegria, a high-school student from Chile, created another successful example of a sensor network to detect and warn of earthquakes. Sebastian's system used a simple seismometer to detect events that could cause destruction, his system passed the information through the Internet via Ethernet and used a buzzer to provide a local warning.

Sensor networks don't have to be as grand as these two examples, however. For example, they can be made to monitor temperatures around a house or keep track of inventory being shipped out of a warehouse. When developing a sensor network, keep in mind of all the development requirements and choose the sensors and communication methods accordingly. For systems that monitor a smaller area, XBee modules can be used to avoid the need to run cabling. In harsh environments, a network that uses cabling might be needed. XBee modules and cable-based systems are great methods for creating stand-alone networks that don't rely on other infrastructure systems but limit the range in which a sensor network can feasibly be created. To increase a senor network to a range that can monitor across a country or the world, it might be preferential to use an existing communication infrastructure, such as the Internet or telephone.

Android is a useful platform to integrate into a sensor network because of the variety of roles it can fill, along with its popularity and ease of development. Android can be used as a method to receive or send sensor information via a web service. Bluetooth can be used to wirelessly obtain data from a factory's sensor network. Android in conjunction with the Open Accessory development kit can provide a portable method to retrieve data from a stand-alone sensor network.

This chapter focuses on building a small sensor network that integrates XBees, Android, and Arduino. The sensor network uses hardware that has been used in other chapters. The Mega ADK, SD breakout, XBee modules, XBee adapters, and an Android device are all required for this chapter. openFrameworks, Eclipse, and Arduino IDEs will also need to be available to complete the sensor network in this chapter.

■ **Caution**   This chapter uses concepts from and builds upon Chapters 3, 4, and 5. I recommend reading these chapters (on openFrameworks, the Android ADK, and XBees, respectively) before continuing with this chapter.

Setting Up a Sensor Network

When starting the development of a sensor network, decide what information needs to be collected. This will help when qualifying sensor types. After determining the information to be collected, make a list of the requirements for the environment that the sensor network is to be deployed in. The environment has the biggest impact on what technologies to use; in an urban environment, power may be more readily available than in a rural or wilderness environment, where power may have to be generated or batteries extensively used. Wireless is probably the easiest type of node to deploy, but may have some reliability issues in environments with high electromagnetic interference; in such cases, shielded cabling may need to be run. The communication method also needs to not interfere with the sensor readings. If RF information is being collected, wireless may have to be avoided or the interference may have to be zeroed out of the information. In some special cases, fiber optics may be the best choice.

The sensor's resolution is one factor that can determine the resolution of the whole network. The resolution can also be determined by the collection rate required by the system being monitored, with the amount of data collected to be sufficient for the application. The requirements need to be considered when starting to develop a sensor network. Systems that monitor machinery may require continuous sensor output every few milliseconds or even seconds, while networks measuring tidal flow may only need to be read every few minutes or even once an hour to achieve sufficient resolution. Some other requirements to plan for are how the collected data will be processed. The network will need sufficient processing power if the data needs to be processed in real time. The network will need to store the data if it's to be processed at a later time than when it is collected.

Sensor networks do not need to be complex or use a lot of hardware in the initial development stages. Usually a sensor network has one gateway for the data and one to a few different node types to collect the data. Building a sensor network can start with a one or two nodes and a gateway and be planned to be expandable. In the initial stages of development, the passing of data is more important than the data itself. The data can be simulated to provide a constant to compare how successful the data transmission is.

The example in this chapter sets up a simple sensor network that demonstrates the integration of some of the technologies and concepts introduced in earlier chapters. The example is not a complete project to make a fully working sensor network.

The example creates a simulated sensor node with three different sensors that transmit predefined data for each sensor to the Mega ADK for logging and further retrieval by the Android device. The XBee modules are set up as router and coordinator in API mode with a baud of 115200. The pan ID needs to match on both XBees, but there is no need for the destination address to be set. The code implements a bit of error correction to ensure that the data is logged properly to the SD card and the serial connections stay synced. The Android device will be set up to pull a log from the Mega ADK and display the data via a graph. The Arduino connects the Android device, SD card, and XBee to create a data gateway. The Arduino also responds to the sensor node to confirm data was received or that the packet was malformed. Figure 8-1 shows the configuration of the Arduino Mega ADK.

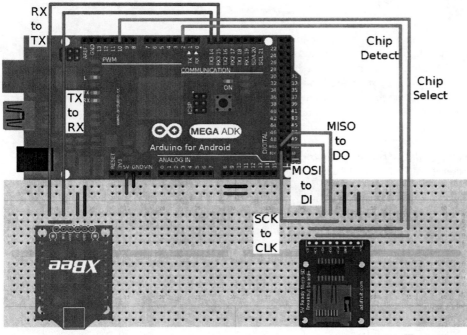

Figure 8-1. *Arduino setup for sensor log node*

As shown in Figure 8-1, the XBee module is connected to serial 3 on the Mega ADK; other connections are TX to RX and RX to TX, with the 5V and GND pins connected accordingly. On the SD adapter, the DI and DO pins are connected to the MOSI and MISO pins on the Mega ADK, CLK is connected to SCK, CS is connected to Arduino pin 10, and CD is connected to pin 2.

Set up the Arduino Mega ADK as shown in Figure 8-1, with the XBee module configured as the router and inserted in the serial adapter, and the coordinator plugged into the USB adapter. Individually testing each component attached to the Mega ADK before developing the code is vital to ensure that the hardware will not present many problems in the debugging stages. To test that the SD card can read and write, open the ReadWrite sketch in File ➤ Examples ➤ SD and add the line pinMode (53, OUTPUT); to make sure the slave select pin will not pull the Arduino out of SPI master mode. Change the line if (!SD.begin(4)) to if "(!SD.begin(10))" to map the SD card to the chosen slave-activation pin. Insert an SD card into the adapter and upload the ReadWrite sketch to the board. Start the serial monitor at baud 9600 and check that the sketch successfully runs.

To test the XBee modules, open the software serial sketch example and modify it to accommodate the serial of the Arduino Mega ADK by changing all occurrences of mySerial to Serial3. Before uploading the sketch, remove the #include and SoftwareSerial code lines at the beginning of the program and change both baud rates to 115200 to match the current XBee configuration. Once the programs is running on the Arduino, plug in the USB explorer to a computer and start the X-CTU software, and try sending the HELLO packet from Chapter 5. The packet is

7E 00 13 10 01 00 00 00 00 00 00 FF FF FF FE 00 00 48 45 4C 4C 4F 7F

The packet should be entered into the packet assembly window in the terminal tab of the X-CTU software. The packet should show up on the serial monitor with a few unreadable characters along with a readable "HELLO." You don't need to test the Android ADK functionality if you've already completed the corresponding exercise in Chapter 5. The coding can begin for the sensor network components once the XBee and the SD card have been successfully tested.

openFrameworks

openFrameworks is used for this setup to create an application to create and transmit known data as a simulated sensor network over a single XBee module connected to a computer. As in Chapter 3, a program is created in a C++ compiler such as Code::Blocks and is made of at least three source files. A copy of the empty example found in openFrameworks directory/apps/myApps can be used as a base for the first part of the sensor network code. You need to modify the main.cpp file to set the drawing window to a smaller size by changing the ofSetupOpenGL function call to create a 276×276-pixel window. Change the call to match the following line of code: ofSetupOpenGL(&window, 276, 276, OF_WINDOW);.

testapp.cpp handles data creation and packet construction, responds to flow control, and graphically draws and indicates what data is being sent. The testapp.cpp code can be replaced with the code from Listing 8-1. The example is made of seven different functions. Part 1 sets up the serial connection declared by the serial object in testapp.h. The serial is connected to the location of the USB serial adapter (COM or TTY, depending on the system) and is connected at 115200 baud. The setup function initializes a destination address of a broadcast for this example, as well as flags needed for program control. Three unsigned byte arrays of 256 bytes are filled with data created by a sine wave–generation equation. The sine waves are zeroed at a value of 127. The sine wave follows the form $y = a + b\sin(k(x - c))$, where a is the vertical transformation, b is the amplitude, c sets the horizontal shift, and k affects the period. The data generated will be drawn to the computer's screen and sent over the XBee module to be eventuality displayed on an Android device.

Listing 8-1. testApp.cpp, Part 1 of 7

```
#include "testApp.h"
void testApp::setup(){
  printf ("Start \n");
  serial.setup("/dev/ttyUSB0", 115200); // change to match where the Arduino is connected
  for (int i = 0; i < 256; i++){
    graph[i] = 127 + (100 * sin((1*(PI/127))*(i-0))); // sine functions
    graph1[i] = 127 + (75 * sin((2*(PI/127))*(i-10)));  // normalized in a 256×256-value area
    graph2[i] = 127 + (50 * sin((3*(PI/127))*(i-40)));
  } // end data fill installation
  for (int i = 0; i < 10; i++){
    destADR[i] = 0x00;  // set the 64-bit broadcast address
  } // end address fill
  destADR[6] = 0xFF; // set network broadcast address
  destADR[7] = 0xFF;
  destADR[8] = 0xFF;
  destADR[9] = 0xFE;
  point = 0; // zero data point indicator
  counts = 0; // used to delay packet send timing
  SensorsSent [0] = false; // packet flags
  SensorsSent [1] = false;
  SensorsSent [2] = false;
  FirstPacketsent = false;
} // end testApp::setup()
```

The next function is the loop that runs constantly during program execution. The update function waits for a set time to pass before trying to send the each of the sensor's data. The time is based upon the amount of times the update function is run and will vary depending on the complexity of the code run. On average, the data is sent in intervals of half a second. Each time a data packet is sent, the code waits for a reply of an "OK" or "BAD," signifying whether it should move on to the next packet or resend the last. Once all three sensors have been sent, the program starts sending the next data position in the array. All three of the sensor's data packets could be sent in one packet, but for this demonstration they are split up to represent different nodes.

Listing 8-1. testApp.cpp, Part 2 of 7

```cpp
void testApp::update(){
  unsigned char DatatoSend[3] ;
  if (counts == 500){
    printf ("sensor 1 \n");
    DatatoSend[0] = 'S';
    DatatoSend[1] = '1';
    DatatoSend[2] =  point;
    DatatoSend[3] = graph[point];
    CreatePacket(DatatoSend, 4);
    WaitForReply();
    SensorsSent [0] = true;
  }
  if (counts == 1000){
    printf ("sensor 2 \n");
    DatatoSend[0] = 'S' ;
    DatatoSend[1] = '2' ;
    DatatoSend[2] =  point;
    DatatoSend[3] = graph1[point] ;
    CreatePacket(DatatoSend , 4 );
    WaitForReply();
    SensorsSent [1] = true;
  }
  if (counts == 1500){
    printf ("sensor 3 \n");
    DatatoSend[0] = 'S';
    DatatoSend[1] = '3';
    DatatoSend[2] =  point;
    DatatoSend[3] = graph2[point] ;
    CreatePacket(DatatoSend , 4 );
    WaitForReply();
    SensorsSent [2] = true;
  }
  if (SensorsSent [0] == true && SensorsSent [1] == true && SensorsSent [2] == true){
    printf ("reset counts move point \n");
    counts = 0;
    point++;
    SensorsSent [0] = false;
    SensorsSent [1] = false;
    SensorsSent [2] = false;
  }
  counts++;
  CheckForIncoming();
} // end testApp::update()
```

The last thing that the update function performs is to check for incoming data on the serial connection. Part 3 is the function that performs the check for incoming packets. The function tries to capture a complete packet from the XBee module and check to see if the packet has the correct checksum before attempting to read what the packet is and performing an action based on the packet's information. The capture length is calculated by the first two bytes received after the packet start byte, not by the amount of available serial data. The buffer is cleared after each packet is captured and read. To attempt to keep the serial data incoming constantly, the buffers are cleared and variables reinitialized if an incoming packet is malformed.

Listing 8-1. testApp.cpp, Part 3 of 7

```cpp
void testApp::CheckForIncoming(){
  incomingPacketChecksum = 0;
  incomingByteLen = 0;
  if (serial.available() && 0x7E == (incomingBuffer[0] = serial.readByte())){
    printf ("Incoming packet \n");
    incomingBuffer[1] = serial.readByte(); // pull packet length
    incomingBuffer[2] = serial.readByte();
    incomingByteLen = incomingBuffer[1] + incomingBuffer[2];
    for (int i  = 3; i <= incomingByteLen + 3; i++){  // receive the rest of the packet's data
      incomingBuffer[i]  = serial.readByte();
      incomingPacketChecksum += incomingBuffer[i]; // add byte to checksum calculation
    }
    incomingPacketChecksum = (0xFF - incomingPacketChecksum);
    incomingByteLen += 3;
    if (incomingByteLen > 0 &&
      incomingPacketChecksum == incomingBuffer[incomingByteLen + 1 ] ){
      printf ("Has Corect Checksum \n");
      ReadPacket();
      serial.flush(true, true); // flush incoming and outgoing serial buffers
    }
    else {
      printf ("Check Sum Error\n");
      serial.flush(true, true);
      incomingByteLen = 0;
      incomingPacketChecksum = 0;
      for (int i = 0; i <= 80; i++){
       incomingBuffer[i] = 0;
      }
    } // end the error else statement
  } //end if (serial.available() && 0x7E ==...
} // end testApp::CheckForIncoming()
```

The function in part 4 reads the packet when called via a switch statement to determent the packet type and associated method of reading. This function responds to three different packet types: an AT command response packet, a transmit response, and a data packet and announces that the packet type is unknown in response to all other packet types. The program uses data packets transmitted for the Arduino to determine if the packet was sent properly; if the packet is returned "BAD," the program resends the packet till an "OK" is returned. This is a simplified method of error correction that is handled by the next function.

Listing 8-1. testApp.cpp, Part 4 of 7

```cpp
void testApp::ReadPacket(){
  switch (incomingBuffer[3]){  // check packet type and perform any responses
    case 0x90:
      dataLength = incomingByteLen - 15;  // reduce to just the data length to get the data
      for (int i = 0; i <= dataLength; i++){
        incomeData [i] = incomingBuffer[i+15]; // phrase out the data from the packet
      }
      if (dataLength == 2 && incomeData[0] == 'O' && incomeData[1] == 'K'){
        printf ("OKAY\n");     // set Okay flag true when a good reply is received
        ReplyOK = true;
      }
      if (dataLength == 3 && incomeData[0] == 'B' && incomeData[1] == 'A' &&
        incomeData[2]  == 'D' && FirstPacketsent){
        ReplyOK = false;  // make sure that the flag is false when a BAD notify is received
        printf ("BAD\n");
        serial.writeBytes (packetBuffer, lastPacketLength); // send last known packet
        WaitForReply();  // wait again for an okay
      }
      break;
    case 0x8B:
      printf ("Transmt Responce\n");
      break;
    case 0x88:
      printf ("Command response %X%X \n", incomingBuffer[8] , incomingBuffer[9]);
      break;
      default: // announce unknown packet type
      printf ("error: packet type not known\n" );
  } // end switch
} // end  testApp::ReadPacket()
```

In part 5, the WaitForReply function is called after sending a packet to the Arduino, and will remain in a loop, constantly polling for new packets. The loop is complete when the reply comes back as a data packet containing an "OK." The program will stop everything else it is doing while in the loop; this could be mitigated with more complexity, such as implementing a timeout. A recursive situation occurs when waiting for a good reply and a "BAD" packet is received, because the wait for reply is called when the resend occurs. The recursive situation is not detrimental to the running of the example and is completely exited when an "OK" is received. The recursive call can cause problems in more complex situations, though, and needs to be handled differently—with the use of timeouts and more robust packet-correction methods.

Listing 8-1. testApp.cpp, Part 5 of 7

```cpp
void testApp::WaitForReply(){
  printf ("Wait for reply \n");
  ReplyOK = false;
    while (ReplyOK != true){
    CheckForIncoming();
  }
} // end testApp::WaitForReply()
```

Part 6 is the function to create and send the packets over the XBee network. A pointer of the data and the length of the data that need to be sent are received when the function is called. The packet is created with the destination address set in the setup function and the pointer containing the data to be sent out. The packet that is created is a transmit request that has no frame ID to limit the number of packets that are worked with for this example. The frame ID can be used in situations where the receiving XBee may fail or go out of range, telling the program whether the packet was received or not. The transmit-reply packet that is generated by the XBee network does not inform the program that the packet was properly received by the Arduino; that is why the "OK" and "BAD" packets are used. The CreatePacket function calculates the checksum needed for the packet as the last step before sending. The function saves the packet length for possible resending and sets the FirstPacketsent flag to true to tell other functions that one packet has been sent; otherwise, the program will fail if a "BAD" packet is received before one packet has been sent.

Listing 8-1. testApp.cpp, Part 6 of 7

```
void testApp::CreatePacket(unsigned char *Outdata, int length){
  printf ("creating packet\n");
  packetBuffer[17+ length] = 0;
  packetBuffer[0] = 0x7E;     // start byte
  packetBuffer[1] = 0;        // 1st length byte will be zero with current limitations
  packetBuffer[3] = 0x10;     // frame type
  packetBuffer[4] =  0;            // frame ID
  for (int i = 5; i <= 14; i++){      // add addresses
    packetBuffer[i] = destADR[i-5];
  }
  packetBuffer[15] = 0;  // set both options
  packetBuffer[16] = 0;
  for (int i = 0; i < length; i++){
    packetBuffer[i + 17] =  Outdata [i];  // add data to packet
    printf ("graph: %X\n",packetBuffer[i+17]); // print sent data to debug console
  }
  packetBuffer[2] = 14 + length;       // set the lower length byte
  for (int i = 0; i <  packetBuffer[2]; i++){ // calculate the checksum
    packetBuffer[17+ length] =  packetBuffer[17+ length] + packetBuffer[i+3];
  }
  // finish packet by adding checksum to the final position
  packetBuffer[17+ length]= 0xFF - packetBuffer[17+ length];
  serial.writeBytes (packetBuffer, (18 + length)); // send the packet
  lastPacketLength = 18 + length;  // save last packet length
  FirstPacketsent = true;  // flag that at least the first packet is sent
} // end testApp::CreatePacket
```

The finishing touch for the openFrameworks code, in part 7, is to create a visual display for quick verification of the position and data being sent. The graph that is generated will be re-created on the Android device. Figure 8-2 shows the approximate graph that is generated using the data generated in the setup function. The draw function is called by openFrameworks after the update function is run and has to generate the view from scratch every time draw is run. The function generates the grid by outlining a 256-pixel area with a square by counting out a 32-pixel line spacing using a for loop. The data is drawn by a for loop that will step through each array of data and draw a series of lines segments connected together corresponding to the data contained in the array. There is a vertical line that is drawn dynamically to indicate the position from which the code is sending data. The position of the data point is incremented when all three simulated sensors have been sent.

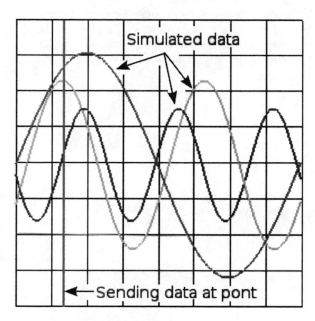

Figure 8-2. *Graph visualization of data being sent*

Listing 8-1. testApp.cpp, Part 7 of 7

```cpp
void testApp::draw(){
  ofBackground (50,50,50);
  ofSetLineWidth (1);
  ofSetColor(0,0,0);
  for (int i = 266; i > 9; i -=32){ // draw the grid
    ofLine(10,i,266,i);
    ofLine(i,10,i,266);
  }
  for (int i = 0; i < 255; i++){ // draw the data
    ofSetLineWidth (2);
    ofSetColor(0,255,0);
    ofLine (i+10,(266 - graph[i]) , i+11 , (266 -graph [i+1]));
    ofSetColor(255,255,0);
    ofLine (i+10,(266 - graph1[i]) , i+11 , (266 -graph1 [i+1]));
    ofSetColor(0,0,255);
    ofLine (i+10,(266 - graph2[i]) , i+11 , (266 -graph2 [i+1]));
  }
  ofSetColor(255,0,0);
  ofLine (10 + point, 10, 10 + point, 266); // draw the position line
  ofSetLineWidth (1);
} // end testApp::draw()
```

The last thing before compiling the code is to declare variables and function prototypes in `testApp.h`. Listing 8-2 describes the class used for the program. For simplicity, a majority of the variables are declared within the class definition. Listing 8-2 needs to replace the one created with the empty application. The code will need a preliminary test before the rest of the project is complete. To test, temporarily comment out the three `WaitForReply` function calls in the update function associated with the packet creation and sending. Compile and run the program, and the red line should increment to a new position after three packets are sent. With the program running, upload the modified software serial sketch to the Arduino Mega ADK that is set up with the connected, required hardware, and check for data printing to the serial monitor. The data is in readable by humans in this from, but shows that the packets are reaching the Arduino.

Listing 8-2. testApp.h

```
#pragma once
#include "ofMain.h"
class testApp : public ofBaseApp{
public:
    // variables and objects
    unsigned char graph[256], graph1[256], graph2[256];
    unsigned char point;
    int counts;
    bool SensorsSent [3];
    bool ReplyOK;
    bool FirstPacketsent;
    unsigned char incomingBuffer[80];
    unsigned char incomeData[64];
    int incomingByteLen;
    unsigned char incomingPacketChecksum;
    unsigned char destADR[10];

 unsigned char packetBuffer [80];
 int lastPacketLength;
 unsigned char dataLength;
 ofSerial serial;
 // openFrameworks-specific functions
 void setup();
 void update();
 void draw();
// sensor network functions to handle packets
 void CheckForIncoming();
 void WaitForReply();
 void ReadPacket ();
 void CreatePacket (unsigned char*, int);
}; // end class testApp
```

The Arduino

The Arduino is the main workhorse of this chapter's example. The Arduino receives packets from other network nodes and processes the information to be logged to an SD card to be eventually retrieved by an Android device. The Arduino programming responds to good incoming data by generating an "OK" reply packet using the address contained within the good incoming packets of the sending node. If a packet is malformed, a broadcast "BAD" packet is sent to the network; the packet is a broadcast because it might not be possible to determine the address of the sending node. Both reply packets keep the simulated sensor network that is made with openFrameworks moving forward and sending data.

The Arduino program waits till the last sensor is received before writing the data to the SD card as a single buffer line. The simple packet-correction method sometimes drops data instead of trying figure out what packets might be missing. The amount of lost data needs to be determined; as a function of the requirements of some projects, it may be more critical that all the data is received.

Listing 8-3 is divided into eight parts. Part 1 sets up most of the variables and libraries needed. Both SD.h and AndroidAccessory.h are used to create the connection to the corresponding SPI devices. Input and output buffers are set for both the serial XBee connection and the SD card read and write. The reply packet that signifies that a packet was not received properly is set as a static byte array, as this packet will be the standard reply for malformed packets. The "BAD" packet is not required to be generated every time it needs to be sent, unlike the "OK" reply packet, which is generated dynamically every time. The SD card output buffer has a set amount of preformatting.

The data contained in the log file is essentially a four-byte string for each sensor: it contains the sensor name, the location of the data in the array of the openFrameworks program, and the actual sensor data. The sensor data is separated by a colon, and a double-colon separates each sensor. The data lines are ended with a carnage return and linefeed character. Each of the remote sensors are designated as S1 through S3, and a local sensor location called L1 has been left in the array to allow for an optimal local sensor attached to the Mega ADK to be processed. A series of Boolean flags are declared for program flow control: one flag contains a blink state to blink the LED and two flags are for ADK connection status.

The last object created is the AndroidAccessory object and uses the same declaration as we used in Chapter 4. As long as the default program has not been set on the Android device, programs associated with a particular accessory name and ID will be given as an autorun option when connected. Using the same accessory lets you avoid an unnecessary upload when starting to integrate the Android device into the sensor network, by allowing the ADK monitor to easily be used as an option for debugging.

Listing 8-3. Data Logger and ADK Handler, Part 1 of 8

```
#include <SD.h> // must be included before AndroidAccessory.h
#include <AndroidAccessory.h>
  static byte badPacket[21] = {0x7E ,0x00 ,0x11 ,0x10 ,0x00 ,0x00 ,0x00 ,0x00 ,0x00 ,0x00 ,
  0x00 ,0xFF ,0xFF ,0xFF ,0xFE ,0x00 ,0x00 ,0x42 ,0x41 ,0x44 ,0x2D };
  byte OutPacketBuffer[80];
  byte incomingBuffer[80];
  int incomingByteLen;
  byte incomingPacketChecksum;
  byte sourceADR[10];      // source addresses holding
  byte incomeData [64];   // phrased data holder
  int dataLength;                 // length of data received
  byte SDinBuffer[34];       // SD buffer is 34 bytes to capture a whole data line
  byte SDoutBuffer[34] =
// pre-format used to contain the data to log
  {'S','1',':',0xFF,':',0xFF,':',':',
   'S','2',':',0xFF,':',0xFF,':',':',
   'S','3',':',0xFF,':',0xFF,':',':',
   'L','1',':',0xFF,':',0xFF,':',':', 0x0A,0x0D};
  int ERRcount = 0;
  int IcomingTime  = 0;
  boolean Blink  = LOW; // blink state holder
  bool lastReply = false; // false bad, true good
  boolean ADKisConnected = false; // so the rest of the code does not have to pull the USB
  boolean LogFileSyncADK = false;
  File LogFile;
```

```
AndroidAccessory ADK("Manufacturer2",
                     "Model2",
                     "Description",
                     "2.0",
                     "http://yoursite.com",
                     "0000000012345678");
```

Part 2 of the Arduino program contains the setup function. Two serial connections are needed: one for the XBee module and one for debugging. Arduino pin 2 is used for card detection and pin 10 is used for SD card slave select. Pins 10 and 13 are set as output, along with pin 53, to make sure the SPI remains in master mode. After the pins and serial are set up, the code remains in a loop, waiting for the SD card to become available, during which the LED produces a slow blink. Once the card is detected, the LED will blink rapidly before making sure that the log file is available. Finally, the setup function initializes the Android connection.

Listing 8-3. Data Logger and ADK Handler, Part 2 of 8

```
void setup(){
  Serial.begin(115200);  // serial to monitor
  Serial3.begin(115200); // serial to XBee
  pinMode(2, INPUT); // pin for SD card detection; can attach interrupt if needed
  digitalWrite (2, HIGH);// pull up for chip detect
  pinMode(13, OUTPUT); // use onboard LED for diagnostics
  pinMode(53, OUTPUT); // make sure the SPI won't enter slave
  pinMode(10, OUTPUT);   // CS pin for SD
  while (!SD.begin(10)) { // wait for SD to be available
    digitalWrite (13, (Blink = !Blink)); // constant blink waiting for card
  }
  delay (100);
  for (int i = 0 ; i <= 10 ; i++) {
    digitalWrite (13, (Blink = !Blink));
    delay (100);
  } // fast blink to show SD card is initialized
  if (SD.exists("sensor.log")) {
    for (int i = 0; i <= 4 ; i++) {
    digitalWrite (13, (Blink = !Blink));
    delay (300);
   }// slow short blink to show file is found
  }
  else{
    LogFile = SD.open("sensor.log", FILE_WRITE);
    LogFile.close();
  } // create log file if none is found
 ADK.begin(); // initialize the Android connection
} // end setup");
```

In part 3, the loop function controls the major flow of the Arduino program. The loop function starts with a confirmation of the presence of the SD card. If there is no SD card inserted, the program blinks the LED and sets flags for use when the SD card is available. When the SD card is available, the program will count the times the loop is run, and if a packet is not received within the set amount of counts, the function will resend the last reply packet type as either "OK" or "BAD." The loop function also checks the availability of the ADK connection, along with checking for new data from Serial3.

Listing 8-3. Data Logger and ADK Handler, Part 3 of 8

```
void loop(){
  if (digitalRead(2) == HIGH){
    digitalWrite (13, HIGH);
    if (IcomingTime >= 25){
      if (lastReply){
        SendOK();
      }
      else{
        Serial3.write (badPacket,21);
      }
      IcomingTime = 0;
    }
    HandleADK();
    CheckForIncoming();
    delay (50);
    IcomingTime++;
  } // end if (digitalRead(2) == HIGH)
  else{
    IcomingTime = 1000;
    bool lastReply = false; // will request a new packet to be set
                            // if node is waiting for reply
    digitalWrite (13, (Blink = !Blink));  // blink when SD card is not available
    delay (100);
  } // end else for if (digitalRead(2) == HIGH)
} // end loop
```

Part 4 is the function to capture incoming packets from the Arduino. It performs the checksum verification. This function is closely related to the receive function created in the openFrameworks portion and described in Chapter 5. The CheckForIncoming function has a bit more control than previous examples to ensure that the packets are properly received. It does this by flushing all of the input and serial connection buffers connected to the XBee module when too many errors have been encountered. This function also initiates the proper reply packet based on the checksum being correct, along with the reading of the packet when a proper packet is received.

Listing 8-3. Data Logger and ADK Handler, Part 4 of 8

```
void CheckForIncoming(){
  incomingBuffer[0] = 0; // clear the first byte of the incoming buffer
  if (Serial3.available() && 0x7E == (incomingBuffer[0] = Serial3.read())){
    incomingBuffer[1] = Serial3.read(); // pull packet length
    incomingBuffer[2] = Serial3.read();
    incomingByteLen = incomingBuffer[1] + incomingBuffer[2]; // calculate packet length
    incomingPacketChecksum = 0; // clear checksum
    for (int i  = 3; i <= incomingByteLen + 3; i++){
      incomingBuffer[i]  = Serial3.read();  // capture packet
      incomingPacketChecksum += incomingBuffer[i]; // calculate checksum
    }
    incomingPacketChecksum = (0xFF - incomingPacketChecksum); // finish checksum
    incomingByteLen += 3;
```

```
    if (incomingByteLen > 0 && incomingPacketChecksum ==
      incomingBuffer[incomingByteLen+1]){
      Serial3.flush(); // done with serial buffer for now
      ReadPacket(); // read and handled the data
      SendOK(); // reply to original sender
    }
    else { // if checksum is bad, perform clean and bad packet send
      ERRcount++; // increment error count
      for (int i = 0; i <= 80; i++){  // clear packet from incoming buffer
        incomingBuffer[i] = 0;
      }
      Serial3.flush(); // clear serial connection
      delay (100);
      // if too many errors encountered, reset serial connection
      if (ERRcount == 10) {
        Serial3.end();   // stop serial completely
        for (int i = 0; i <= 10; i++) {  // blink for verification
          digitalWrite (13, (Blink = !Blink));
          delay (50);
          ERRcount = 0; // reset error count
        }
        Serial3.begin(115200); // restart serial connection
        delay (30);
      }
      Serial3.write (badPacket,21); // send BAD reply
      lastReply = false; // set last reply ad bad flag
    }  // end else checksum bad
  } // end if (Serial3.available() && 0x7E
} // end void CheckIncoming()
```

Part 5 reads a proper incoming packet using a switch statement and recognizes three packet types. The three packet are a data packet, an AT command response, and a transmit response. The transmit and AT command response both print to the serial monitor when they are detected and perform no other work on those types. When a data packet is received, the address of the sending node is placed in an array for use in the SendOK function, which will be called after this function returns to CheckForIncoming. Data is also phrased from the data packet and placed in an array to be used for prepping the format and containment in the log file on the SD card.

Listing 8-3. Data Logger and ADK Handler, Part 5 of 8

```
void ReadPacket(){
  IcomingTime  = 0;  // received a good packet-reset time
  switch (incomingBuffer[3]){  // check packet type and perform any responses
    case 0x90:  // data packet
      dataLength = 0;
      for (int i = 4; i <= 13; i++){  // get both addresses of the source device
        sourceADR[i-4] = incomingBuffer[i];
      }
      dataLength = incomingByteLen - 15;  // reduce to just the data length to get the data
      for (int i = 0; i <= dataLength; i++){
        incomeData [i] = incomingBuffer[i+15]4data from the packet
      }
```

```
      if (dataLength == 4){ // send data to the preparation function if length is proper
        PrepareDataForSD();
      }
      break;
    case 0x8B:  // if packet is a transmit response, perform action
      Serial.println ("Transmit Response");
      break;
    case 0x88: // inform of information from command response
      Serial.print("Command response :");
      Serial.print (incomingBuffer[8], HEX);
      Serial.println (incomingBuffer[9],HEX);
      break;
    default: // announce unknown packet type
      Serial.println ("error: packet type not known");
  } // end Switch Case
} // end void ReadPacket
```

In part 6, the next function preps the data to be contained in the SD card and that's ready for passing to the Android device. When data is received and parsed from the incoming packets, it is sent to this function and placed in the SD buffer according to the sensor's number. This function will place all three sensors into the respective locations, and when the last sensor is received, the SD buffer is written to the SD card for storage. The data is sorted with a switch that looks at the second position of the incomeData array, which contains the sensor number associated with the sensor data. Once the third sensor is received, the SD buffer is printed to the serial connection to the computer for debugging, and the SD buffer will be sent to the Android device if connected and the data in the log has been synced.

The method of logging the data after the third sensor has been received sometimes misses some of the other sensors. In more professional setups, the program should make a request for the missing sensor data from the network, but for this demonstration it is not necessary. This function can also be used to pull a local sensor to add extra sensor data to the log. When the SD buffer is ready, the code opens the file for writing and finds the last position by seeking to the end based upon the file size, and closes the file when finished. The positions that are associated with the sensor data are reset to the initialization values returning back to the calling function.

Listing 8-3. Data Logger and ADK Handler, Part 6 of 8

```
void PrepareDataForSD(){
  switch (incomeData[1]){
    case '1':
      SDoutBuffer[3] =  incomeData[2];
      SDoutBuffer[5] =  incomeData[3];
      break;
    case '2':
      SDoutBuffer[11] =  incomeData[2];
      SDoutBuffer[13] =  incomeData[3];
      break;
    case '3':
      SDoutBuffer[19] =  incomeData[2];
      SDoutBuffer[21] =  incomeData[3];
      // a local sensor can be pulled and added to the SD buffer at the L1 location
      LogFile = SD.open("sensor.log", FILE_WRITE);  // open file for writing
      LogFile.seek(LogFile.size()); // find end of file to append
```

```
      if (LogFile) {
        LogFile.write (SDoutBuffer,34);
        Serial.write (SDoutBuffer,34);
        if (ADKisConnected && LogFileSyncADK){
          ADK.write (SDoutBuffer,34);
        }
      } // end if (LogFile)
      LogFile.close();
      SDoutBuffer[3]  =  OxFF;  // reset SD buffer
      SDoutBuffer[5]  =  OxFF;
      SDoutBuffer[11] =  OxFF;
      SDoutBuffer[13] =  OxFF;
      SDoutBuffer[19] =  OxFF;
      SDoutBuffer[21] =  OxFF;
      break;
  } // end switch
}// end void PrepareDataForSD()
```

Part 7 is the function that creates and sends an OK reply and is called when a good packet is received from the XBee network. The packet is created dynamically to be able to send the reply packet to the originating sensor node. The packet is formed in the same fashion as every XBee API transmit request that has been generated thus far. The packet is formed in a buffer with the proper formatting before being sent. The packet's data is constant; the only change is that of the address.

Listing 8-3. Data Logger and ADK Handler, Part 7 of 8

```
void SendOK(){
  delay (50);
  byte length = 2;
  byte Outdata[2] = {'O', 'K'};
  OutPacketBuffer[17 + length] = 0; // clear checksum byte
  OutPacketBuffer[0] = 0x7E;    // start byte
  OutPacketBuffer[1] = 0;       // 1st length byte will be zero with current limitations
  OutPacketBuffer[3] = 0x10;    // transmit request frame type
  OutPacketBuffer[4] =  0;          // frame ID
  for (int i = 5; i <= 14; i++){    // add addresses
    OutPacketBuffer[i] = sourceADR[i-5];
  }
  OutPacketBuffer[15] = 0 ;         // set both options
  OutPacketBuffer[16] = 0 ;
  for (int i = 0; i < length; i++){
    OutPacketBuffer[i + 17] =  Outdata [i];  // add data to packet
  }
  OutPacketBuffer[2] = 14 + length;      // set the lower length byte
  for (int i = 0; i <  OutPacketBuffer[2]; i++){   // start calculating errorsum
    OutPacketBuffer[17+ length] =  OutPacketBuffer[17+ length] + OutPacketBuffer[i+3];
  }
  // finish packet by adding checksum
  OutPacketBuffer[17+ length]= OxFF - OutPacketBuffer[17+ length];
  Serial3.write(OutPacketBuffer, (18 + length));
  lastReply = true;
}// end void SendOK()
```

In Part 8, the last function included in the Arduino sketch handles the Open Accessory connection. This function is pulled at a regular interval to check for incoming data from the Android device. When the Android device is connected, a Boolean flag is set to true to avoid running the isConnected function too often by other functions that need to know when the Android device is connected. A predetermined set of bytes are used as commands from the Android device to allow for syncing of the log information, deleting the log, or disconnecting the Android device from the Arduino. The command for syncing the data is an ASCII a; when this command is issued from the Android device, the Arduino will read the log file 34 bytes at a time and send the information to the Android device for further processing. When a command of a b is received, the Arduino will stop sending updated information to the Android. The log file will be deleted when a command of c is received. If the Android device is not connected, the two flags that control the sending of updated data to the Android device are set to false.

Listing 8-3. Data Logger and ADK Handler, Part 8 of 8

```
void HandleADK(){
  if (ADK.isConnected()) {
    delay (100);
    ADKisConnected = true;
    if (ADK.available() > 0){      // check for incoming data
      switch (ADK.read()){
        case 'a': {
          Serial.println('a');
          File LogFile = SD.open("sensor.log");
          If (LogFile) {
            while (LogFile.available()) { // read bytes into buffer
              for (int i = 0; i < 34; i ++){
                SDinBuffer[i] = LogFile.read();
              }
              ADK.write (SDinBuffer, 34);
            } // end while (LogFile.available())
            LogFileSyncADK = true;
            LogFile.close();
          }  // end if (LogFile)
          break;
        } // end case 'a':
        case 'b':
          LogFileSyncADK = false;
          break;
        case 'c':
          SD.remove("sensor.log");
          break;
      }// end switch (ADK.read())
    } // end if (ADK.available() > 0)
  }  // end if (acc.isConnected())
  else{
    ADKisConnected = false;
    LogFileSyncADK = false;
  }
}// end HandleADK()
```

When all the code is complete for the Arduino sketch, compile and upload it to the Arduino Mega ADK with the SD adapter and the XBee module connected. The openFrameworks program needs to be started to ensure that the WaitForReply function calls are uncommented and the program is recompiled. Insert an SD card into the Arduino and power on the setup. When the Arduino is powered on, the openFrameworks program should start to send data and move through the data arrays. The serial monitor can be used to see the data being written to the SD card after three sensors have be sent and received.

Now that the data is being logged to the SD card, the ADK monitor program that was created in Chapter 4 can be used to verify that the data is getting sent to the Android device. While the Arduino and openFrameworks are running, plug the Android device into the host side of the Mega ADK and wait till the Android program detects the event. A command can be sent to the Mega ADK when an a is sent; in this case the log data should be printed to the Android screen. The data should match the printed data on the Arduino serial monitor and should update at about the same time while connected.

■ **Note**   Before the Android program is complete, you can verify the data on the SD card by using a hex editor to read the sensor.log file when the SD card is read by a computer.

The Android Application

In this section, we'll make the Android program display the data in a more human-readable format. The example adds a chart that graphs the data in a fashion similar to the openFrameworks code. The layout of the program is shown in Figure 8-3. The graph is drawn at the top of the screen above the monitor box. Making the graph is a bit difficult to do from scratch, so a library is used to add the functionality. The library that is going to be used is called AChartEngine. The chart library adds the ability to make scatter plots, pie charts, and line or bar graphs that can be created dynamically and can be pinched, zoomed, and scrolled. The binary distribution of the library needs to be downloaded from www.achartengine.org.

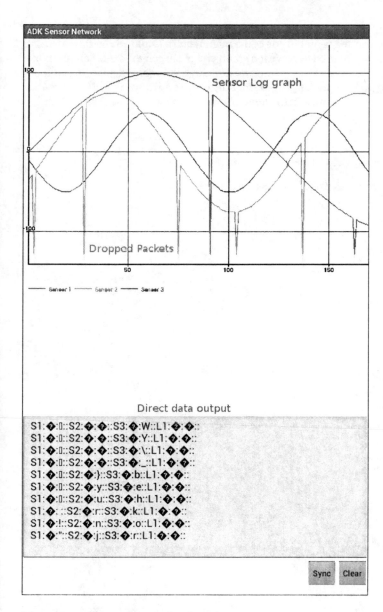

Figure 8-3. *The running Android application*

The program that this example creates uses the same framework that was created in Chapter 4. A new project can be created in the Eclipse IDE and the framework section copied over using the same method as the original setup. To use the library, create a folder named libraries in the RES folder in the project's workspace, and drag and drop the achartengine-1.0.0.jar file into the newly created folder. Right-click the added JAR file in the workspace and select Build Path ➤ Add to Build Path from the pop-up menu to make the library fully ready for use. The JAR file will move from the location copied to the Referenced Libraries workspace folder when it is properly added to the build path.

The Javadocs of the AChartEngine library can be a great help on how to use it (see www.achartengine.org). Note that this example only focuses on one possible implementation of the chart engine and only uses the line graph setup.

The Android application needs a different `main.xml` file and a `strings.xml` file. Listing 8-4 is the `main.xml` file that needs to be created. The graph is created in a nested layout inside of the main relative layout within the `main.xml` file. The `LinearLayout` tag defines the space that will be used to place the graph created at run time. An Edit text box is used to display the incoming data from the Arduino and has the same functionality as the data-display box for the ADK monitor program. Two buttons are also created in the `main.xml` file for the layout: one to sync the data stored on the SD card and receive current updates while plugged in, and the other to clear the data from the screen. Both buttons are set up to call a respective function in the activity class.

Listing 8-4. main.xml

```xml
<?xml version="1.0" encoding="utf-8"?>
<RelativeLayout xmlns:android="http://schemas.android.com/apk/res/android"
    android:id="@+id/relativeLayout1"
    android:layout_width="fill_parent"
    android:layout_height="fill_parent"
    android:layout_weight="0.72" >
    <LinearLayout
        android:id="@+id/chart"
        android:layout_width="fill_parent"
        android:layout_height="500dp"
        android:layout_alignParentTop="true"
        />
    <EditText
        android:id="@+id/incomingData"
        android:layout_width="wrap_content"
        android:layout_height="250dp"
        android:layout_above="@+id/syncbutton"
        android:layout_alignParentLeft="true"
        android:layout_alignParentRight="true"
        android:scrollbars="vertical"
        android:clickable="false"
        android:cursorVisible="false"
        android:focusable="false"
        android:focusableInTouchMode="false"
        android:gravity="top"
        android:inputType="textMultiLine|textNoSuggestions"
        android:hint="@string/hint" />
    <Button
        android:id="@+id/clear"
        android:layout_width="wrap_content"
        android:layout_height="wrap_content"
        android:layout_alignParentBottom="true"
        android:layout_alignParentRight="true"
        android:onClick="clearScreen"
        android:text="@string/clear" />
    <Button
        android:id="@+id/syncbutton"
        android:layout_width="wrap_content"
        android:layout_height="wrap_content"
        android:layout_alignParentBottom="true"
```

```
            android:layout_toLeftOf="@+id/clear"
            android:onClick="SyncData"
            android:text="@string/sync" />
</RelativeLayout>
```

Listing 8-5 is the strings.xml file and defines the new application name, a hint for the Edit text box, and the name of the two buttons. As stated in Chapter 4, putting the information in the strings.xml file saves you from having to go to every instance that will be used to change a name. When this application is loaded on the Android device, it will have a different name than that of the ADK monitor, but will still respond to the same accessory name declared in the Arduino sketch. Sharing the same information is not a problem if the default program option on the autorun pop-up menu is not selected. The Android device will give a series of options if there are multiple programs that use the same accessory. If the multiple options are undesirable, change the declaration to a new accessory name in the Arduino sketch, and change the accessory_filter.xml file in the Android project to reflect the changes.

Listing 8-5. strings.xml

```
<?xml version="1.0" encoding="utf-8"?>
<resources>
    <string name="app_name">ADK Sensor Network</string>
    <string name="hint">Data from Arduino board will be displayed here</string>
    <string name="sync">Sync</string>
    <string name="clear">Clear</string>
</resources>
```

New objects for the chart engine need to be imported for you to use the graphing capabilities in the application. Listing 8-6 shows the new imports needed for the chart that will be used. ChartFactory and GraphicalView make up the main core of the chart engine. There is a data class that contains the data in a series for the graph using Cartesian x- and y- coordinates for the point's position. XYMultipleSeriesDataset is used for a class that will contain all the series data that will need to be displayed on the screen. XYSeriesRenderer and XYMultipleSeriesRenderer are needed to get the data rendered properly. The import android.graphics.Color is used to get classes that predefine colors such as red, green, and blue to make color use a bit easier. The import android.widget.LinearLayout will allow the blank layout to be accessible for adding the graph to the layout space defined in main.xml. Add the import in Listing 8-6 to the beginning of the ADK framework from Chapter 4.

Listing 8-6. New Imports for Using the AChartEngine Library

```
import org.achartengine.ChartFactory;
import org.achartengine.GraphicalView;
import org.achartengine.model.XYMultipleSeriesDataset;
import org.achartengine.model.XYSeries;
import org.achartengine.renderer.XYMultipleSeriesRenderer;
import org.achartengine.renderer.XYSeriesRenderer;
import android.graphics.Color;
import android.widget.LinearLayout;
import android.widget.View;
import android.widget.Button;
import android.widget.EditText;
```

Listing 8-7 defines the new variables that need to be added to the framework to define the chart and the data that will be drawn to the screen. The first two new variables declare the multiple-series data set and the renderer. The data-set variable contains the three series that will make up the data from the sensors. The renderer uses the data set to display the data and is used by the SensorChartView class's repaint function. Options for the renderer are set in the SetupGraph function, described later. Each piece of the sensor's data is contained in a simple XYSeries variable declared with the name on creation and will have data added to it as it is received from the Arduino board. The linear layout has to be declared so that the registerUIobjects function can add the graph to the view for the user. The buttons and the Edit text box are added in the same way as the ADK monitor. The last six variables are used to store information for the placement within the graph and the beginning limits to display, along with a Boolean to inform functions of the status of the synchronization with the Arduino board. Add the variables in Listing 8-7 to the program after the beginning of the activity class and before the first function.

Listing 8-7. New Variables for the Android Sensor Network Application

```
// chart variables
private XYMultipleSeriesDataset SensorData = new XYMultipleSeriesDataset();
// the XYMultipleSeriesRenderer spans two lines in the book
private XYMultipleSeriesRenderer SensorRenderer = new XYMultipleSeriesRenderer();
private XYSeries Sensor1CurrentSeries = new XYSeries("Sensor 1");
private XYSeries Sensor2CurrentSeries = new XYSeries("Sensor 2");
private XYSeries Sensor3CurrentSeries = new XYSeries("Sensor 3");
private GraphicalView SensorChartView;
// chart container and other UI objects
private LinearLayout layout;
private Button buttonSync;
private Button ScreenClear;
private EditText DataFromArduino;
// chart control variables
double[] limits = new double[] {0, 500000,-127,127}; // for chart limits
double x = 0;
double y = 0;
double xCount = 0;
double lastMinX = 0;
boolean Sync = false;
```

Listing 8-8 is the function that registers the user interface objects to the code. Both of the buttons and the text box are set to the defined objects in main.xml, as was done in prior Android applications. The chart is a bit unusual because the chart view must be added to the linear layout; this is done by adding the output of ChartFactory's getLineChartView function to the SensorChartView variable. Some information has to be included with the getLineChartView function call—the instance of the program along with the data set and renderer that will be used with the chart need to be passed to the function. Then the SensorChartView variable id added to the linear view before this function is finished.

Listing 8-8. New registerUIobjects Function

```
private void registerUIobjects(){
  buttonSync = (Button) findViewById(R.id.syncbutton);
  ScreenClear = (Button) findViewById(R.id.clear);
  DataFromArduino = (EditText)findViewById(R.id.incomingData);
  layout = (LinearLayout) findViewById(R.id.chart);
  // the next line spans two in the book
```

```
SensorChartView = ChartFactory.getLineChartView(this, SensorData,
SensorRenderer);
layout.addView(SensorChartView);
}// end registerUIobjects
```

The SetupGraph function defined in Listing 8-9 sets the options for how the graph will be rendered to the screen, and also links the individual data series to the graph. The overall options that are set include the color of the axes, the text size, the axes' minimums and maximums, and the pan limitations. The color of the data series is controlled by individual renderers that are added to the multi-series renderer variable. There are a lot of options that can be set for the graph; be sure to check out the Java reference documentation at www.achartengine.org/content/javadoc/index.html for more in-depth information. The SetupGraph function needs to be called from the onResume function of the framework. Add the code line SetupGraph(); after the super.onResume(); line in the function. The SetupGraph function is called from this function to ensure that the graph will be set up correctly every time the program resumes.

Listing 8-9. Function That Defines How the Graph Is Drawn

```
public void SetupGraph(){
    // set chart-drawing options
    SensorRenderer.setAxisTitleTextSize(10);
    SensorRenderer.setChartTitleTextSize(10);
    SensorRenderer.setLabelsTextSize(10);
    SensorRenderer.setLegendTextSize(10);
    SensorRenderer.setMargins(new int[] {10, 10, 10, 0});
    SensorRenderer.setAxesColor(Color.WHITE);
    SensorRenderer.setShowGrid(true);
    SensorRenderer.setYAxisMin(-127);
    SensorRenderer.setYAxisMax(127);
    SensorRenderer.setXAxisMin(0);
    SensorRenderer.setXAxisMax(100);
    SensorRenderer.setPanLimits(limits);
    // add the three series to the multi-series data set
    SensorData.addSeries(Sensor1CurrentSeries);
    SensorData.addSeries(Sensor2CurrentSeries);
    SensorData.addSeries(Sensor3CurrentSeries);
    // set color options for the data lines to match graph openFrameworks
    XYSeriesRenderer Sensor1renderer = new XYSeriesRenderer();
    Sensor1renderer.setColor(Color.GREEN);
    XYSeriesRenderer Sensor2renderer = new XYSeriesRenderer();
    Sensor2renderer.setColor(Color.YELLOW);
    XYSeriesRenderer Sensor3renderer = new XYSeriesRenderer();
    Sensor3renderer.setColor(Color.BLUE);
    // add the sensor graph with set options to the graph
    SensorRenderer.addSeriesRenderer(Sensor1renderer);
    SensorRenderer.addSeriesRenderer(Sensor2renderer);
    SensorRenderer.addSeriesRenderer(Sensor3renderer);
} // end SetupGraph
```

The message handler function that is linked to the thread that is created to check for incoming data from the Arduino is where the program dynamically updates the graph. Because the data is well formatted at the point it is sent from the Arduino, and the data is consistently sized, the parsing is pretty straightforward—we have only to look at specific places in the data buffer. This is only possible if the data transition is reliable; in a more refined setup, a verification step should be used to check that the transition is what is expected. The connection between the Android device and the Arduino is decently reliable, so this example does not add the verification complexity.

Once the data is received from the Arduino, the three sensors' data is pulled from the 34-byte array and added as the y value to the appropriate series of data. Because the data that was sent to the Arduino from openFrameworks was normalized to a unsigned byte, you have to normalize the data back to a zero value of the sine wave function by subtracting 127 from the sensor value to make the byte signed. The x value is controlled by a count that is incremented every time a data transition is received; the same count value is added to all three series. A special function is called after the data is added to the graph to check if the data is outside of the view; if so, it will scroll to the last position, keeping the current incoming data always in the view area. The old data is not lost as the graph scrolls, and can be viewed by scrolling back to the left.

After the graph is printed to the screen, the entire data buffer is appended to the text box to add an extra view for possible debugging. The information in the text box could be accessed for further processing, such as saving the data to a file on the Android device. A decent tutorial on reading and writing to the storage of an Android device can be found at www.java-samples.com/showtutorial.php?tutorialid=1523. This tutorial can be modified to work with this example because the data is printed to a text box. Listing 8-10 replaces the existing incoming data handler within the framework.

■ **Note**   Some online examples for AChartEngine call for a separate thread to be created to be able update the chart dynamically for new data. This is not necessary for ADK applications, because of the existing thread used to respond to incoming information from the Mega ADK. This thread provides an event to update the graph when new data is received.

Listing 8-10. Incoming Data Handler Function

```
Handler IncomingDataHandler = new Handler() {
  @Override
  public void handleMessage(Message msg) {
    BufferData IncomingBuffer = (BufferData) msg.obj;
    byte[] buffer = IncomingBuffer.getBuffer();
    // pull and add sensor data to the graph
    byte sen1 = (byte) (buffer[5] - 127);
    byte sen2 = (byte) (buffer[13] - 127);
    byte sen3 = (byte) (buffer[21] - 127);
    Sensor1CurrentSeries.add(xCount,  sen1 );
    Sensor2CurrentSeries.add(xCount,  sen2 );
    Sensor3CurrentSeries.add(xCount,  sen3 );
    // check if a scroll is needed
    refreshChart();
    xCount++;
    if (SensorChartView != null) {
      SensorChartView.repaint();
    }
    // add data buffer to text box
    String str = new String(buffer);
    DataFromArduino.append(str);
  }// end handleMessage(Message msg)
};// end Handler IncomingDataHandler = new Handler()
```

The refreshChart function described in Listing 8-11 provides the mechanism to scroll the graph when the current incoming data exceeds the view area on the screen. The scroll is accomplished by checking if the current x value count is greater than the highest value of the graph being drawn. When the count is greater, the function increments the minimum x value and sets the values of the minimum and the new maximum to the graph, creating the scrolling effect.

Listing 8-11. Function to Keep the Graph Focused on the Most Current Data

```
private void refreshChart() {
  // check if a shift of the graph view is needed
  if (xCount > SensorRenderer.getXAxisMax()) {
    SensorRenderer.setXAxisMax(xCount);
    SensorRenderer.setXAxisMin(++lastMinX);
  }
  SensorChartView.repaint();
}
```

■ **Caution** The graph will fail to redraw when the Android device rotates to a new orientation. This happens because the application has not been programmed to handle the screen-rotation event.

Listing 8-12 shows the last two functions needed to complete the Android application. The first function is the clearScreen function, associated with the Clear button. The clearScreen function sends a command of an ASCII b to the Arduino to inform it that the Android device is no longer synchronized. The clearScreen function then performs an operation to reset the graph and the text box back to their initial settings.

The SyncData function is associated with the Sync button on the user interface; it first checks whether the data is currently synchronized to avoid resending the data when the button is clicked multiple times. The SyncData function send an ASCII command of a to the Arduino, initiating the transfer of the sensor.log file located on the SD card attached to the Arduino. The transfer is captured by the running thread that is checking for incoming data. The Arduino transfers 34 bytes at a time to the Android device, and the information of the three sensors is added to the graph. While the Arduino is connected and the data has been synchronized, new data will be transferred to the Android device and recorded to the log file on the SD card.

Listing 8-12. Clear-Screen and Sync-Data Button Events

```
public void clearScreen(View v) {
  byte[] BytestoSend = new byte[1];
  BytestoSend[0] = 'b';
  write(BytestoSend);
  Sensor1CurrentSeries.clear();
  Sensor2CurrentSeries.clear();
  Sensor3CurrentSeries.clear();
  xCount = 0 ;
  lastMinX = 0 ;
  SensorRenderer.setYAxisMin(-127);
  SensorRenderer.setYAxisMax(127);
  SensorRenderer.setXAxisMin(0);
  SensorRenderer.setXAxisMax(100);
  Sync = false ;
  SensorChartView.repaint();
  DataFromArduino.setText(null);
}// end clearScreen

public void SyncData(View v) {
  if (!Sync){
    byte[] BytestoSend = new byte[1];
```

```
    BytestoSend[0] = 'a';
    write(BytestoSend); // sends buffer to the ADK
    Sync = true;
  }
} // end void SyncData(View v)
```

After the updates described in this example are added to the ADK framework and a final check for errors is done, the application can be uploaded to a target Android device. Start and run the openFrameworks program and the Arduino without the Android connected, and let them run for a while to build some data in the log file. When a sufficient amount of data is sent, connect the Android device without restarting the Arduino. A pop-up menu should appear, asking for permission to run a program. Select the ADK Sensor Network program. Synchronize the data when the program is ready, and observe the graph and compare to the one drawn by the openFrameworks program. The red line in the openFrameworks program should match the last position of the Android graph.

■ **Note**   The Android application may have to be forcefully stopped each time it is run because the thread sometimes does not stop properly. More robust thread handling is required for final products.

Summary

The example series in this chapter showed one method of integrating Android into a sensor network and provided a review of other concepts introduced in other chapters of this book. The possible combinations of what the sensor network observes and measures and the different technologies that can be used to achieve a final product are limitless. The example series is not intended to be a final product, but a starting point for further exploration into sensor networks and integration. An extra challenge that can be tackled with this chapter's concepts is using a third XBee module and another USB adapter connected to a different computer to add three more simulated sensors. The most important thing about sensor networks, Arduino, and Android is that you should explore the technology to get more familiar with more advanced techniques so you can use them in future projects.

■ ■ ■

## CHAPTER 9

Using Arduino with PIC32 and ATtiny Atmel Chips

Transitioning from standard to custom Arduino hardware can save space and money. Custom boards can add new capabilities to projects through increased speed, memory, and pins, as well as new features. This chapter will look at chips and boards on a spectrum from the power and complexity of the Leonardo to the inexpensive simplicity of the ATtiny. It will examine the unique capabilities of the chipKIT environment based on the Microchip's PIC32 series micro-controller. Then the chapter will demonstrate some unique libraries and features of the chipKIT environment, including support for scheduling timers, which make object detection with Infra-Red (IR) simple. As an example using the Atmel ATtiny environment, you will program a secret knock to operate a servo motor, which will open and close a small wooden box.

Arduino and Nonstandard Environments

Arduino is both a physical specification and a software abstraction layer. Since the Arduino API functions so effectively, it has been ported to many different platforms and microcontrollers. chipKIT is one of the earliest of these platforms and the first one that supported compiling code for both itself and Arduino. Multiplatform Arduino means that that the Arduino environment can compile code for multiple families of different chips. The multiplatform IDE (MPIDE) can compile Arduino code for Atmel chips and the multiple-platform PIC32.

There is now a broad choice of Arduino-compatible options, including faster and slower chips, with a range of available numbers of pins, and a variety of other features. This spectrum of complexity results in a spectrum of price points. For example, the Arduino Due has an ARM Cortex 3 chip that enhances Arduino performance and has capabilities at similar levels to that of the chipKIT.

These high-performance options work best for some purposes. For example, such an option would be ideal if you were trying to create a project that causes 26 small boxes to blink Morse code, listen with piezos, or unlock boxes. You could customize the projects to include a low-cost chip that has a custom circuit board to make the project affordable. Using these additional environments through the Arduino API allows you to use a high-end prototype. With the Arduino advantage of quick code prototyping, you can make a smooth transition for porting a project from a standard Arduino Uno and put the project on a smaller and less expensive ATtiny family of chips.

Lastly, I will be showing how to program smaller chips like the ATtiny85 from a standard Arduino. You will examine how to make the Arduino a programmer for the ATtiny85 chip—a technique that can be used for the entire ATtiny family, and for many other chips. You will also use the MPIDE to create a PIC32 Arduino-inspired project.

The MPIDE and chipKIT PIC32

chipKIT is an Arduino-derived variation that uses significantly faster hardware and has much more memory. In this section, you will explore bigger, high-end options. The reference boards for the chipKIT environments are the Digilent chipKIT Uno32 (shown in Figure 9-1) and the chipKIT Max32. The platform has been around long enough that there are chipKIT-compatible boards, such as the chipKIT FubarinoSD and chipKIT Fubarino Mini. These boards all fall in the same price range as the Arduino Uno and the Arduino Mega, but they have significantly improved performance. The Arduino Due board is comparable in speed.

Figure 9-1. *Chipkit Reference Board the Uno32 by Digilent Inc*

The chipKIT home page is at http://chipkit.net, and the documentation for the project is located at http://chipkit.net/category/chipkit-projects. Support and discussion of the project is at the chipKIT forum, at http://chipkit.org/forum. Lastly, the MPIDE source code and bootloader are located at https://github.com/chipKIT32/chipKIT32-MAX. Table 9-1 gives a comparison of the two boards.

Table 9-1. *Comparison of the Built-In Features of the chipKIT Max32 and the Arduino Mega*

Features	chipKIT Max32	Arduino Mega
CPU performance	80 MHz	16 MHz
Core	32 bit	8 bit
Flash memory	512 KB	256 KB
SRAM/program memory	128 KB	8 KB
Digital I/O	83/5 PWM	54/14 PWM
Analog I/O	16	16
RTCC	Yes	No
Ethernet	Yes, with add-on shield	No
USB	USB 2.0 FS, device/host, OTG	
CAN controllers	2	0
Timers	16/32 bit	8/16 bit
Comparators	2	1
I2C	5	1
SPI	2	1
UART	6, with IrDA	4

Digilent has created additional libraries to take advantage of the unique hardware. In addition to the standard Arduino SPI, there are some improved SPI libraries, including Digilent SPI (DSPI) and Open Source Serial Peripheral Interface hardware with SPI support. Software SPI (SoftSPI) is a software implementation of SPI that allows any pin to be used for SPI communication. Software Pulse Width Modulation Servo (SoftPWMServo) ensures that every pin can be used. It also has improved timer support with the Core Timer Service, and a Task Management service. I will demo those features later in this section.

■ **Note**   The editor is a derivation of the ArduinoThis ChipKit Max32 board in Table 9-1 has many features which put it on the same playing field as the Arduino Due. Additional features like Ethernet, and Car Area Network(CAN) Bus allow for less expensive shields that bring out these features to pins on Ethernet, or CAN Bus shield. More chip details can be found at http://www.chipkit.org/wiki/index.php?title=ChipKIT_Max32.

Another thing in common with the Arduino Due is power issues. There are many pins on the ChipKit Max32 that are 5v tolerant, but not all are. Here are some caveats when powering pins:

- The PIC32 MCUs on these boards have an operational voltage of 3.3V. The ChipKit MAX32, UNO32, and u32 boards are 5V tolerant, meaning you can input 5V to get a digital or analog reading without burning out the chip. However, these chips only output a maximum of 3.3V. Some 5V components may not recognize 3.3V.

- The readings will be made by default in the range of 0–3.3V instead of 0–5V. So, you will have to change the values in your own code or libraries in order to obtain the correct range. This may include using a logic level converter for a 5V device. However, many components are already 3.3V compatible, so, for example, you will not need a logic level converter for chipKIT or Arduino Due boards. The Arduino revision 3 shield specification includes an IOREF pin. If your code checks this pin value, you can enable the appropriate level converter for your board.

- For I2C, there needs to be external pull-up resistors. The PIC32 does not have internal pull-up resistors for every digital pin, so it is best to not use them. You can also design shields or breadboard projects by including the needed pull-up resistors, typically 2–2.7kΩ. This helps make a shield or project compatible with the Arduino Leonardo, which also does not have pull-up resistors on the I2C pins.

■ **Note**   The editor is a derivation of the Arduino IDE, and it acts and performs the same as the Arduino 1.0 editor. However, at the time of writing, it supports the Arduino 0023 core.

Digilent Incorporated has created additional libraries to take advantage of the unique hardware. In addition to the standard Arduino SPI, there is Digilent Serial Peripheral Interface (DSPI) for hardware based SPI support. Additionally, there is an official Software SPI (SoftSPI) is a software implementation of SPI that allows any pin to be used for SPI communication. It is common when using shield to have a conflict with a pin that is already using SPI. Being able to use software create a new SPI pin gets around that conflict.

Software Pulse Width Modulation Servo (SoftPWMServo) ensures that every pin can be used. The SoftPWMServo library allows for any pin on a ChipKit board to support servos.

It also has improved timer support with the Core Timer Service, and a Task Management service. The Core Timer Service will let you work on timing issues with micro second resolution. Whereas the Task Management Service will let you work at millisecond resolution. We will use the Task Management Service to do object detection with in timed intervals that will not interfere with your code in the main loop. Also, it will not require polling the sensors in your loop code.

Example: Object Detection using the Task Manager service

In this example, you will use one chipKIT Uno32, two IR LEDs, and one IR sensor. The example uses the ChipKit Task Manager to register two tasks that blink the IR LEDs at specified intervals. Figure 9-2 shows the project breadboard layout. The sensors are connected to pins 5, and 6. The IR sensor is connected to pin 2 which is an interrupt pin. This will allow the IR sensor to immediately trigger upon the detection of IR.

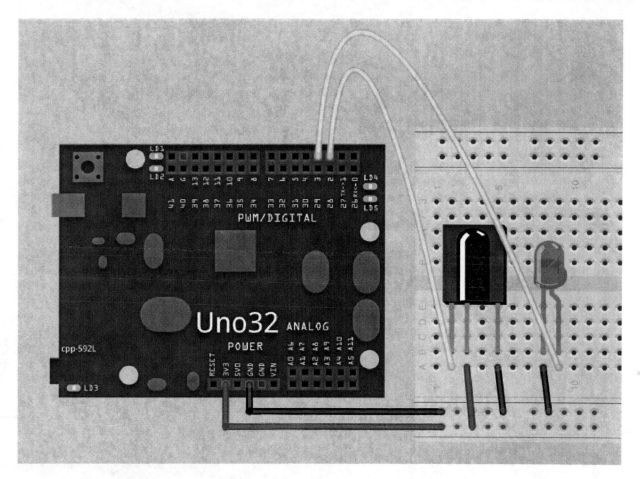

Figure 9-2. *Uno32 IR LED sensor and emmiter wiring example*

The code in Listing 9-1 is loaded using MPIDE. The chipKIT Uno32 is both a listener and broadcaster. It blinks and receives information about whether or not reflections from the IR LEDs. The code is non-blocking, so you can simultaneously perform other actions while it is working. It is possible to operate a servo and respond to objects detected in the front, left, or right of the sensor.

Listing 9-1. IR Object Detection Using the Task Manager Code Example

```
/*
* Object Detection with the Core Task Manager Service
 * Determine with one sensor which where an object is
 * 2 - 4 IR LEDs
 * 1 IR Sensor
 */

//PIN_INT1 for the ChipKit UNO32 is Pin 2
#define pinInt PIN_INT1
```

```
#define SENSOR1_PIN 2
#define EMITTER1_PIN 5
#define EMITTER2_PIN 6
#define BEATS 6
```

In listing 9-2 the interrupt pin is defined as PIN_INT1. This is a generic way to refer to interrupt 1. Depending on what kind of ChipKit you use these can map to different pins on the hardware. For a ChipKit Uno32 these map to pin 2. If you wanted to use a different interrupt you could use:

Listing 9-2. define hardware values

```
PIN_INT0        38
PIN_INT1        2
PIN_INT2        7
PIN_INT3        8
PIN_INT4        35
```

When ever you switch to a different board you will want to double check which pins correspond to the correct interrupt.

```
int emmiter1_id;
int emmiter2_id;

unsigned long blink1_var;
unsigned long blink2_var;
```

In listing 9-3 the the required ChipKit Task Manager variables are defined emmiter1_id, and emmiter2_id are the task identifier variable that are used to register the task. The blink1_var, and blink2_var are the the data variables that are passed into the task function and represent the current time information.

Listing 9-3. ChipKit Task Manager Library require variables

```
volatile boolean emitter1State = LOW;
volatile boolean emitter2State = LOW;
volatile boolean prevEmitter1State = LOW;
volatile boolean prevEmitter2State = LOW;

volatile boolean detected = LOW;
volatile boolean e1detected = LOW;
volatile boolean e2detected = LOW;

volatile unsigned long emit1Count = 0;
volatile unsigned long emit2Count = 0;
volatile unsigned long detectCount = 0;
```

The meta data about the task are defined. This includes detection count, current emitter status, previous emitter status, and which emitter was detected. These values will be adjusted in the task manger functions, and the when the detection interrupt is triggered.

Listing 9-4. Emmiter data defined and initialized with default values

```
volatile int phaseA = 0;
volatile int phaseB = 0;
volatile int prevPhaseA = -1;
volatile int prevPhaseB = -1;
volatile int measureA = 0;
volatile int measureB = 0;
volatile int prevMeasureA = -1;
volatile int prevMeasureB = -1;
```

A measure is defined as the basic container of a set number of intervals that can be thought of as beats per measure. As each of these beats is stepped through the phase of the measure is updated. The default configuration is 6 beats per measure. Every time a task is activated it increases the phase until it reaches the end of the measure and the measure and phases start over again.

Listing 9-5. The measeure and the phase of the measure are defined and initialized

```
//Prototypes
void blink_emitter1(int id, void * tptr);
void blink_emitter2(int id, void * tptr);
void readIRSensor();
void blink(int);
```

In Listing 9-6 the prototypes are required because the functions are defined after the loop code. So the prototypes have to be listed.

Listing 9-6. Prototypes of the functions used by the interrupt system, and the task manger code.

```
void setup() {
  Serial.begin(115200);
  delay(2000);
  // initialize the digital pin as an output.
  // Pin PIN_LED1 has an LED connected on most Arduino boards:
  pinMode(pinInt, INPUT);
  //debugging LED, shows when pulse found
  pinMode(PIN_LED1, OUTPUT);
  digitalWrite(PIN_LED1, HIGH);
  pinMode(SENSOR1_PIN, INPUT);
  pinMode(EMITTER1_PIN, OUTPUT);
  pinMode(EMITTER2_PIN, OUTPUT);

  digitalWrite(EMITTER1_PIN, LOW);
  digitalWrite(EMITTER2_PIN, LOW);
  //blink before timers and interrups
  blinkAll(6);
```

In Listing 9-7 the code uses the defined hardware and configure it corectly for the starting state of the project. This includes a diagnostic called blinkAll. One you see all the LEDs blinking, the hardware is configured correctly and is ready to detect the IR pulses.

Listing 9-7. Configuration code the hardware.

```
attachInterrupt(SENSOR1_PIN, readIRSensor, RISING);
emmiter1_id = createTask(blink_emitter1, 13, TASK_ENABLE, &blink1_var);
emmiter2_id = createTask(blink_emitter2, 13, TASK_ENABLE, &blink2_var);


}
```

In Listing 9-8 the code attaches the interrupt to the pin it is checking to see if it changes. When the pin is in a rising state, meaning that it goes from a LOW state to a HIGH state perform a callback to the readIRSensor function. This guarantees that as soon as the sensor detects an IR pulse it triggers immediately without the need to constantly check in your loop code a pulse came in.

The next section of code in Listing 9-8 uses the createTask function to set up the task of blinking led emmiter1. The task id is stored in emmiter1_id. Any time a manipulation of the task is required this id can be used to reference the task. In the function the first portion is the callback function blink_emmiter1. Blink_emmiter1 is called in a 13 millisecond interval. TASK_ENABLE forces the task start right away, and the task data is stored in blink1_var. The same logic applies for the second emitter. At this point the device is sensing and blinking with no code in the main loop used to control these events. This way your code is always remains specific to your goal, and only needs to respond to a detection of an IR pulse.

Listing 9-8. Create and activate the interrupt, and the tasks that control the IR leds.

```
void loop() {
  digitalWrite(PIN_LED1, LOW);

  if (detected) {
    Serial.print("{ \"IRDetect\": ");
    Serial.print(detectCount);
    Serial.print(" ,\"measureA\": ");
    Serial.print(measureA);
    Serial.print(" ,\"measureB\": ");
    Serial.print(measureB);
    Serial.print(" ,\"phaseA\": ");
    Serial.print(phaseA);
    Serial.print(" ,\"phaseB\": ");
    Serial.print(phaseB);
    Serial.print(" ,\"Emmit1\": ");
    Serial.print((int)emitter1State);
    Serial.print(" ,\"prevEmmit1\": ");
    Serial.print((int)prevEmitter1State);
    Serial.print(" ,\"count\": ");
    Serial.print(emit1Count);
    Serial.print(" ,\"Emmit2\": ");
    Serial.print((int)emitter2State);
    Serial.print(" ,\"prevEmmit2\": ");
    Serial.print((int)prevEmitter2State);
    Serial.print(" ,\"count\": ");
    Serial.print(emit2Count);
```

The current statue of the system is reported on by using the serial output to show the status of the system in JSON format.

Listing 9-9. The main loop reports on the status of the system in a JSON format via serial.

```
  if(emitter1State) {
    prevEmitter1State = emitter1State;
    Serial.print(" ,\"Obj\": \"Right\"");
  }
  if (prevMeasureA == measureA) {
    if (e1detected && e2detected)
    {
      Serial.print(" ,\"Obj\": \"Front\"");
    }
  }
 if(emitter2State) {
    prevEmitter2State = emitter2State;
    Serial.print(" ,\"Obj\": \"Left\"");
  }
  Serial.println("}");
  prevMeasureA = measureA;
  prevMeasureB = measureB;
  prevPhaseA = phaseA;
  detected = false;
 }

}
```

Listing 9-10 shows the detection logic. If only emitter1 is detected in a measure there is an object on the left. If only emitter2 is detected in a measure then an object on the right is detected. If in the measure both emitter1, and emmiter2 are detected there is an object in front of the device.

Listing 9-10. The detection logic is defined by what is detected in a single measure.

```
void readIRSensor() {
  digitalWrite(PIN_LED1, HIGH);
  if(emitter1State) {
    emit1Count++;
    detectCount++;
    detected = true;
    e1detected = true;
  }
  else if (emitter2State) {
    emit2Count++;++;
    detectCount++;
    detected = true;
    e2detected = true;
  }
}
```

Listing 9-11. readIRsensor function is defined.

```
void blink_emitter1(int id, void * tptr) {
  if(phaseA >= BEATS) {
    phaseA = 0;
    measureA++;
    e1detected = false;
  }

  if (phaseA== 1) {
    emitter1State = true;
    phaseA++;
    digitalWrite(EMITTER1_PIN, emitter1State);
  }
  else  {
    emitter1State = false;
    phaseA++;
    digitalWrite(EMITTER1_PIN, emitter1State);

  }
}

void blink_emitter2(int id, void * tptr) {
  if(phaseB >= BEATS) {
    phaseB = 0;
    measureB++;
    e2detected = false;
  }
  if (phaseB == 3) {
    emitter2State = true;
    phaseB++;
    digitalWrite(EMITTER2_PIN, emitter2State);
  }
  else
  {
    emitter2State = false;
    phaseB++;
    digitalWrite(EMITTER2_PIN, emitter2State);
  }
}
```

Listing 9-12. Blink_emitter1 and blink_emitter2 task are defined.

```
void blinkAll(int loops)
{
  for (int ii = 0; ii < loops; ii++)
  {
    digitalWrite(PIN_LED1, HIGH);
    digitalWrite(EMITTER1_PIN, HIGH);
    digitalWrite(EMITTER2_PIN, HIGH);
    delay(250);
    digitalWrite(PIN_LED1, LOW);
```

```
      digitalWrite(EMITTER1_PIN, LOW);
      digitalWrite(EMITTER2_PIN, LOW);
      delay(250);
   }
}
```

Blink all is used as diagnostic function

The code sends timed infrared pulses that are then detected by an IR sensor, so you can debug it and determine which port is sending data. Connect the chipKIT Uno32 and open the serial monitor in the MPIDE. Then power up or connect the USB to the FubarinoSD, and it will start transmitting. You should now see frequency counts per second in your serial MPIDE monitor, and you can perform line-of-sight infrared object detection or detect remote beacon.

In this project the code is depends very little on what occurs in the loop. The only loop code that is used is to make a decision about where the object is that was detected. Knowing the object position can cause your robot or device to respond in several different ways including avoidance or point towards it in case you were choosing to move a camera to look at what was detected. By using these advanced features of interrupts with the Core Task Manager, service complicated tasks become much easier.

Arduino Support for the ATtiny Family

There are two main ATtiny cores for Arduino. One is maintained by David Mellis at the Hi-Low Tech MIT web site (http://hlt.media.mit.edu/?p=1695), and the other is a Google Code project called ATtiny core, at http://code.google.com/p/arduino-tiny/. This chapter will use the ATtiny core project from Google Code, as it includes support for a wider array of chips, features, and pins.

The ATtiny chips arrive from the factory with fuses set for less than 1 MHz, so you have to decide at what speed you want your chip to run. The ATtiny85 runs at 1 MHz, but it can be configured to run at 8 MHz, 16 MHz internally, or 20 MHz with a crystal or oscillator. The first step in programming these chips is to burn the fuse configuration to support the clock that you will use.

■ **Note**   If you don't burn the bootloader, or if you set it to the wrong speed, your chip will not perform at the expected speed.

You can do this in the Arduino IDE by selecting the chip and the speed from the Tools menu, as shown in Figure 9-3.

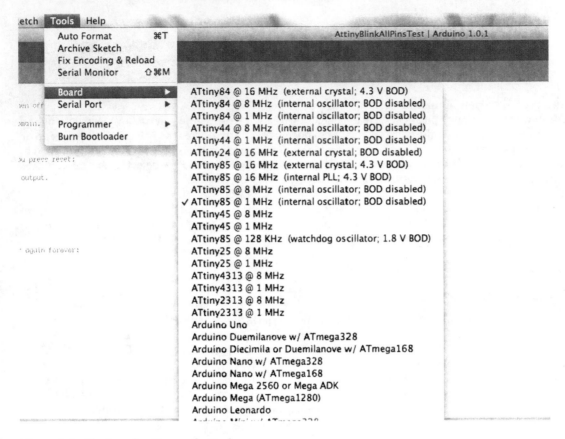

Figure 9-3. *The Board option on the Tools menu*

Next, select the Burn Bootloader option, as shown in Figure 9-4. This will trigger Avrdude to program the correct options in your chip.

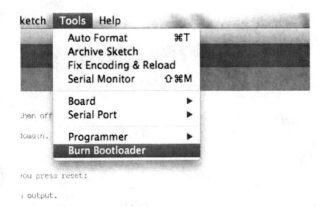

Figure 9-4. *The Burn Bootloader option*

While the Atmel family of chips is compatible with Arduino, its pin-numbering scheme is different. Let's look at the features and specifications of the ATtiny chips in Tables 9-2, 9-3, and 9-4, paying particular attention to the pin numbering, as diagrammed in Figures 9-5, 9-6, and 9-7.

The Atmel family consists of the following chips:

- ATtiny 85, 45, and 25

- ATtiny 84, 44, and 24

- ATtiny 4313 and 2313

ATtiny 85/45/25

Table 9-2 shows the chip specifications for the ATtiny 85, 45, and 25.

Table 9-2. *Chip Specifications for the Arduino ATtiny 85/45/25*

Chip	Flash	EEPROM	SRAM	PWM	ADC	Digital I/O
ATtiny85	8KB	128 bytes	128 bytes	2	3	6
ATtiny45	4KB	256 bytes	256 bytes	2	3	6
ATtiny25	2KB	512 bytes	512 bytes	2	3	6

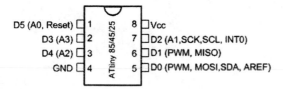

Figure 9-5. *Pin layout of the ATtiny 85/45/25*

Pin 7 supports I2C, and pin 5 supports SCL and SDA, as shown in Figure 9-3. This support is maintained through the TinyWire library. The code can be found at `http://arduino.cc/playground/Code/USIi2c`.

ATtiny 84/44/24

Table 9-3 shows the chip specifications for the ATtiny 84, 44, and 24.

Table 9-3. *Chip Specifications for the Arduino ATtiny 84/44/24*

Chip	Flash	EEPROM	SRAM	PWM	ADC	Digital I/O
ATtiny84	8KB	128 bytes	128 bytes	4	8	11
ATtiny44	4KB	256 bytes	256 bytes	4	8	11
ATtiny24	2KB	512 bytes	512 bytes	4	8	11

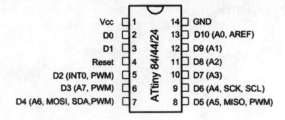

Figure 9-6. *Pin layout of the ATtiny 84/44/24*

I2C is supported on pin 7, and SDA and SCL are supported on pin 9, as shown in Figure 9-4.

ATtiny 4313 and 2313

Table 9-4 shows the chip specifications for the ATtiny 4313 and 2313.

Table 9-4. *Chip Specifications for the ATtiny 4313 and 2313*

Chip	Flash	EEPROM	SRAM	PWM	ADC	Digital I/O
4314	4KB	256 bytes	256 bytes	4	0	18
2313	2KB	128 bytes	128 bytes	4	0	18

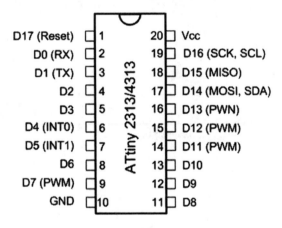

Figure 9-7. *Pin layout of the ATtiny 4313 and 2313*

These chips do not have a standard serial interface, so the normal Arduino bootloader does not work with these chips. You must manually set the chip configuration in one step, and then you can program the chip using an in-system programmer. The protocol is SPI.

Each of these chips has the following:

- MISO
- MOSI
- Vcc

- GND
- SCK
- RESET

Using the Arduino as an ISP Programmer

An *in-system programmer (ISP)* is a device that can program other chips. There are several system programmers available. I recommend the Adafruit USBTinyISP, which you can download at https://www.adafruit.com/products/46. In this case, as shown in Figure 9-8, you want to use the Arduino as an ISP programmer, which allows you to wire it directly, and to create a custom PCB, or to make a shield for quick programming.

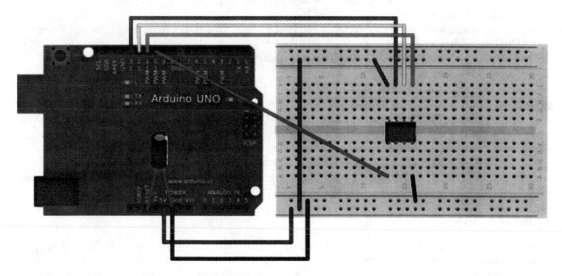

Figure 9-8. *The Arduino Uno as an ISP programmer*

The ATtiny in the example is the ATtiny85. Other ATtiny chips can be programmed the same way as long as the correct ISP pins are mapped. The example in Figure 9-6 also shows a corresponding circuit board that you can create.

Since an Arduino resets when connected via a serial port, you will need to disable the reset pin in order to avoid a reset when programming. This can be done in a couple of way—you can either use a 10µF capacitor from the reset pin to the ground or a 124Ω resistor to pull reset high to the 5V pin.

Analog pins are numbered from 1,2 and 3. They correspond to the pins 7, 3, and 2 on the chip, but are referenced in this way: ADC1 is 1, ADC 2 is 2, and ADC 3 is 3. Since they are already properly initialized, do not set the pin mode for analog pins. All the digital pins can be referenced via their pin number on the data sheet.

■ **Note**   It is possible to program an ATtiny that is configured for 1 MHz, as 8 MHz will cause the delay functions to be extra slow.

It is also important to note that internal analog reference is usually 1.1, but it is possible to set it to other values too; however, you must not apply an external voltage to the AREF pin, or else you will short out the op amp in the ADC.

Given these features, it is possible to program the ATtiny using an Arduino by configuring an Arduino Uno or another board with the Arduino ISP sketch and wiring the boards to each other, which I will demonstrate in the following example.

Project: Secret Knock Box

In this example, you will use a secret-knock example to open a small box with a servo. The idea is to detect a knock and then trigger a servo to open the box. Then you can then use a double-knock to close the box. The box remains closed until the secret knock is identified. This technique has been used to open doors and boxes and to trigger events based on a knock code. I used them in my Morse's Secret Box project, where tapping Morse code opened the box. The laser-cut designs for these boxes can be found online at http://github.com/ricklon/morsessecret. A custom circuit board for the project, called the ATtiny Servo, is available as well, at https://github.com/ricklon/attinyservo.

This project is typically done with a larger chip or a standard Arduino Uno. However if you were to make 20, 30, or even a thousand of these boxes the cost and complexity would be very high. This makes it impractical to sell a project for a profit, or efficiently reduce the complexity of project. It is a good idea to prototype on an Arduino Uno which on average costs $35.00 per unit. In this case, though, you want to use the ATtiny85, which costs around $1.29, or approximately $0.75 in quantities of 25.

The options for this chip are somewhat limited, so if Servo.h is unavailable, there are other servo options available. However, because there is only one timer on the chip, there is a conflict with the Arduino standard Servo Library. Other servo options are available, but the very basic option is to operate the servo manually by programming the chip to send the servo pulse commands. This solution works well, and is modeled by this project.

This chapter introduces a project that uses a knock sensor to tap a secret code. LEDs are used to show a knock occurred, and was detected. When the correct code is sensed a command is sent to move a servo to open a box lid. An ATtiny85 is used because it has a small form factor, and the additional electronics can fit in extremely small spaces.

What the Device Does

When you program a knock pattern into the device, the system listens for the knock, and the servo is triggered to open the box. Additionally, there is a programming mode where you can set the knock and use some LEDs for feedback on the programming process. This project transforms the code from just a stand alone sketch to a library that can be used in many projects.

Bill of Materials

For this project, you will need the following:

- Servo
- Piezo
- Two LEDs
- One button
- Two resistors (220kΩ)
- One 6MΩ resistor

The project is small enough to be a simple do-it-yourself PCB or a breadboard, as in Figure 9-9; it can also use dead bug–style wiring.

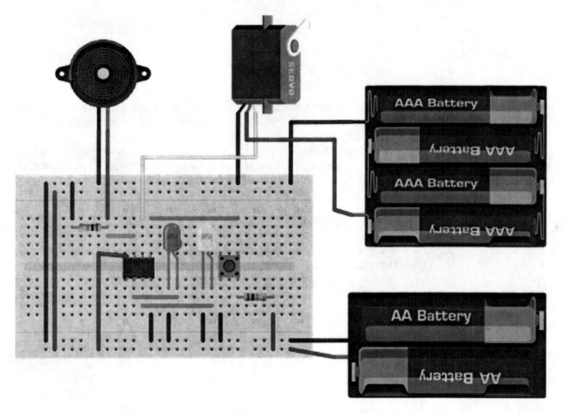

Figure 9-9. *Circuit diagram of the knock box*

The Arduino sketch is called KnockUnlock.ino, and includes a servo.h library and a SecretKnock.h library. The servo.h library simply configures the servo to move at a specific pulse for a specified number of milliseconds. The SecretKnock.h library defines an object, which allows for the configuration of an initial secret knock and the appropriate feedback pins to reprogram the knock sequence.

Listing 9-13 is the main sketch.

Listing 9-13. Main Sketch of Secret Knock Box

```
#include "SecretKnock.h"
#define SERVO_PIN 1

int initKnocks[MAX_KNOCKS]= { 50, 25, 25, 50, 100, 50, 50, 0, 0, 0, 0, 0, 0, 0, 0, 0, 0, 0, 0, 0};

SecretKnock sKnock;

void setup() {

sKnock.begin(initKnocks);

}
```

```
void loop() {

  sKnock.checkKnock();

}
```

The current configuration detects a "shave and a haircut, two bits" type of knock. It sounds like "dah, dit, dit, dah, dit, pause, dit, dit", and can be visualized like "_.._. .." You can change this to any knock combination by defining the pauses in the antiknocks. The pause ratio is used to determine if there are any matching knocks.

Most of the work is completed in the SecretKnock object. First, the pin configurations include the servo—the green LED is pin 3, the red LED is pin 4, the piezo's knock sensor is analog pin 1, the program button is pin 0, and the servo pin is #define SERVO_PIN 1, which is digital pin 1.

Then the secret knock properties are defined, as in Listing 9-14.

Listing 9-14. Definging the Properties of the Secret Knock

```
threshold = 500;            // Minimum signal from the piezo to register as a knock
rejectValue = 25;           // If an individual knock is off by this percentage of a knock we
                               don't unlock.
averageRejectValue = 15;    // If the average timing of the knocks is off by this percent we
                               don't unlock.
knockFadeTime = 200;        // milliseconds we allow a knock to fade before we listen for
                               another one. (Debounce timer.)
lockTurnTime = 650;         // milliseconds that we run the motor to get it to go a half turn.
lockMotor = 2;
knockComplete = 1200;       // Longest time to wait for a knock before we assume that it's finished.
```

Once this is complete, the code is ready to perform checkKnock() in the main loop() function. Once the first knock is detected, it will seek to match a knock pattern.

The enclosure can be any kind of box that you want; you use the servo as a lock that opens when the secret knock triggers the move-servo code.

You can program the code into the ATtiny85 using the technique demonstrated in Listing 9-13, but be sure to disconnect the servo.

The servo code, as shown in Listing 9-13, is simplified to manually pulse the servo to make it move. This technique requires the chip to keep pulsing for the length of time it takes to move the servo. The result is that only one servo at a time can be active. Even if you were to configure multiple servos, you could only move one at a time.

The key to reading the knock sensor is inside of the checkServo() function. This is analogRead(knockSensor), which checks if the piezo is greater than the trigger threshold. If so, the code will start listening for a knock pattern.

A knock pattern is recognized by the ratio of pauses within a certain tolerance. The code that makes that comparison appears in Listing 9-15.

Listing 9-15. The Code That Identifies the Secret Knock

```
// Sees if our knock matches the secret.
// returns true if it's a good knock, false if it's not.
// to do: break it into smaller functions for readability.
boolean SecretKnock::validateKnock()
{
  int i=0;
```

```
  // simplest check first: Did we get the right number of knocks?
  int currentKnockCount = 0;
  int secretKnockCount = 0;
  int maxKnockInterval = 0;                   // We use this later to normalize the times.

  for (i=0;i<MAX_KNOCKS;i++){
    if (knockReadings[i] > 0){
      currentKnockCount++;
    }
    if (secretCode[i] > 0){                   // todo: precalculate this.
      secretKnockCount++;
    }

    if (knockReadings[i] > maxKnockInterval){    // collect normalization data while we're looping.
      maxKnockInterval = knockReadings[i];
    }
  }

  // If we're recording a new knock, save the info and get out of here.
  if (programButtonPressed==true){
    for (i=0;i<MAX_KNOCKS;i++){ // normalize the times
      secretCode[i]= map(knockReadings[i],0, maxKnockInterval, 0, 100);
    }
    // And flash the lights in the recorded pattern to let us know it's been programmed.
    digitalWrite(greenLED, LOW);
    digitalWrite(redLED, LOW);
    delay(1000);
    digitalWrite(greenLED, HIGH);
    digitalWrite(redLED, HIGH);
    delay(50);
    for (i = 0; i < MAX_KNOCKS ; i++){
      digitalWrite(greenLED, LOW);
      digitalWrite(redLED, LOW);
      // only turn it on if there's a delay
      if (secretCode[i] > 0){
        delay( map(secretCode[i],0, 100, 0, maxKnockInterval));
// Expand the time back out to what it was, roughly.
        digitalWrite(greenLED, HIGH);
        digitalWrite(redLED, HIGH);
      }
      delay(50);
    }
    return false;      // We don't unlock the door when we are recording a new knock.
  }

  if (currentKnockCount != secretKnockCount){
    return false;
  }
```

Listing 9-16 compares the relative intervals of the knocks, not the absolute time between them. So, for example, the door should open regardless of whether you carry out the pulsing pattern slowly or quickly, as long as the pattern is correct. This makes the timing less tricky, which, while making it less secure, can also make the box less picky about your tempo, which may be slightly off.

Listing 9-16. Code Comparing the Intervals of Knocks

```
int totaltimeDifferences=0;
int timeDiff=0;
for (i=0;i<MAX_KNOCKS;i++){ // Normalize the times
  knockReadings[i]= map(knockReadings[i],0, maxKnockInterval, 0, 100);
  timeDiff = abs(knockReadings[i]-secretCode[i]);
  if (timeDiff > rejectValue){ // Individual value too far out of whack
    return false;
  }
  totaltimeDifferences += timeDiff;
}
// It can also fail if the whole thing is too inaccurate.
if (totaltimeDifferences/secretKnockCount>averageRejectValue){
  return false;
}

return true;

}
```

The code in Listing 9-16 uses the knock reading array to hold the pattern of knock pauses.

Summary

Transitioning from standard Arduino to a professional approach is a big step. Knowing how to use a high-speed, 32-bit, and feature-rich MCU is critical in moving toward creating high-end projects for video, audio, and peer-to-peer communication. Additionally, working with the low-end Atmel chips cuts costs and allows you to work on projects with multiple small parts. For example, you can create a set of Arduinos, using the ATtiny85, that blinks a single code per block. It is much cheaper to use the ATtiny85, and the form factor is small enough to keep the project relatively small.

CHAPTER 10

Multiprocessing: Linking the Arduino for More Power

Certain projects may not lend themselves well to an individual Arduino, because of possible limitations with the hardware, such as a processor's speed or limited memory. Multiprocessing can add greater functionality to a system; this is commonly seen with Arduino in the form of coprocessors connected via shields such as the Ethernet shield. Coprocessor-style shields share their functionality with the Arduino to offload complex processes, but still allow the Arduino to have the main control. Multiprocessing is normally associated with high-level computing when it is infeasible to make a single device perform at required speeds. The principles of supercomputing can be applied to microcontrollers. This chapter explorers the fundamental hurdle of multiprocessing by examining reliable communication between two or more processors.

Processors can be of same type or unique to best match the type of work being performed. For instance, the Arduino may not be meant for digital signal processing (DSP) itself, but when combined with a DSP chip, it can control the DSP and make use of the data coming from the DSP. The development of a sensor package may fit well within the abilities of one Arduino, and the package could use a basic serial connection. A different communication method may need to be used if 100 packages have to be working at the same time within the same system. Controlling a mass LED display built with smaller LED units would employ numerous identical units to make a much larger display, which would be difficult for a single piece of equipment to achieve.

Multiprocessor systems can be broadly categorized by the coupling between devices. *Loosely coupled* systems require a communications package be used between devices, such as the Xbee module to communicate via wireless or the Ethernet shield. Even if the secondary device is built into the same physical device, the use of a middleman requires that the processors use extra resources maintaining the additional communication hardware. However, while loosely coupled processors can lose a great deal of efficiency by adding the extra layer for communication, changing from one protocol to another, they do have the advantage of being able to traverse great physical distances.

Tightly coupled systems take advantage of methods designed for high bandwidth that are built within the processor, such as HyperTransport. Some server processors have HyperTransport built directly within the processor to be able to communicate directly with other processors without having to use other communication hardware. Tightly coupled multiprocessing setups operate at short distance to maximize the available bandwidth. Usually distances of a few inches to a few feet separate processors before the increase in transmission line impedance makes separated hardware-based communication methods more viable. Tightly coupled systems can also share common resources such as memory with greater ease than can be done with loosely coupled systems. Tightly coupled systems usually have a protocol for flow control and addressing between processing units. The protocols that are used within tightly coupled systems are usually simple when compared to loosely coupled systems because data corruption is limited by careful engineering of the physical connections, lowering the need for complex error correction.

This chapter focuses on chip-to-chip, tightly coupled systems. Several methods exist to connect one chip to another, and they are categorized as either *serial* or *parallel*. In recent times, parallel alone has been decreasing in use because of the increase in the reliability and speed that serial now provides. A parallel methodology combined with serial communications has been coming out in the form of technologies such as SATA, PCI express, and USB 3.0.

The lower count of the used pins makes serial methods more viable for microcontroller work. Out of the three common communication methods that are implemented in the Arduino, only two are viable for use for multiprocessing: I2C and Serial Peripheral Interface (SPI).

I2C and SPI have the advantage over serial because they offer the ability to connect multiple devices over a data bus. The I2C and SPI serial communication standards are natively available within the Arduino without any extra hardware and are excellent choices for chip-to-chip communication. Unlike regular serial, which uses two separate lines for each connected device, I2C and SPI share the same data transmission lines and are also synchronous communication methods, both using a shared clock line, which helps with the reliability of transmitted data. SPI is capable of running faster than I2C, but SPI uses more digital connection when adding more end devices. The added digital connections are used to address the individual connected devices. Concentrations of the differences between SPI and I2C need to be taken into account when deciding which method will meet the requirements of a project.

I2C

I2C is a great choice for connecting processors, sensors, and accessories. It has a significant amount of support from multiple hardware vendors, at least in part because of its low pin count to connect multiple devices. I2C requires only two lines, a serial clock and a serial data line, shared between multiple end devices. It has advanced features including flow control, addressing, master/slave both able to control data transmission, and clock stretching to allow interoperability of slower devices.

I2C has some disadvantages that keep it from being a direct choice for chip-to-chip communications:

- I2C is only capable of half-duplex transmission and the bus speed is lower to allow for two-way communications.

- I2C has a large address space and allows you to create large networks. An increase in the number of devices can be problematic, however, because as the number of devices go up, the data line can become saturated with transmissions, choking the serial transmission and increasing the number of data collisions.

- I2C has a deterministic method to deal with collisions between devices, so data should not be lost unless the end device waiting to send fills its entire buffer with data before it can take control of the data line, which is possible on busy networks.

Other problems can occur with communications between two distant endpoints within a large network. Capacitance of the data and clock lines can be increased when a line grows in size, due to the data and clock on I2C connections being pulled high. The change in capacitance directly affects the rise and fall time of the digital signal, requiring slower bus speeds to accommodate the delay in the state change. The capacitance is negligible with short-run wire distances, but requires extra consideration on larger systems if a higher data rate is required. There is more bandwidth loss in I2C inherently because the protocol has built-in handshaking and reply packets.

I2C may be a sufficient solution for chip-to-chip communication if only a few devices neesd to be connected or the amount of data being transferred is minimal. I2C was earlier described in Chapter 6; refer to the example there for the basic techniques for implementing I2C communications with Arduino.

■ **Note** Hardware that is labeled as having a "two-wire interface" is similar to I2C, with some key differences. Diligence should be used when selecting components, especially if the two standards are to be used in conjunction to ensure compatibility.

Serial Peripheral Interface

SPI is almost the same as serial communication, being capable of full-duplex communication while providing synchronous connection between devices. SPI offers the following advantages:

- It can achieve very high speeds and is normally implemented between one master and one or more slaves.

- There is no clock limit set by the SPI standard, and it is limited only by the hardware's maximum clock speed.

- The clock is shared between SPI devices, eliminating the need for the devices to be individually clocked. The master SPI device controls the clock and is similar to the method used by I2C.

- SPI slave devices do not have the ability to temporally hold the clock that is inherent for I2C devices.

- SPI has defined a range of connection types: three-wire, which uses a bidirectional data line (a half-duplex method); the more common four-wire; and five-wire, which adds a data-ready line to provide the ability for a slave device to inform the master that data needs to be transferred.

■ **Note**   The lack of defined protocols can be problematic when integrating multiple devices, as each device can implement unique protocols, possibly making interconnectivity difficult. A router can be used to bridge dissimilar SPI protocols by translating and passing data from one SPI network to another. Manufacturer data sheets should contain all the information needed to develop such a router. The lack of defined protocols is also an advantage in that it provides flexibility to tailor protocols to the application.

There are a lot of abbreviations used in this chapter, so Table 10-1 acts as a handy reference guide.

Table 10-1. *SPI Abbreviations*

Abbreviation	Definition
SCK (serial clock)	The clock signal generated by the SPI master associated with data transfer
SS (slave select)	A logical high or low signal line used to select one or multiple devices
MOSI (master out slave in)	A shared data line on all SPI devices in a network; this is the output of the master's shift register and the input of the slave's
MISO (master in slave out)	A shared data line on all SPI devices in a network; this is the input of the master's shift register and the output of the slave's
CLI (clear interrupts)	Clears the global interrupt enable flag
SEI (set interrupts)	Sets the global interrupt flag
ISR (interrupt service routine)	Used to define event handling on the processor
SPCR (SPI control register)	An 8-bit register that defines a majority of SPI functionality and configuration

(*continued*)

Table 10-1. (*continued*)

Abbreviation	Definition
SPIE (SPI interrupt enable)	Turns on interrupt handling for SPI events
SPE (SPI enable)	Turns SPI core on or off
DORD (data order)	Sets the data order of a transfer to most-significant-bit-first or least-significant-bit-first
MSTR (master/slave select)	Enables the master mode in the SPI core
CPOL (clock polarity)	Defines the clock polarity when idle
CPHA (clock phase)	Determines when data is set and when it is read in correlation to the rise and fall of the clock
SPR1, SPR0, SPI2X (SPI clock rate select)	Used together to determine the clock divider and speed of the SPI network
SPSR (SPI status register)	Stores flags regarding the SPI transfer; also holds the SPI2X value
SPIF (SPI interrupt flag)	Is set when an event triggers the SPI interrupt and is cleared on read
WCOL (write collision)	Is written when data is written to the SPDR during a transfer
SPDR (SPI data register)	Holds the incoming and outgoing data of an SPI transfer

Connecting Two Devices

The place to start with SPI is to use the SPI master library. The slave will be demonstrated through direct manipulation of the registers because the SPI library does not implement a slave mode. It will be easier (and necessary) to work with SPI using the registers for both master and slave when developing new protocols. The following list describes the class functions associated with the SPI library:

- `SPI.begin()`: This starts the SPI on the Arduino *and* sets input/output (I/O) of the SPI default pins.

- `SPI.end()`: This turns off SPI but does not change the pin modes.

- `SPI.setBitOrder()`: This passes `LSBFIRST` or `MSBFIRST`. The master and slaves must be set the same for proper communication, and in most cases this is arbitrary. Some hardware will require a specific bit order, so you should reference a data sheet when using the Arduino with SPI hardware that cannot be configured.

- `SPI.setClockDivider()`: The Arduino is cable of running at several different speeds by setting a divider of the main clock. This is useful when connecting devices that cannot operate at the Arduino maximum speed. Increasing the clock divider lowers the clock speed and is also useful for troubleshooting connections, by preventing noise or crosstalk on the line from being sampled as a data. The changes in clock speed can correct for lines that have high-capacitance issues. Table 10-2 lists the available options that can be set.

■ **Note**   The slave devices must be capable of running at the end clock speed of the master. If the clock is too fast, the slave devices may attempt to read the clock and data but will fail.

Table 10-2. *Clock Divider Settings with Resulting Speed*

Command	Divide By	End Clock Speed
SPI_CLOCK_DIV2	2	8MHz
SPI_CLOCK_DIV4	4	4MHz
SPI_CLOCK_DIV8	8	2MHz
SPI_CLOCK_DIV16	16	1MHz
SPI_CLOCK_DIV32	32	500kHz
SPI_CLOCK_DIV64	64	250kHz
SPI_CLOCK_DIV128	128	125kHz

■ **Caution**   The Atmel data sheet states that a minimum clock divider of 4 should be used. Significant transmission errors occur when attempting to communicate at 8MHz.

- SPI.setDataMode(): This determines how the clock is configured and read. The data lines are sampled in relation to the clock cycle. This setting is similar to serial baud rate, and all devices must be set the same for communication to take place. Table 10-3 shows the data modes and when data is sampled in relation to the clock polarity. When mode0 is used, the clock will idle low, and data will be sampled when the clock rises. Mode1 shares the same clock polarity as mode0, with the sample happening when the clock falls to the idle state. Mode2 and mode3 mirror mode0 and mode1, but with the clock set to high when idle. Mode2 samples the data when the clock falls and mode3 samples when the clock goes high. The default for the Arduino is mode0.

Table 10-3. *SPI Data Transmission Modes*

Command	Mode	Sample on Clock Edge	Clock Polarity When Idle
SPI_MODE0	0	Leading	Low
SPI_MODE1	1	Trailing	Low
SPI_MODE2	2	Leading	High
SPI_MODE3	3	Trailing	High

■ **Note**   Since the SPI clock will remain idle for a majority of the time, even when transmitting, you should use mode0 or mode1 if possible in power-conscious designs.

- SPI.transfer(): Calling this function and passing data will both send and receive 1 byte over the SPI lines. This function will return the incoming byte from the active slave. This is a full-duplex transfer; as one bit shifts out of the master, it is received by the slave, and the slave simultaneously sends a bit to the master.

Setting Up a Master SPI Device

For Listing 10-1, two Arduino-compatible boards are required (Unos were used for the example). For other Arduinos, refer to the board's pin map and connect to the appropriate pins. You'll also need an external LED because the SPI communication uses pin 13. The SPI master simplifies the pin mapping by setting the pins automatically, regardless of the board. SPI is electrically a straight-through protocol. The four standard lines of SPI—MISO (master in slave out), MOSI (master out slave in), SCK (serial clock), and SS (slave select)—should be wired together. You'll also need to share a common ground between devices and power, either separately or from one board to another. Table 10-4 describes the standard pin configuration.

Table 10-4. *SPI Default Pin Configuration*

Master			Slave	
MOSI	Output	→	MOSI	Input
MISO	Input	←	MISO	Output
SCK	Output	→	SCK	Input
SS	Output	→	SS	Input

The SS line on the master is not tied to any particular pin, and multiple can be used at the same time, one for each additional device. When using different SS connections, the original SS needs to be declared as an output. If the SS is an input and drops low, the device will lose its configuration as a master and become a slave.

Listing 10-1 includes code for both an SPI master and slave. The master uses the SPI library, and the slave is written directly addressing the SPI registers on the Arduino. The code for the slave will be recycled for the second example, later in the chapter. Before beginning, you should mark the Arduinos as designating master or slave. A marker with ink that comes off easily with rubbing alcohol can be used on the USB connector.

Listing 10-1. SPI Master Sketch

```
#include <SPI.h> // Include the SPI library for master
byte dataToSend;
byte dataToReceive;
boolean blink = LOW;

void setup() {
  pinMode(8,OUTPUT); // Blink
  pinMode(10,OUTPUT); // Set the slave select pin to output for the master
  digitalWrite(10, HIGH); // Set the slave select pin high
  SPI.begin(); // Start SPI
  Serial.begin(115200);
  delay(500); // Allow connected devices to initialize
}// End setup

void loop() {
  while (Serial.available() > 0) {
    dataToSend = Serial.read(); // Read a byte in from serial
    transferSPI(dataToSend); // Sent that byte
  }
```

```
    digitalWrite(8, (blink = !blink));    // Blink LED life check
    delay(1000);
}// End loop

byte transferSPI(byte dataToSend) {
    digitalWrite(10, LOW); // Turn the slave select on
    delay(1); // The slave takes a moment to respond to the slave select line falling
    dataToReceive = SPI.transfer(dataToSend); // Begin full-duplex data transfer
    digitalWrite(10, HIGH); // Turn the slave select off
     Serial.write(dataToSend); // Echo sent data
    Serial.println();
    Serial.write(dataToReceive); // Display byte received
    Serial.println();
}// End transferSPI
```

Verifying the Code

The code in Listing 10-1 needs to be uploaded to a single Arduino that will be designated as master. The SPI functionality is handled by the library, and with only the SPI.begin() used, the default settings are all used from the Arduino. To verify that the code is working properly, set up the LED to pin 8 and connect the MOSI pin 11 to the MISO pin 13, creating a data loopback. The SS and SCK can be left alone for this test. The master connected to itself should echo the characters sent through the serial connection. As it shifts a byte out normally to a slave, it shifts a byte in. This process is held in lockstep by the SCK, which normally causes the slave to simultaneously send and receive a bit until the whole byte is swapped. When plugged into itself, the master will expect a bit from the slave every time it sends one. Once you have verified that the Arduino can properly send and receive data, it is ready integrate the slave into the SPI setup.

Interrupting Vectors

In order to respond to the incoming data from the master, the slave will need to react very quickly to the SS going low. The SS pin could be constantly polled in the loop, but this would take a lot of time, and as the code grows in complexity, it would become altogether impossible for the slave to react quickly enough. To achieve the proper response time to the master's control, an internal interrupt needs to be implemented. The Arduino has several interrupt vectors that each has a specific trigger. Generally, both the SREG and the specific interrupt must be set. The simplest way to manipulate the SREG is to use the built-in commands cli(); and sei();. cli(); turns global interrupts off, and sei(); turns them on. When they are on, any enabled interrupts will be followed and make use of the code within an attached ISR (interrupt service routine) function. When an interrupt occurs, the current instruction will complete and the code that was running will stop and wait for the interrupt to finish. When working with new code in an interrupt, it may be helpful to do something observable in the main loop—that is, to have a simple method to verify that the interrupt is exiting properly and the loop is proceeding.

When designing code that includes interrupts, you need to take special care to determine if other code in the program will fail while the interrupt is running. This may include code that itself is time sensitive or perhaps shares a global variable with the interrupt, whereby data loss would occur by following the interrupt. In these cases it is best to turn interrupts off until the code has executed. This can be accomplished by the command cli();. Remember the interrupts need to be turned back on after the critical code has executed to be used again later. This, again, is accomplished by using the sei(); command. When multiprocessing, the behavior of other devices must also be accounted for. The fact that interrupts are turned off on one device does not prevent the remaining devices from acting as normal. With SPI, this could be handled through a software layer protocol. Simply have the slave echo the first byte back to the master before the master continues transmission. This will tell the master that the slave is ready and listening.

The SPI interrupt vector is called when the SREG and SPI interrupt enable are on and the SPI interrupt flag is set by the SS line going low. These registers are explained in the next section in detail. When these three conditions are met, the device will jump to ISR(SPI_STC_vect). ISR(SPI_STC_vect) is similar to a function, but has some key differences. The compiler does not see this as a normal function, so code may be optimized on compile. To protect against this, data types may have the property _volatile added when in doubt. The biggest difference is that nothing may be passed to an ISR upon calling it and no data will be returned. ISR cannot call as a normal function; only the internal interrupt handler may call it when conditions are met. Global variables can be used within the ISR and will be usable upon exit. Otherwise, using memory space and pointers is also an option, though greater in complexity.

SPI by the Registers

There is no library functionality for an Arduino to run as a slave device at the time of writing. You can create a slave by directly addressing the registers that control SPI. This method will be used in Listing 10-2 to create a slave device and will be used in subsequent examples. The functionality of SPI is controlled within three 8-bit registers. This does not include manipulating the data direction registers or the SREG for global interrupts, which will also be required for a proper SPI device to be written in a register. The three SPI registers are the SPCR (SPI control register), SPSR (SPI status register), and SPDR (SPI data register). The layouts of these three registers are shown in the Figure 10-1.

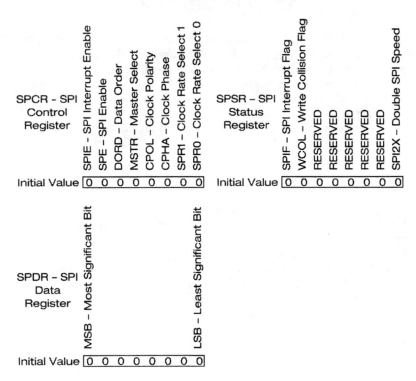

Figure 10-1. *SPI register structure*

The SPIE (SPI interrupt enable) in the SPCR enables the SPI interrupt vector when SREG is also enabled. This allows the device to respond quickly when data is ready to transmit and is an absolute must for a slave device. SPI is a highly time-sensitive protocol; the master will transmit data when it is ready and assumes that the slave is waiting. The slave cannot delay the master and will cause problems when not properly synchronized with the master. It is possible for the slave to begin listening to the transmission partway through, which will result in lost data. In addition to using interrupts, the master may also include a short delay before the first byte in a string of bytes is transmitted, which helps ensure that the slave is ready and waiting.

The SPE (SPI enable) is required for any SPI communication to take place, and in conjunction with the MSTR will automatically configure some pin directions as either input or output. Pins that are still user configured must be set manually. When the MSTR bit is set, the device is in master mode, only forcing MISO to input, so the MOSI, SCK, and SS should be manually set. If the MSTR is left off, the device is a slave, and all SPI lines except MISO are set as input. Depending on the nature of the project's code, it may not be necessary to set the MISO as output, in which case the slave is set to a receive-only mode. This may be useful in a situation where you need to push data or a command to multiple devices at once but do not need anything returned from the slave. In these cases it may even be possible to use a single SS line that is common to all devices if the data being sent is the same for all end devices. Otherwise, the MISO must be set to output on the slave to allow for full-duplex communication. SPI pin modes are outlined in Table 10-5 for master and slave.

Table 10-5. *SPI Master vs. Slave Pin Modes*

	Master	**Slave**
MOSI	User set	Force input
MISO	Force input	User set
SCK	User set	Force input
SS	User set	Force input

Returning to the DORD that was skipped over in the SPCR, this bit controls the order in which the bits of the SPDR are transmitted. The default setting is 0 and will shift the MSB of the SPDR first and the LSB last. If set to 1, then the reverse will happen—the LSB will be sent first and the MSB last. It is important that these agree on both the master and the slave.

CPOL and CPHA on the master device determine how the clock is to be generated, as well as when data is to be shifted to and from the SPDR. A slave device will use these to control how it responds to the clock signal from the master. The slave will sample the data line when triggered and set the outgoing bit on clock setup. We saw a full explanation of the clock modes earlier in the chapter. The CPOL and CPHA settings for each mode are listed Table 10-6.

Table 10-6. *SPI Clock-Generation Modes*

	CPOL	**CPHA**
Mode 0	0	0
Mode 1	0	1
Mode 2	1	0
Mode 3	1	1

The last two bits of the SPCR, SPR1 and SPR0, set the clock divider along with the last bit of the SPSR, SPI2X, which is a clock multiplier. Setting the SPI2X will double the clock rate; this, combined with the available speeds from SPR1 and SPR0, yields a range of clock dividers from 2 to 128. It is worth noting again that the Atmel data sheet states that the minimum clock divider that should be used is 4. In practice, attempting to use a clock divider of 2 should return corrupt data. The speed settings are listed in Table 10-7.

Table 10-7. *SPI Clock-Generation Multipliers*

	SPCR		SPSR
Divider	SPR1	SPR0	SPI2X
2	0	0	1
4	0	0	0
8	0	1	1
16	0	1	0
32	1	0	1
64	1	0	0
128	1	1	0

The SPSR has two remaining settings left: the SPIF (SPI interrupt flag) and the WCOL (write collision). The SPIF is set when a serial transmission has completed. It can be cleared in a number of ways, including by reading the SPSR followed by accessing the SPDR. This feature allows a while loop to execute until the serial transfer is completed. This prevents you from having to read the SPDR before the byte is actually received, and if you are in a sequence of loops, it prevents you from writing the SPDR while a transmission is in progress. Should the SPDR be written during a serial transmission, the WCOL will be set to a logical one. This is not generally preferable, so should be avoided. The WCOL is cleared in the same fashion as the SPIF.

Let's now see the slave sketch (Listing 10-2).

Listing 10-2. SPI Slave Sketch

```
byte dataToEcho; // Declare a global variable to be used in interrupt
boolean blink = LOW;
void setup() {
  Serial.begin(115200);
  DDRB |= 0b00010001;    // MISO LED(8) Output
  PORTB |= 0b00000100;   // Set slave select HIGH
  SPCR |= 0b11000000;    // Turn SPIE and SPE on
  SPSR |= 0b00000000;    // Default SPI settings
  sei(); // Enable global interrupts
}// End setup

void loop() {
  digitalWrite(8, (blink = !blink));   // Blink LED life check
  delay(1000);
}// End loop

ISR(SPI_STC_vect) {
  cli(); // Turn interrupts off while running sensitive code
  while (!(PINB & 0b00000100)) { // Enter while loop if slave select is low
    SPDR = dataToEcho; // Load the SPI data register with data to shift out
    while (!(SPSR & (1 << SPIF))); // Wait till data transfer is complete
    dataToEcho = SPDR; // Read the incomming data. This byte will be sent next interrupt.
  }
  sei(); // Turn interrupts back on when done
}// End ISR for spi
```

Verifying the Code

Connect the slave to the master as per Figure 10-2, with pins 13 through 10 connected together between the two Arduinos for SPI, and connect a separate LED to pin 8.

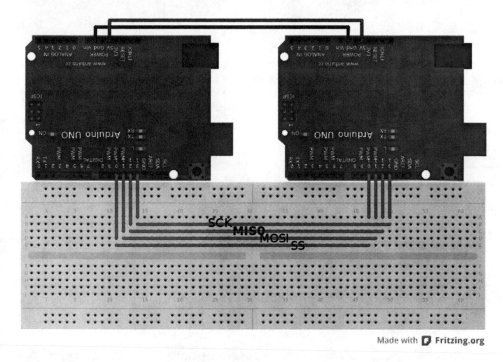

Made with 🔲 Fritzing.org

Figure 10-2. *Arduino-to-Arduino SPI connections*

Once you've made the physical connections and powered the boards, open a serial connection via USB to the master. When you enter a single character through serial, that character will be sent to the slave device, and at the same time receive a byte from the slave. Note that when echoing data, the slave will always be one byte behind; a null byte will be received back from the first SPI transfer. When the second byte is sent, the first byte will then be echoed. Should more data from a slave be expected, the master can transmit null bytes until the expected data is all received. In the case of a slave that echoes, the master will need to send one additional trailing null byte to get back the full string that it sent. The data sent and received should look like Tables 10-8 and 10-9. Table 10-9 shows a null byte being sent at the end of a transmission string.

Table 10-8. *Data Transfer Shifting*

Transfer #	1	2	3	4	5	6
Sent	S	A	M	P	L	E
Received	-	S	A	M	P	L

Table 10-9. *Null Byte at the End of the String*

Transfer #	1	2	3	4	5	6	7
Sent	S	A	M	P	L	E	-
Received	-	S	A	M	P	L	E

The transfer between master and slave is procedural and requires the connection to be maintained consistently between the devices. The communication in the sample code follows the steps in Table 10-10. The example sends one byte at a time as Table 10-10 shows; however, large strings can be sent within a loop. The use of loops for sending data is demonstrated in Listing 10-3, along with an alternative method to create master device by using registers.

Table 10-10. *Master and Slave Communication Steps*

Master	Slave
1. Drop slave select low	1. Begin listening to master
2. Write data to be sent	2. Write data to be sent
3. Full-duplex transfer	3. Full-duplex transfer
4. Read received data	4. Read received data
5. Slave select high	5. Return to idle

Multiple Slaves

Developing a master through register manipulation is a logical next step to developing tightly controlled protocols. The next feature I'll address, though, is connecting to multiple slaves. Under a normal four-wire SPI connection, the addition of slaves beyond the first requires additional SS lines controlled by the master. The MISO, MOSI, and SCK are shared lines between all devices on an SPI network; however, the SS line will be separated under all but the most unusual SPI networks. This allows the master to select one slave at a time, and a slave that is not signaled will ignore the communication.

Master in Register

While in most cases, the SPI library will suffice in the creation of a master SPI device, it will fall short when creating more complex protocols. For that reason, and to gain a better understanding of the SPI, writing the master code in register is the next step and is shown in Listing 10-3.

Listing 10-3. Master Code Register Sketch

```
const int bufferSize = 64; // Sets the size of the txBuffer and the rxBuffer
byte txBuffer[bufferSize]; // Created to hold data waiting to be sent to the slave
byte rxBuffer[bufferSize]; // Created to hold incoming data received from the slave

void setup() {
  Serial.begin(115200);
  DDRB |= 0b00101101; // LED(8) MOSI SCK SS Output
  PORTB |= 0b00000100; // Set slave select HIGH
```

```
  SPCR |= 0b01010000; // This is the SPI control register. SPE (bit 6) enables SPI, and MSTR (bit 4)
sets device as master
  SPSR |= 0b00000000; // Default SPI settings and interrupts
}

void loop() {
  if (Serial.available() > 0) {
    int count = 0;
    delay(50); // Allow serial to complete receiving
      while (Serial.available() > 0) {
        txBuffer[count] = Serial.read(); // Dump serial buffer into the txBuffer
        count++;
      }
    PORTB &= 0b11111011; // Turn the slave select on
    transferSPI(count);
    PORTB |= 0b00000100; // Turn the slave select off
  }
  // Blink code
  PORTB |= 0b00000001;
  delay(1000);                 // Wait for a second
  PORTB &= 0b11111110;
  delay(1000);                 // Wait for a second
}

int transferSPI(int txBytes) {
  int count = 0;
    while (count < txBytes) {
      SPDR = txBuffer[count]; // Writing to the register begins SPI transfer
      while (!(SPSR & (1 << SPIF))); // While until transfer complete
      rxBuffer[count] = SPDR; // Read newly received byte
      count++;
    }
  displayBuffer(count);
}

int displayBuffer(int nBytes) { // Write txBuffer and rxBuffer to the screen
  Serial.write (txBuffer, nBytes);
  Serial.println();
  Serial.write (rxBuffer, nBytes);
  Serial.println();
}
```

Verifying the Code

To use the master code from the second example, connect it to an Arduino running the slave code from the first example. This will be in the normal fashion, straight through, as per Figure 10-2. Verification of code consists of running a serial connection and sending data. The data will be echoed in the same fashion as the first example. This code implements one major difference: it takes all incoming serial data and loads it into an array so that the SPI transmission can be completed in series with greater efficiency. The SS line goes low and stays low until all data in the txBuffer has been sent and the rxBuffer is filled.

Symmetric Architecture Bipolar Bus

SPI is in many ways an elegant solution for chip-to-chip communication; however, it has significant drawbacks that limit its use:

- The first problem is that as the number of slave devices increases, so does the number of SS lines. This can certainly be a problem for pin-intensive projects. Without extra logic such as a MUX, even the Mega can run out of pins.

- The second problem is that the SPI architecture is not resilient to changes. It will work as configured, but you must take great care of design when adding or removing nodes. There is no real hot-swap ability native to SPI. And, should the master device become compromised, the whole network will collapse. When a slave device needs to request data transfers, you need to add a data-ready line. The data-ready signal output from the slave tells the master that data needs to be transferred. To add a data-ready line we will need additional connections for each additional slave. All data-flow control is placed on the master, which can limit the functionality of the master, as it may need to spend a significant amount of processor resources to monitor and handle communication.

- Finally, one slave cannot communicate directly with another. Even if the master were to route the data from one slave to another, there would be a great loss of efficiency, as the data would have to be transmitted twice. The solution to all these problems is a custom protocol.

Douglas Bebb of MAD Fellows developed a bus architecture as an open standard to better serve in chip-to-chip communication. This architecture and protocol is called the *Symmetric Architecture Bipolar Bus (SABB)*. It is a standard in active open development and goes beyond functionality on the Arduino, but can be fully demonstrated on any Arduino board. On the Arduino, it is built on the SPI block, and so uses registers and methodologies discussed earlier, but takes best practices and turns them on their head.

Again, for reference, SPI defines a standard that has unique master/slave devices, full-duplex transmission, and a shared serial clock. Much is left undefined when using SPI, which is both an advantage and drawback. SABB is designed to be more robust while still allowing flexibility. The highlights of SABB include the following:

- Full-duplex communication

- Synchronous serial

- Roleless devices

- Hot-swap capabilities

- Individual addressing capabilities

- Address-broadcasting capabilities

- Backward compatibility to SPI

- Modular and redundant design

- Four-wire bus (no extra SS or data-ready lines needed for extra devices)

The logical and electrical connections in SABB are similar to SPI, with the exception that the SS line is shared between all SABB-enabled devices. Figure 10-3 shows a logical block diagram of this feature.

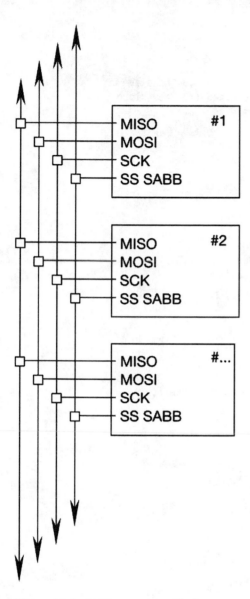

Figure 10-3. *SABB connection block*

SABB by the Code

Possibly the most significant feature of SABB is the scrapping of master/slave topography. This topography is a huge limitation on a bus, and so for a number of reasons has been engineered out. All devices connected using SABB share the same code. While only one device can control the data lines at once, each device has the ability to do so. Note that while SPI allows communication between a master and a slave, the slaves do not have the ability to directly communicate. This barrier is removed, as there is no slave/master relationship. Any device may communicate to any other device on the network. Flow control is first determined on a hardware level, and then once the bus is held by a device, software flow control takes over. The flow control used in Listing 10-4 is limited to the ability of each device to be addressed.

Listing 10-4. SABB

```
const byte myAddress = '2'; // Address range from 0 - 255
const int bufferSize = 64; // 64 matches the size of serial buffer
byte txBuffer[bufferSize]; // Created to hold data waiting to be sent to the slave
byte rxBuffer[bufferSize]; // Created to hold incoming data received from the slave
volatile byte rxBufferSlave[bufferSize]; // Holds data when used as slave
volatile boolean flag = true; // Change LED state flag

void setup() {
  Serial.begin(115200); // Open serial connection
  PORTB |= 0b00000100; // Set SS HIGH
  while (!(PINB & 0b00000100)); // Wait to initialize if SS held LOW externally
  initSPI(); // Prepare to connect to the network
  txBuffer[0] = 0b00000000; // Load tx buffer with a null byte
  transferSPI(1); // Send null byte to release waiting devices
  initSPI(); // Set idle state for board to board communication
  Serial.println("Ready"); // Alert that device is fully initialized
}
void loop() {
  if (Serial.available()) {
    delay(1000); // Wait a sec to receive serial data
    int count = 1; // Store data begining 2nd byte in array
    txBuffer[0] = 0b00000000; // Send null byte first
    while (Serial.available()) {
      txBuffer[count] = Serial.read(); // Dump serial buffer into the txBuffer
      count++;
    }
    Serial.flush(); // Clear serial buffer
    transferSPI(count); // Sends and receives data as master
    printBuffer(count); // Prints data that was sent and received
    initSPI(); // Return to idle state
  }
  if (flag == true ){ // Flag sets true when addressed by master
    PORTB = (~(PINB << 7) >> PINB7); // Change the LED state
    flag = false; // Clear the flag
  }
}
void initSPI() { // Sets idle state of connection
  DDRB |= 0b00000001; // LED Output
  DDRB &= 0b11000011; // MOSI MISO SCK SS Input
  PORTB |= 0b00000100; // Set slave select HIGH
  PORTB &= 0b11000111; // MISO MOSI SCK LOW
  SPCR = 0b11000000; // SPIE, SPE, SLAVE, MODE0, CLOCK DIV_4
  sei(); // Global interrupt enabled
}
int printBuffer(int nBytes) { // Display data tx and rx when master
  Serial.println();
  Serial.write (txBuffer, nBytes);
  Serial.println();
```

```
  Serial.write (rxBuffer, nBytes);
  Serial.println();
}
int transferSPI(int txBytes) {
  cli(); // Turn global interrupts off
  SPCR |= 0b00010000; // Set SPI master
  DDRB |= 0b00101100; // MOSI SCK SS output
  DDRB &= 0b11101111; // MISO Input
  PORTB &= 0b11111011; // Turn the slave select on
  int count = 0;
  delay(50); // Wait for connected devices to enter interrupt; 50 is a very safe number
  while (count < txBytes) { // Loop until all data has transferred
    SPDR = txBuffer[count]; // Begin byte transfer by writing SPDR
    while (!(SPSR & (1 << SPIF))); // Wait for transfer to complete
    rxBuffer[count] = SPDR; // Read incoming byte
    count++;
  }
  PORTB |= 0b00000100; // Set SS HIGH
}
ISR(SPI_STC_vect) { // SPI interrupt vector
  int count = 0;
  if (!(PINB & 0b00000100)) { // Enter if SS is LOW
    while (!(PINB & 0b00000100)) { // While SS is LOW
      while (!(SPSR & (1 << SPIF))); // Wait till data transfer complete
      rxBufferSlave[count] = SPDR; // Read SPDR
      if (rxBufferSlave[0] == myAddress) {DDRB |= 0b00010000;} // If address matches set MISO to
Output
      SPDR = rxBufferSlave[count]; // Write data to send to SPDR
      count++;
    }
  if (rxBufferSlave[0] == myAddress) {flag = true;} // If address matched set LED change flag
  initSPI(); // Return to idle connection
  }
}
```

Verifying the Code

For Listing 10-4, you'll need to connect at least two Arduinos together, as per Figure 10-4. Many more Arduinos may be used; when more Arduinos are used, the advantage of SABB over SPI becomes apparent. Each connected device needs a unique address that is set in the code before the sketch is compiled and uploaded. Electrically, the connections between boards are nearly the same as a standard configuration of SPI. A pull-down resistor is needed for the data lines to prevent cross talk. An external pull-up resistor may also be added to the chip-select line, though this is not required. Figure 10-4 shows the specific connections and resistor values.

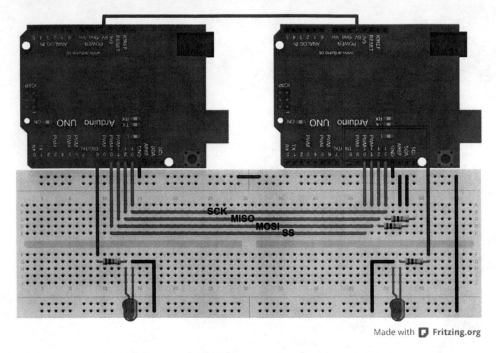

Figure 10-4. *SABB connection diagram (note the pull-down resistors)*

When loading the code to each board, be sure to assign a unique address to each. No other changes need to be made to the code. Finally, connect to at least one of the boards through a serial terminal. From this point, you can send a string to the board. This string will be sent to any devices connected on the bus. The first byte will be examined for a matching address, and if a match occurs, that device will echo the data it receives. Both the data sent and the data received will be displayed from the sending device. Also, the code is set to change the state of an LED whenever it is addressed in a communication sequence. This provides two ways to demonstrate a successful transfer.

After the code is verified, add another Arduino if possible; you can do this on the fly, as functionality for hot-swap is included in this code example.

Connecting SABB to SPI

While this example does not demonstrate communicating to a conventional SPI device, this is possible, and one can be added. Since the SPI block will remain idle when not activated by the chip-select line going low, conventional SPI devices can share the same bus lanes as SABB. You can make a device running SABB a master in an SPI network by following proper procedure. Figure 10-5 shows a block diagram demonstrating one connection possibility of SPI sharing a SABB data bus. This relation between SABB and standard SPI allows for every SABB-enabled device to share standard SPI devices if the SS lines are connected to each SABB device that requires the resource.

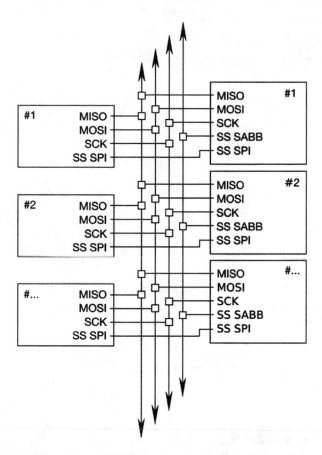

Figure 10-5. *Connection methods; SPI sharing with SABB*

The first step is to drop the chip-select line low between SABB devices. A null byte is sent to all devices on the bus instead of a matching address or broadcast. Now, as long as this common chip-select line remains low, none of the devices sharing the SABB device will attempt to hold the data lines. After this step, an SPI device may be used in slave mode. While SABB does not require additional chip-select lines between devices, SPI does. A chip-select line per slave to be connected should be used. Connect the SPI device to the MISO, MOSI, and SCK of the SABB device and the dedicated chip-select line as well. When this unique chip-select line is pulled low, SPI communication can take place. To release the lines, raise the chip-select lines.

Conversion to Mega

Consistent with other chapters, the code for this chapter was written to support the Arduino Uno. Should the need arise, you can convert from Uno code to Mega relatively simply. The Mega, having more I/O pins and more program space, could be replaced by multiprocessing smaller boards. While this is certainly a viable option, the Mega uses a chip set with more features than the Uno. The Mega may also be an attractive solution because of its density of I/O pins per device.

The first step is to identify the pins and ports that will be used on both devices. When using the SPI core, we are locked into using specific but unique pins from one board to another. Both devices use PORTB for SPI, but the bit position in the register is unique, as is the order. This confusion stems from design considerations on the part of Atmel in assigning PORT definitions. It is then abstracted again by Arduino, in the mapping of the pins on the board to the chip set. Once the pins and ports are identified, it is a good idea to create a cross-reference chart, as shown in Tables 10-11 and 10-12.

Table 10-11. *PORTB Register with SPI Pins*

	PB7	PB6	PB5	PB4	PB3	PB2	PB1	PB0
Uno			SCK	MISO	MOSI	SS		
Mega					MISO	MOSI	SCK	SS

Table 10-12. *Arduino SPI Pin Reference*

	Uno		Mega	
SS	PB2	Pin 10	PB0	Pin 53
MOSI	PB3	Pin 11	PB2	Pin 51
MISO	PB4	Pin 12	PB3	Pin 50
SCK	PB5	Pin 13	PB1	Pin 52

The final step is to find all references to the PORT, PIN, and DDR registers in the Arduino code. When addressing the entire register, be mindful of the pins not used for SPI. These values should be left unchanged and should be masked accordingly. Commonly used values may be simpler to declare globally as a constant so that only one value needs to be changed when converting code. It is also a good idea to adopt code conventions that include thorough commenting. This is especially important when writing registers and using bitwise operations as it can greatly simplify debugging.

Physical Best Practices

These are just a few design considerations when designing the physical layer. When working within an electrically noisy environment, interference on the transmission lines may cause corrupted data. Wire lengths and PCB connection tracks should be kept to a minimum; this reduces the "electrical size" of the transmission lines, limiting the amount of interference induced into the system. This will also prevent high impedance and capacitance on the lines from causing problems, though on a high-quality line, it is possible to get as much as 6 feet out of a transmission line. Remember that all SPI lines that are electrically connected should have lengths totaled.

Shielding is the next consideration and especially simple to implement when using external transmission lines. Since connected SPI devices should use a common ground, adding shielding to a transmission line is as simple as using a shielded cable and connectors, and then running the ground through the shielding. On a board, a grounded metal shield or ground plane can be used to keep electromagnetic radiation out. This is likely only a concern when placing a board near large radiation sources. In less noisy environments, ribbon cable is a great choice. In most circumstances this will be adequate and has several advantages. Ribbon cable is cheaper than shielded cable. It also gives you the ability to add crimp connectors anywhere along the cable with no special tools.

Branches of a transmission line may be different lengths; however, the line lengths should be the same or at least kept close. This means the MISO line should be the same length as the SCK line, which should be the same as the MOSI line. A difference of a couple inches won't significantly impact a transmission line, even at the highest speed available on the Arduino.

Summary

There are many was to connect chips together, and this chapter only focused on a small area of multiprocessing communication methods. It introduced SPI and SABB, which utilize the fastest communication available on the Arduino, allowing you to create more complex projects and devices.

■ ■ ■

## CHAPTER 11

Game Development with Arduino

Game development on the Arduino can push both the hardware resources and the developer's imagination to their potential. Games can be simple or extremely complex, challenging skills or even telling a story. This chapter explores game development as it is related to the Arduino. Games can come in all forms, from a few LEDs testing skill or luck to a full graphical side-scroller made with the help of the Gameduino.

The Arduino is a great platform to get started with when first getting in to game development, being easy to program and expand upon. Modern computer games are incredibly complex and are targeted at a large number of different end devices; they usually involve a lot of development and have game engines that are difficult to understand. This makes it difficult for individual developers to complete these types of projects on their own. With Arduino, developers can build great games, and test and distribute their games with greater ease than with modern computer and console games.

Games Suitable for the Arduino

The average processing power of microcontrollers makes them well suited for the development of coin-operated (coin-op), medal, redemption, and merchandiser-style arcade games. Here are some examples of these types of games:

- Coin-op are games usually table sports played on a table (for example, air hockey and pool) that charge a fee for one complete game.

- Coin pushers and slot machines are examples of medal games.

- Redemption games include alley roll and whack-a-mole; these games give tickets to be traded for prizes.

- Claw cranes are in the game category of merchandisers, which give the prize directly to the player.

- The pinball machine is another popular arcade game. This style game is in the same category as the medal and redemption games, but dates back (in its current form) to the 1950s.

These arcade games became quite popular at video arcades in the early to mid-1990s, just after the peak of video arcades themselves and are still used and developed for modern arcades.

■ **Note** Arcade owners began to use coin-op, redemption, medal, and merchandiser games to keep the arcade industry alive after the widespread availability and acceptance of game consoles and personal computers lowered arcade attendance. I'll refer to these types of games as *arcade games* to avoid any confusion with video arcade games, such as Space Invaders, Centipede, and Pac-Man.

Arcade games are akin to robotics development because of the heavy use of motors and sensors to measure and move game play along. Both arcade and video arcade games rely heavily on the game play being balanced, requiring them to be simple to understand and play but difficult to master. Users must be able to easily identify the game mechanics of an arcade game before choosing to play. The game whack-a-mole, for example, has a mechanism that is easily identifiable by both the game's descriptive name and watching others play—but it has a challenge that pits hand-eye coordination to speed. The game play in home consoles and on personal computers can spend more time teaching a user the unique mechanics of the game in the early stages. An example of a game that teaches a complex game mechanism in the early stages is Valve Corporation's first Portal game; the game uses each level to teach only one part of the mechanism at a time, until all the basic components can be used to solve more difficult puzzles.

The development of arcade games employs a different skill set than that of computer or console games. The skills of problem development, storytelling, programming, and graphic design are common among most digital game development fields. Arcade games make use of carpentry, hardware integration, and electrical engineering. Carpentry is used to make the cabinets that house the actual arcade games. The Behemoth game company, makers of Castle Crashers, posted a video that demonstrates an arcade cabinet being constructed in time lapse (see `www.youtube.com/watch?v=MJ6Lp2GqHoU`), to give you an example of how much is involved. Carpentry is a skill that can be acquired with a little practice and a trip to the local book store for a plethora of information on the subject. Arcade game cabinets are usually the flashiest part of the entire game, designed to entice people to play. They usually make sounds, blink lights, and are covered in graphics or eye-popping colors.

The distinctly average power of a microcontroller's capabilities for complex video graphics is why other methods of attracting the player are used such as intense cabinet design flashing lights and sounds to make games attractive for play instead of relying on the game graphics the way computer games do. Arcade game cabinets also integrate the game surface and playing area into the cabinet; pinball and alley roll are great examples of the game surface being included in the cabinet. Video arcade games use cabinets for reasons similar to arcade games, but the game play is performed on a screen mounted in the cabinet.

The skill of hardware to software integration will be familiar to any Arduino developer that uses sensors, motors, and lights in other developments. Arcade games can perform many types of hardware integration—for example, using sensors to determine if an object has reached a goal. Game play can use motors and solenoids to manipulate and move physical objects. LED displays can be used to keep score. Each arcade game has different requirements on the type of hardware needed and how it connects.

Another type of game that is well-suited to the Arduino is the board game. Using electronics in a board game is great for adding game depth that may not be available via any other method. Milton Bradley's Omega Virus and Dark Tower are both classic games that demonstrate how electronics can be integrated into a board game, adding a unique game play experience.

Electronics can also be used in pen-and-paper role-playing games (RPGs)—for example, you could use the simulated RFID reader from Chapter 6 in a cyber-style RPG to have players "hack" and intercept access codes for certain game elements. Vintage video games have seen a comeback in the form of stand-alone controllers that integrate one or more games into the controller to provide an easy connection to a display.

This chapter shows you how to build two proof-of-concept games: one that uses 11 LEDs, 11 resistors, and a button; and one that uses the Gameduino and a button.

The games are designed to be simple while demonstrating concepts of game development. This chapter's hardware requirements are an Arduino Uno or compatible device with a standard pin interface, some LEDs and buttons, and a Gameduino. The Gameduino is graphic coprocessor shield that enables the Arduino to control sprite based games. The Gameduino shield can be acquired at many online retailers, such as Adafruit Industries, Seeed Studio, and SparkFun electronics.

A Simple Game

Game play is one of the most important parts of game development and is crucial to making a fun and entertaining game. After a game concept has been brainstormed, building a proof of concept of a game is an important step to iron out details and mechanics. The proof of concept can help determine if the game is feasible early in the development process. Simple tests of working concepts are also useful to figure out if the challenges are too difficult for anyone to complete. Testing concepts is vital, especially if a game mechanism is going involve components that rely on physics or mechanical contraptions such as a ball toss or claw retrieval. You should develop each game mechanism as best you can before integrating it with other systems, building each and testing for bugs before setting the final product into motion. The extra components that make up an arcade game (such as artwork, coin mechanisms, ticket dispensers, and attractive cabinet accoutrements) can be integrated later in the development process.

The game that you will set up in section is a simple game that challenges reaction time by making the player stop a sweeping series of LEDs at a specified point within the series. The game is called Stop It, and the main part of this game is the display with the sweeping of a single-light LED from one side of a series to the other. The challenge for this game is the amount of time a player has to react. The game appears to move faster when the time a single LED is on before the next one lights up is lowered. To achieve a level completion the player has to press a button while a specified LED is on. Stop It will use 11 LEDs and a single button; the winning LED is in the middle, and five LEDs are on either side.

After each level is complete or *micro-win*, Stop It will decrease the time each LED is on before moving on to the next stage. A micro-win will flash an alternating pattern on the LEDs, and after 11 micro-wins, a more elaborate pattern will flash, signifying a *big win*. If an attempt fails, Stop it will reset back to the first level, and the succession to the big win will be restarted. The flash of the LEDs is the reward for the proof of concept. If Stop it were to be developed in to a full arcade game, the reward would have to be greater than just flashing lights. For example, you might add 1 point to a score or money to a jackpot for every micro-win, and reward the player with tickets for each big win. Stop it will also need a risk for the user to place up front to attempt to play. For example, a number of tokens could be accepted via a coin acceptor before the player is allowed play.

Proof of Concept

Stop It's proof-of-concept setup is described in Figure 11-1, with 11 1kΩ resistors connected to 5V power and then to the anode side of 11 LEDs. The cathode side of each LED is connected to pins 3 through 13—one cathode per pin. The LEDs will be on when the pin is pulled low, instead of when the pin is high. Turning on the LEDs by grounding is a best practice for lowering the amp draw though the microcontroller. A button is connected to ground on one side and pin 2 on the other so that the interrupt can be utilized to determine when the player has made an attempt to win. Serial is not used for this code, but the pins are left alone so that the serial can be used to communicate to other modules. It is possible to use a couple of shift registers to lessen the pin usage of the Arduino and allow for other devices to connect to digital pins. This example does not use shift registers, keeping the parts requirement to a minimum.

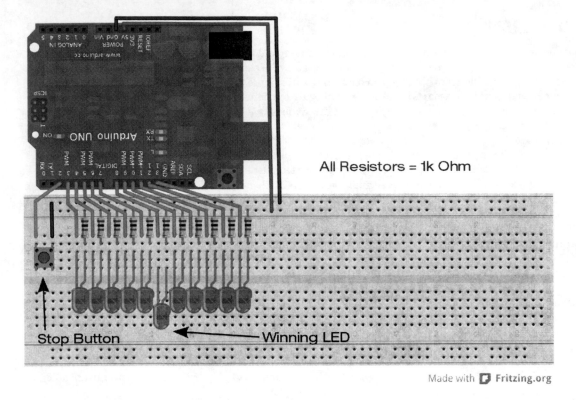

All Resistors = 1k Ohm

Stop Button ← Winning LED

Made with **F** Fritzing.org

Figure 11-1. *Stop it's proof-of-concept setup*

There are two common methods to accomplish the sweep of an LED in a series:

- The first uses an array to hold the state of each LED and uses a loop to perform a series of digital writes to each individual pin.

- The other method is to directly manipulate the pin registers.

The register method is used for Stop it because it simplifies the program's logic. Register manipulation was introduced in Chapter 6 to create a fast 10-bit digital-to-analog converter. The method for changing the pin state is the same: a single integer is used to hold the pattern that will be used to turn on or off the pins using bitwise shifts along with AND masks to turn the entire register at once. Stop it's code, shown in Listing 11-1, is broken up into 11 parts and contains 12 functions.

Coding Stop It

Part 1 of Listing 11-1 sets up the variables for Stop it and the pins' data direction. The proof of concept has five variables in total: one integer, one byte, and three Booleans. The integer is used to manipulate the pattern of the LEDs; this variable is used for everything that will be displayed to the user, and also to determine the direction of the sweep and whether a win has been archived. The byte variable is used to determine the level and to increase the speed of the sweep. The Booleans are used as flags to tell what direction the sweep needs to travel, and tell if a win condition has been achieved and if the button has been pressed.

Listing 11-1. Stop It's Code, Part 1 of 11

```
int LEDshift = 0x0001;      // holds the LED pattern
boolean RightLeft = false; // true for right
boolean Win = false;        // when true, a win state has be achived
boolean button = false;     // flag if the button has been pressed
byte level = 0;             // curent level holder

void setup() {
  DDRD = DDRD | B11111000; // pins 3 - 7 set data direction
  DDRB = DDRB | B00111111; //  pins 8 - 13
  digitalWrite(2,HIGH);    // pull up so the input can be signaled on a low transition
}
```

The code for part 2 of Stop it is the function to perform the LED sweep. The moveLED() function is called from the main loop. The function first checks if the ON LED is at the first or last LED of the display. The check is performed by AND masking the LEDshift variable. If the mask equals anything other than zero, then the check is true, and depending on which mask is true, you set the flag RightLeft to the proper direction. The function then checks the RightLeft direction variable to bit shift the LEDshift over one every time the moveLED() function is called. The function then calls the displayLED() function.

Listing 11-1. Stop It's Code, Part 2 of 11

```
void moveLED() {
  if (LEDshift & 0x0002) {
    RightLeft = false;
  }
  if (LEDshift & 0x0800) {
    RightLeft = true;
  }
  if (!RightLeft ) {
    LEDshift = LEDshift  << 1;
  }
  if (RightLeft) {
    LEDshift = LEDshift   >> 1;
  }
  displayLED();
} // end  moveLED
```

The displayLED() function is part 3 for Listing 11-1. This function is responsible for changing the actual pin states to control the LEDs. When the displayLED() function is called, the LEDshift variable is parsed and split to match to the pins that are connected to the LED array. To get the LEDs that are connected to pins 3 through 7, the LEDshift variable is masked against a number that correlates to the position of the bits needed, and the result is then shifted to the left by two positions so that the final result is in the proper position for the pins. Before the total result is written to the register, a NOT operation is performed so that the pins will be in the proper state for the LED.

Listing 11-1. Stop It's Code, Part 3 of 11

```
void displayLED() {
  PORTD = ~((LEDshift & 0x003E) << 2); // format and place the proper bits into the registers
  PORTB = ~((LEDshift & 0x0FC0) >> 6); // portd = low portb = hi
}
```

Part 4 is the function that will be used for the interrupt when the player attempts to stop the LED. This function is held in a loop while the button attached to pin 2 is depressed. The `while` loop of this function helps to debounce the interrupt because delays do not work inside of interrupts. The function sets the button flag, signifying that the player has made an attempt to stop it. A check of the `LEDshift` variable verifies that the winning LED is on; this is done by an AND mask. If the proper LED is on, the flag is set to `true`; otherwise, the flag remains `false` and will trigger a win or a loss condition when returning from this function.

Listing 11-1. Stop It's Code, Part 4 of 11

```
void Button(){
  while (digitalRead(2)== LOW) {
    button = true;
    if ((LEDshift & 0x0040)) {
      Win = true;
    }
    else {
      Win = false;
    }
  } // end while
} // end button
```

Part 5 is the function to check if a button event is a win or a loss. This function is called from the main loop only when a button flag is `true`. The level gets incremented if a win or a big win is achieved. A big win is achieved when the LED has been stopped 11 successful times. This function calls the `flashWin()` function for every successful stop and the `BigWin()` function for 11 in a row. The level is incremented for every win. If the player does not stop the LED on the winning point, the function will call the `notWin()` function to reset the levels and provide the player with the feedback that they have lost.

Listing 11-1. Stop It's Code, Part 5 of 11

```
void checkWin() {
  if (Win) {
    if (level < 10) {
      flashWin();
    }
    if (level >= 10) {
      BigWin();
    }
    IncreaseLevel();
  }
  if (!Win) {
    notWin();
  }
  resetPlay ();
} // end checkWin
```

`flashWin()` is the function that makes up part 6 of the code for Stop it. This function is a reward for the player. A binary pattern is first loaded in to the `LEDshift` variable of alternating 1s and 0s. Then a loop is used to invert the `LEDshift` variable, turning 1s into 0s and vice versa. The pattern is displayed by calling the `displayLED()` function and waiting until the player can see the pattern before continuing through the loop a total of ten times.

Listing 11-1. Stop It's Code, Part 6 of 11

```
void flashWin() {
  delay (100);
  LEDshift = 0xFAAA;
  for ( int i = 0 ; i < 10; i++) {
    LEDshift = ~LEDshift;
    displayLED();
    delay (100);
  }
} // end flashWin
```

The BigWin() function of part 7 is called when the player makes 11 successful wins. This function first calls the flashWin() function and then loads a new pattern, starting from the center LED and radiating outward, turning on all the LEDs. The function does this four times before finishing up with another flashWin().

Listing 11-1. Stop It's Code, Part 7 of 11

```
void BigWin () {
  flashWin();
  for (int i = 0 ; i < 4 ; i++) {
    LEDshift = 0x0040; // turn on the center LED
    displayLED();
    delay (100);
    for (int i = 0 ; i < 6 ; i++) {
      LEDshift = LEDshift  | (1<< 5 - i); // radiate from the center by a logical OR of the 1s
                                          // into the
      LEDshift = LEDshift  | (1<< 7 + i); // LEDshift variable
      displayLED();
      delay (25);
    }
  }
  flashWin();
} // end BigWin
```

Every game has to have a condition for not winning. Part 8 of Listing 11-1 is the notWin() function. The notWin() function resets the level back to zero and sweeps the LED from right to left. The loop to display the pattern shifts the LEDshift variable to the left by 1, and then increments the variable till the loop is finished.

Listing 11-1. Stop It's Code, Part 8 of 11

```
void notWin() {
  level = 0;
  delay (100);
  LEDshift = 0x0001;
  for ( int i = 0 ; i < 11; i++) {
  LEDshift = LEDshift << 1;
    LEDshift++;
    displayLED();
    delay (100);
  }
} // end notWin
```

Part 9 is the DspLevel() function, which informs the player what level they are now on. This function is called before the game starts the next level. This function works in the opposite way to the notWin() function, by shifting from left to right. In the loop, 1 is added to the high bit of the LEDshift variable by an OR of 0x1000, then bit shifting the variable LEDshift to the right by 1. The loop will run as many times as there are levels.

Listing 11-1. Stop It's Code, Part 9 of 11

```
void DspLevel() {
  LEDshift = 0x0000;
  for (int i = 0 ; i <= level ; i++) {
    LEDshift = LEDshift | 0x1000; // add 1 to the high bits of LEDshift
    LEDshift = LEDshift >> 1 ;
    displayLED();
    delay (50);
  }
  delay (500);
} // end DspLevel
```

In part 10 of Listing 11-1 are the two functions to handle the resetting of game play for each level after the reward and loss patterns are displayed. Listing 11-1 also includes a function to increment the level after a win condition. The resetPlay() function first calls the DspLevel() function, and then resets all of the game condition variables to their initial state. The level variable is not reset in this function, but is a condition of a loss.

When the IncreaseLevel() function is called, the level variable is incremented by 1. This function also handles the reset to level 0 if the player can make it past level 15; the reset is done by an AND mask. The level variable helps set the speed of the LED sweep and needs to be kept below a certain number; otherwise, the time the LED stays on goes negative and can halt the Arduino. The level reset in this function is also independent of the loss condition reset.

Listing 11-1. Stop It's Code, Part 10 of 11

```
void resetPlay () {
  DspLevel();
  Win = false;
  button = false;
  LEDshift = 0x0001;
  RightLeft = false;
}

void IncreaseLevel() {
  level++;
  level = level & 0x0F;// reset level when greater than 15
}
```

The last function (shown in part 11 of Listing 11-1) is the main loop that sets the game into motion and ties together all the functions of Listing 11-1. The first thing the loop() function does is to detach the interrupts so that the player cannot cause false wins or losses. The interrupts are not turned off by the noInterrupts() function, because that would stop the delay() function from working. Once the interrupts have been turned off, the button press and win state flags are checked for handling. After the check for a win or loss, the loop() function moves the ON LED to the next LED in the current direction it is traveling. The moveLED() function handles the movement and direction changes of all the LEDs. After the new LED is on, the interrupt for the button() function is turned back on, followed by a call to a delay.

The time the delay provides is the amount of time that any one LED is on before going to the next LED in the display; this is also the amount of time the player has to react to stop the LED sweep. The time for the delay is set by subtracting the level times 6 from 100. With the first level being equal to 0, the delay will be 100 ms, and every subsequent level shortens the time by 6 ms. the big win occurs after level 11 has been passed; that level has a time of 40 ms between LEDs. This delay sets the difficulty of getting a win a larger delay make the game easier and smaller is more difficult. The difficulty needs to be balanced for the intended audience, and is usually determined by age for arcade games. Games that are for children are often really easy for adults.

■ **Note**   It is important that the delay never goes negative; otherwise, the program will freeze up. Stop it allows a level up to 15 before resetting at a delay 10 ms; at this delay time, it is unlikely that a human player can achieve a win.

Listing 11-1. Stop It's Code, Part 11 of 11

```
void loop() {
detachInterrupt(0);
if (button == true) {
 checkWin();
}
moveLED();
attachInterrupt(0, Button, LOW);
delay  ( 100 - (level*6));
}
```

Verifying the Code

Stop it is ready to play after an Arduino is connected to the LEDs and button, as per Figure 11-1 (shown previously in the chapter). Upload all 11 parts of Listing 11-1 as a single Arduino sketch. Once the upload is finished, the game should start sweeping one LED from one side of the display. Depending on the color of the LEDs used, the display may be reminiscent of the front of a certain black 1980s sports car with artificial intelligence.

Begin the game by testing your skill, and try to Stop It on the center LED by pressing the button when the center LED is ON. The code should react as describe earlier. Since it may not be easy to test all the way to a big win, this game has a developer (or cheat mode) built in. To enter developer mode and ensure that the code is behaving properly, connect the ground side of the switch to the cathode side of the winning LED. Developer mode will make the button only trigger the interrupt when the center LED is on. Developer mode makes it possible to cycle though all of the levels and back to the first one.

Dirty Little Tricks,

Not to detract from the excitement of developing arcade games, but it is worth mentioning the unfair advantage known as rigging that some arcade games might have built into them. Such rigging only allows prizes to be won after certain conditions are met other than those presented within the game (some games never allow prizes to be won at all). This is like the belief that slot machine will only pay out a jack pot when it has received a certain dollar amount. Because arcade games are not regulated the same way as gambling machines, the possible use of rigged mechanisms has led to some controversy about legalities. Rigging is an unfortunate practice that takes away from a game's entertainment value and in some places can be illegal. Rigging may come up when developing a redemption or merchandiser game for a client.

It is best practice to make a game as fair as possible but it is up to the developer's judgment. Players will feel cheated when a rigged game is discovered. If the players have an enjoyable gaming experience, they will return to play more games. Games can be challenging, and as long as the players skill is the only factor keeping the player from winning.

As a game developer be-careful about developing games that are chance based and give prizes, as this can be considered a gambling machine and is highly regulated. But don't be afraid to develop games that provide prizes; it is usually the monetary value of the prize and the frequency that a prize can be won that determines if a game is classified as a gambling machine. A game that always gives a ticket, a piece of candy or a small toy just for starting the game and the game gives more prizes out the longer the player plays is usually not considered gambling because something is awarded for every play and in some cases just putting in a token will award some tickets. Alley roll is an example of this; most alley roll games will provide one ticket for getting the ball to the other end, but if the ball makes it into a scoring ring, more tickets are awarded. However, it is always best to research the laws and regulations when building games that give out prizes.

Adding Better Displays and Graphics

A lot of unique games can be made with displays made of arrays of LEDs, mechanical flip dots, character LCDs, or small LCD panels. The games made with displays of these styles can sometimes lack the extra shine that may be desired from a television or a computer monitor. The Arduino with a couple of resistors can drive a television using the TV out library (`www.arduino.cc/playground/Main/TVout`), but is only capable of providing black-and-white images and only works with devices that have an RCA connection. To have the power to drive more complex graphics, additional hardware—a graphics processing unit (GPU)—is required.

The Gameduino was designed to be a GPU for the Arduino and is a shield that provides a graphics platform that can create complex graphics and animations. The Gameduino's processor is programmed in to a Xilinx Spartan Field Programmable Gate Array (FPGA) and can connect to any microcontroller that is capable of SPI communication, even though it is packaged as a standard Arduino shield. The Gameduino can output video to a VGA-comparable display at 400×300 pixels with 512 colors, and can fully draw sprites, bitmaps, and backgrounds and generate stereo sound. The Gameduino is compatible with computer monitors with at least 800×600 resolution. The graphics capabilities of the Gameduino are very similar to 1980s video game consoles and older arcade games. The Gameduino also includes a secondary coprocessor that is independent of the main graphics functionality and is used to generate bitmaps for wireframe effects and control the video registers to create split-screen games.

The use of the Gameduino offloads all the graphics and display functions from the Arduino, leaving the Arduino free to control the game logic, handle user input, and track game progress. The Arduino initializes the Gameduino by copying to RAM all image data, sound data, and, if necessary, programming for the secondary processor to the Gameduino's memory. The Gameduino has 32 KB of internal memory and is split up into background images, sprite images, and program space.

This chapter just introduces the Gameduino basics to show you how to build a functional game. Gameduino reference material is available at `www.excamera.com/sphinx/gameduino/` and has samples and tutorials for more complex game feature, such as split screen and 3D wireframe. Download the quick-reference poster for working with the example in this section from the above site. The Gameduino is available at many online retailers, such as SparkFun Electronics, Adafruit Industries, and Jameco electronics.

Gameduino Library

The Gameduino is a SPI device that you can run the with standard SPI communication practices mentioned in Chapter 10. But for ease of getting games working quickly, the Gameduino library will be used for this section, and is available on the Gameduino's website (`www.excamera.com/files/gameduino/synth/sketches/Gameduino.zip`). The library installs in the standard Arduino location and needs to be modified to work with the Arduino 1.0.1 and above IDE.

To make the Gameduino library compatible, the include "Wprogram.h" in the beginning of GD.cpp needs to be changed to include Arduino.h; this can be done in any text editor.

The following list is a reference of the most common functions that will be used from the Gameduino's library. All of the functions can be called with a preceding GD. before the function call.

- begin(): Starts a connection to the Gameduino; returns true if successful.

- rd(address): Returns a byte read from the Gameduino's memory located at address.

- wr(address, data): Writes a byte of data to the Gameduino's memory at specified address.

- rd16(address): Same as rd(), but reads 16 bits from memory, instead of 8 bits, at address and address +1.

- wr16(address, data): Writes 16 bits to memory.

- fill(address, data, amount): Copies 1 byte to consecutive memory addresses up to amount.

- copy(address, data pointer, amount): Copies data from the Arduino's memory to a Gameduino address.

- setpal(palette, RGB): Sets the character color palette.

- RGB(R, G, B): Converts RGB byte values to 15-bit encoding for the Gameduino.

- sprite(sprite #, position x, position y, image #, palette, rotation, collision): Tells the Gameduino to draw a sprite to the display. Table 11-1 describes the parameters for drawing sprites to the display.

Table 11-1. *Arguments for the sprite() Function*

Parameter	Description
sprite #	Onscreen sprite number that addresses the individual sprite value between 0 and 255
position x	Horizontal sprite position value between 0 and 511; 0 is the left edge of screen
position y	Vertical sprite position on the screen value between 0 and 511; 0 is the top edge of screen
image #	Selects a background sprite to display from The Gameduino's RAM value between 0 and 63
palette	Color palette to use when rendering the sprite value between 0 and15
rotation	Sets the rotation and flip of the sprite
collision	Sets the collision detect flag

- `sprite2x2(sprite #, position x, position y, image #, palette, rotation, collision)`: Sets a 2×2 sprite to be drawn at the center four corners; uses same parameters as `sprite()`.

- `ascii()`: Loads Gameduino's standard font.

- `putstr(position x, position y, string)`: Prints a string encapsulated in quotes at the position (x, y). Needs `ascii()` to be run first to load the default font.

- `voice(voice #, wave type, frequency, left volume, right volume)`: Sets a tone to be played out of the Gameduino's audio port. Table 11-2 describes the `voice()` parameters.

Table 11-2. *Arguments for the voice() Function*

Parameter	Description
`voice #`	Individual hardware voice number used to output sound; takes a value between 0 and 63
`wave type`	Waveform (0 is sine wave, 1 is noise)
`frequency`	Frequency in quarter-Hertz (e.g., 100 Hz is 400)
`left volume, right volume`	Amplitude of the wave output per channel; takes a value between 0 and 255; total volume for all voices should be less than or equal to 255

Some of the functions require a memory address to be able to read or place data into the Gameduino. The library also defines some keywords that are helpful when calling functions that deal with memory addresses. Table 11-3 provides the name, address, and descriptor; the keywords referenced are the common memory locations for developing games.

Table 11-3. *Useful Keywords Specific to the Gameduino's memory sructure and begging adresse locations. memory addresses * Byte length = total bytes in memory*

Keyword	Address	Description
`RAM_CHR`	0x1000	Screen characters (256 ×16 = 4096 bytes)
`RAM_PAL`	0x2000	Screen character palette (256×8 = 2048 bytes)
`RAM_SPR`	0x3000	Sprite control (512×4 = 2048 bytes)
`RAM_SPRPAL`	0x3800	Sprite palettes (4×256 = 2048 bytes)
`RAM_SPRIMG`	0x4000	Sprite image (64×256 = 16384 bytes)
`PALETTE16A`	0x2840	16-color palette RAM A (32 bytes)
`PALETTE16B`	0x2860	16-color palette RAM B (32 bytes)
`PALETTE4A`	0x2880	4-color palette RAM A (8 bytes)
`PALETTE4B`	0x2888	4-color palette RAM A (8 bytes)
`VOICES`	0x2a00	Voice controls

A New Stop It

Building on top of other working projects is a great way to help simplify the development of more complex projects. The game for this section takes the idea of Stop it and expands it into the second dimension. The new game, called Stack It, as almost the same challenge as Stop It, but instead of requiring the player to stop a scrolling LED, Stack it uses scrolling sprites that need to be stopped when the current moving sprites are in the same position as the past sprites. Stack it speeds up and moves to the next level up the screen instead of displaying the level between each win.

There are two mechanisms of difficulty:

- The speed of the row

- The number of sprites that need to be matched

If the player misses the position of the previous row, the game removes sprites for the next level until the player has no more sprites left to play. Figure 11-2 shows the game play of Stack it with the last level still in play. The first level is always a gimme; it allows the player to decide where to start the stack and then continue through 16 levels to a big win.

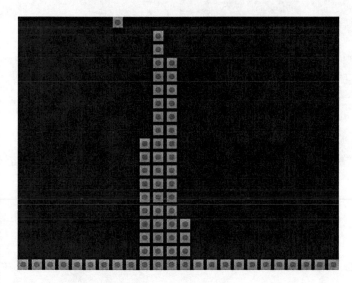

Figure 11-2. *Stack it's game play*

The hardware setup for Stack it includes the Gameduino and a button; Figure 11-3 shows the setup for the Arduino. You need to plug the Gameduino into the Arduino, making sure to align the pins and one lead of a button connected to ground, and the other lead connected to pin 2 in the headers of the Gameduino. The Gameduino only uses digital pins 9, 11, 12, and 13. Pin 9 is the slave select and is unavailable for any other function. Pins 11, 12, and 13 are the standard SPI connections and can be used to connect other SPI devices, such as SD cards. The power for the Gameduino comes from the 3.3V, 5V, and ground of the Arduino and requires no extra connectors. The Gameduino can be connected to a monitor or a television with a VGA port.

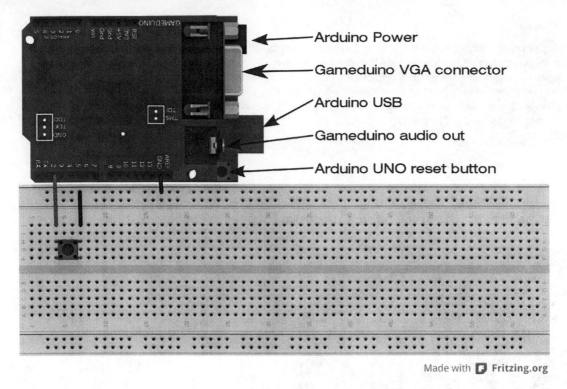

Figure 11-3. *Stack it's hardware configuration*

■ **Note**   Some televisions may not be compatible with the Gameduino's signal. For best results, use a monitor that is capable of 800×600 resolutions and has 4:3 aspect ratio. You can try a VGA-to-HDMI converter if no analog display inputs are available.

Art

When developing a game, the art and graphics usually don't get finished till the all the game mechanisms are working. On the Gameduino, however, some graphics need to be available for display so that the game mechanisms can be developed. The graphics can be a placeholder or a simplistic version of what might be the final graphic. If game is a side-scroller, the player controls a main character that is an animated sprite. For initial development, the sprite can be just a single frame of the animation. Stack it only uses one sprite and the background doesn't move.

Art for the Gameduino uses a special format that needs to be converted from an existing file or hand coded. Each sprite is 16×16 pixels. The Gameduino does not store each sprite with the color information, but instead uses a separate color palette and draws sprites to the screen in a way similar to color-by-numbers. The Gameduino offers three palette types 4, 16, or 256 and describe the amount of different colors that the palette can hold. The use of the palettes saves memory because each color needs 16 bits and is in ARGB1555 format and if the color information was saved in every pixel, 64 sprites would need 32 KB of memory, as compared to the 16.5 KB used by the separate color palette. Figure 11-4 illustrates the ARGB color format used to create color; bit 15 is the flag for transparency and each of the five bits for R, G, and B. The Gameduino is little-endian when it comes to memory; the lower bits (0 through 7) need to be copied to the address and the higher bits (8 through 15) are copied to the address plus 1.

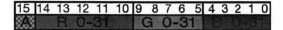

Figure 11-4. *ARGB 1555 color format*

The sprite used for Stack it is illustrated in Figure 11-5, using the coding to the 4-color palette. Each sprite maps 1 byte to the color palette per pixel. One sprite can be made with a 265-color palette, two sprites with a 16-color palette, and four sprites with a 4-color palette. Using the 4-color palette allows more sprites to be in memory, because it takes 2 bits to map to a color, and 8 bits are available. Each 2 bits of the sprite map can describe a different color used; this is good for space saving and making animated sprites. When multiple sprites are combines in one map, they can be added to the screen by changing the palette argument when calling the `sprite()` function. Larger graphics can be made by placing two or more sprites side by side on the screen.

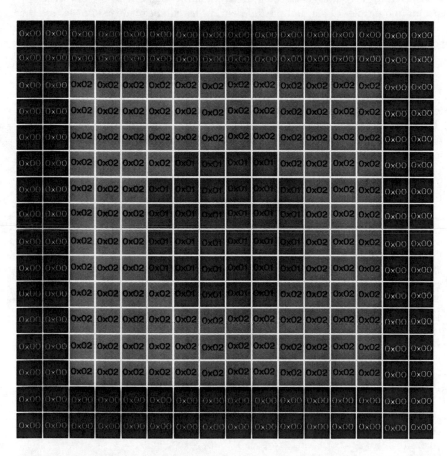

Figure 11-5. *Stack it' s sprite with palette coding*

Figure 11-6 illustrates the color palette used for Stack it. It consists of the colors black, red, green, and blue. Any color value can be used, however There is a limit to amount of different colors that the palette can hold. Stack It's sprite only uses three of the four colors available. You can give sprites transparent pixels by setting bit 15 to 1 on one of the colors. When transparency is used, the color information for R, G, and B are ignored and only one color needs to be transparent. Transparency allows for background colors to show; this is useful for non-square character sprite move over a changing background the background.

Pallet Position	0x00	0x01	0x02	0x03
Color code	0x0000	0x007C	0x03F0	0x001F

Figure 11-6. *Four-color palette using black, red, green, and blue (from left to right)*

The Gameduino Tools Online page (http://gameduino.com/tools) offers three great tools that convert image files to the proper coding to avoid hand coding sprites, backgrounds and lossy images. The tool also provides an Arduino sketch to quickly check the sprites on the display before putting them in a game. The tool provides a .h file that contains the converted image. The three types of conversions tools background, sprite sheets and lossy image conversion requires an image to convert. The sprite sheet tool also has options for the sprite size and color palette type.

The easiest way to get started making sprites is to use GIMP (www.gimp.org/)—free, open source image manipulation software that is capable of creating PNG files. When creating a new sprite image, it is best to work at the actual pixel size and with dimensions in multiples of 16. Multiple different sprites can be made in one file, and the conversion tool will divide them up according to the settings. Note that the conversion tool may not always get the colors perfect and manual manipulation of the palette may be required in the Arduino sketch.

Coding Stack It

To get started coding Stack it, create a new sketch and add a new file within the Arduino IDE by pressing Ctrl+Shift+N, and enter **cube.h** when prompted. Listing 11-2 contains the converted image from the Gameduino image tool—the variables names in cube.h are generated by the image tool. Listing 11-2 uses only the image information and does not include the function that is autogenerated by the image tool. Two static arrays are declared in cube.h. The first is cube_sprimg[], which is the mapping to the color palette, and the other is cube_sprpal[]. The bytes set in both cube_sprimg[] and cube_sprpal[] are in the order they will be loaded into the Gameduino's memory. Because of the little-endian mode of the Gameduino, the palette has the lower byte of the color set before the higher byte.

Listing 11-2. Sprite Code for Stack It

```
static PROGMEM prog_uchar cube_sprimg[] = {
0x00,0x00,0x00,0x00,0x00,0x00,0x00,0x00,0x00,0x00,0x00,0x00,0x00,0x00,0x00,0x00,
0x00,0x00,0x00,0x00,0x00,0x00,0x00,0x00,0x00,0x00,0x00,0x00,0x00,0x00,0x00,0x00,
0x00,0x00,0x02,0x02,0x02,0x02,0x02,0x02,0x02,0x02,0x02,0x02,0x02,0x02,0x00,0x00,
0x00,0x00,0x02,0x02,0x02,0x02,0x02,0x02,0x02,0x02,0x02,0x02,0x02,0x02,0x00,0x00,
0x00,0x00,0x02,0x02,0x02,0x02,0x02,0x02,0x02,0x02,0x02,0x02,0x02,0x02,0x00,0x00,
0x00,0x00,0x02,0x02,0x02,0x02,0x01,0x01,0x01,0x01,0x02,0x02,0x02,0x02,0x00,0x00,
0x00,0x00,0x02,0x02,0x02,0x01,0x01,0x01,0x01,0x01,0x01,0x02,0x02,0x02,0x00,0x00,
0x00,0x00,0x02,0x02,0x02,0x01,0x01,0x01,0x01,0x01,0x01,0x02,0x02,0x02,0x00,0x00,
0x00,0x00,0x02,0x02,0x02,0x01,0x01,0x01,0x01,0x01,0x01,0x02,0x02,0x02,0x00,0x00,
0x00,0x00,0x02,0x02,0x02,0x01,0x01,0x01,0x01,0x01,0x01,0x02,0x02,0x02,0x00,0x00,
0x00,0x00,0x02,0x02,0x02,0x02,0x01,0x01,0x01,0x01,0x02,0x02,0x02,0x02,0x00,0x00,
0x00,0x00,0x02,0x02,0x02,0x02,0x02,0x02,0x02,0x02,0x02,0x02,0x02,0x02,0x00,0x00,
0x00,0x00,0x02,0x02,0x02,0x02,0x02,0x02,0x02,0x02,0x02,0x02,0x02,0x02,0x00,0x00,
0x00,0x00,0x02,0x02,0x02,0x02,0x02,0x02,0x02,0x02,0x02,0x02,0x02,0x02,0x00,0x00,
0x00,0x00,0x00,0x00,0x00,0x00,0x00,0x00,0x00,0x00,0x00,0x00,0x00,0x00,0x00,0x00,
0x00,0x00,0x00,0x00,0x00,0x00,0x00,0x00,0x00,0x00,0x00,0x00,0x00,0x00,0x00,0x00,
};

static PROGMEM prog_uchar cube_sprpal[] = {
0x00,0x00,  0x00,0x7c,  0xe0,0x03,  0xff,0xff,
};
```

With the sprite for Stack it ready, the game-play code can be added. Stack it shares a similar concept with Stop it and also shares similar coding methods for the game mechanisms. Listing 11-3 is entered in to the main part of the sketch and is broken up into seven parts. Part 1 of Stack it sets up the variable decorations, includes, and the setup() function. The Gameduino library (GD.h), SPI library (SPI.h), and cube header (cube.h) needs to be included to have access to the functions used by Stack It. The cube.h file is included with quotes instead of < >, signaling the compiler to look for a local file in the sketch folder instead of searching for the header file in a library location. The order of the library includes is important; the SPI.h include comes before cube.h, and GD.h is the last include.

Listing 11-3. Stack It's Sketch, Part 1 of 7

```
#include <SPI.h>
#include "cube.h"
#include <GD.h>

long cubeMove[18];
boolean RightLeft;
boolean Win = false;
boolean button = false;
int level = 0;

long initPattern = 0x0000001f;

void setup() {
  pinMode(2,INPUT);
  digitalWrite(2,HIGH);
  GD.begin();
  GD.copy(PALETTE4A, cube_sprpal, sizeof(cube_sprpal));
  GD.copy(RAM_SPRIMG, cube_sprimg, sizeof(cube_sprimg));
  resetPlay();
} // end setup
```

The integer that was the LEDshift variable in Stop it is changed to a long array; this is to account for the increased number of elements that can be displayed on the screen. The array is declared as size 18 so that every level can be accounted for when displaying the sprites. The flags for the win, direction, and button press serve the same function as those used in Stop It. A variable that stores the initial pattern that will be used for the first level of the game is created here. The binary pattern of the variable is used when displaying the sprites. The pattern of the bits can be used to make the game more challenging the more bits that are placed consecutively will provide an easier challenge, allowing for the player to miss the target more often. The bit pattern does not have to be consecutive making the game more interesting. Remember that the Gameduino can only have 256 sprites on the screen at any given moment, so choose an initial pattern that will keep the sprite count below 256. There are 17 levels of Stack it, but 18 array positions—one of the array positions is used to create a base at the bottom of the screen below the first level and will use 24 of the available sprites.

The setup() function prepares the Arduino pin that will be used for the button, and is similar to the setup function as used in Stop it. The setup function adds the initialization of the Gameduino and copies the sprite and palette to memory. The memory locations used is the first four-color palette and the start of the sprite RAM section. The image is copied from the cube.h variables. The final step in the setup() function is to call resetPlay() to make sure the game is ready to play.

The function for part 2 is responsible for shifting the row of sprites from one side of the display to the other. The RowShift() function is almost identical to the moveLED() function for Stop it; it checks for when the bit-shift reaches the existents of the screen changing the bit-shift direction. The only change accounts for the increased bits used for the position, and the level determines what position of the array is currently in play.

Listing 11-3. Stack It's Sketch, Part 2 of 7

```
void RowShift() {
  if (cubeMove[16-level] & 0x00000001){
    RightLeft = false;
  }
  if (cubeMove[16-level] & 0x00800000){
    RightLeft = true;
  }
  if (!RightLeft ){
    cubeMove[16-level] = cubeMove[16-level]  << 1;
  }
  if (RightLeft){
    cubeMove[16-level] = cubeMove[16-level]  >> 1;
  }
} // end row shift
```

The function that is responsible for displaying the game to the player is the same in functionality as the display function for Stop it, but is executed differently. The use of the Gameduino allows for dynamic positioning of game elements within the 400×300 pixel viewing area, and there are no registers to directly manipulate. Part 3 is the function for displaying all the sprites to the screen. The cubeMove array is used to hold the patterns that need to be displayed. Every time the displaySprites() function is called, it will display all the current values of cubeMove; A value of 1 equals a sprite, and a sprite will be displayed according to position within the array. The array is two dimensional there is a vertical and a horizontal component; the array position is the vertical and the individual bits within the variable makes up the horizontal position. Stepping through the array is done with one for loop, while a nested for loop shifts though the bits of the variable. When there is a 1 in the variable, a sprite is displayed, and when there is a 0, the loop continues to the next step. The position of the sprite on the screen is determined by what step each for loop is at, the sprite is 16×16 pixels. The step count of the for loops is multiplied by 16 so the sprites will be place side by side on the screen. A counter that is incremented when a 1 is found to keep track of the number of sprites being displayed and is used to create a dynamic sprite count for the Gameduino.

Listing 11-3. Stack It's Sketch, Part 3 of 7

```
void displaySprites() {
  int spriteNum = 0; // start sprite count at 0
  for (int y = 0 ; y < 18 ; y ++ ) { // loop though the array for y positon
    for (int x = 0 ; x < 24 ; x ++) {  //  loop though the variable for x positon
      if ((cubeMove[y] >> x) & 0x00000001) { // check current variable position for a 1
        GD.sprite(spriteNum, (x* 16)+7, (y*16)+7 ,0, 8 , 0);
        spriteNum++;
      } // end if
    } // end for loop x
  } // end for loop y
} // end displaySprites
```

The buttonInterrupt() and WinState() functions implement part 4. buttonInterrupt() is called when the player attempts to win the current level and move on to the next. The interrupt is activated in the same fashion as in Stop it. buttonInterrupt() waits in a loop while the button is depressed and calls the WinState() function to determine if the player has won or not. The check for a win condition has been moved to a separate function to allow for possible other functions to check for win conditions outside of the player's control. A win state is true if there is at least 1 bit in common between the current level and the prior level. The first level of the game is compared against the foundation bits in the cubeMove array. The first level is always a gimme, and allows the player to decide where the stack starts. If there are no common bits, the win state is false and the game is reset.

Listing 11-3. Stack It's Sketch, Part 4 of 7

```
void buttonInterrupt  () {
  while ( digitalRead(2)== LOW) {
   WinState();
  }
} // end buttonInterrupt

void WinState() {
  button = true;
  if ((cubeMove[16-level] & cubeMove[17-level])) {
    Win = true;
  }
  else {
    Win = false;
  }
} // end WinState
```

Part 5 performs actions based on the win state when the player presses the button and increases the level. If the win state is true, then the prior level is masked with the current to determine the amount of sprites that are in common. If some of the sprites are not directly above the prior level, they get removed, and the new amount of sprites is copied to the next level, making it more difficult for the player along with decreasing the time the player has to react. If the win state is false, the game simply resets. The IncreaseLevel() function works like the one for Stop it, but the masking of the level count is unavailable because of the array. An if statement is used in place of the mask, and when the level reaches 17, the final pattern within cubeMove() is displayed and the game is reset. A reward function can be called at the point the level is maxed.

Listing 11-3. Stack It's Sketch, Part 5 of 7

```
void checkWin() {
  if (Win) {
    // check prior level and set curent level to any misses and copy to next level
    cubeMove[15-level] = cubeMove[16-level] = cubeMove[16-level] & cubeMove[17-level];
    IncreaseLevel();
  }
  if (!Win) {
    resetPlay ();
  }
  button = false;
} // end checkWin

void IncreaseLevel() {
  level ++ ;
  if (level >= 17) {
    // display winning pattern and reset play
    displaySprites();
    delay (200);
    resetPlay();
  }
} // end IncreaseLevel
```

The resetPlay() function of part 6 ensures that the game is set back to the beginning and ready for a new attempt. The cubeMove array is first zeroed and loaded with the initial state. The Gameduino then needs the sprite buffer cleared, because sprites with a higher number than that currently produced from the cubeMove pattern will remain on the screen. A loop is used to step through all 256 possible sprites and tell the Gameduino to draw blank sprites off the screen.

Listing 11-3. Stack It's Sketch, Part 6 of 7

```
void resetPlay () {
  for (int i = 0 ; i < 17 ; i ++) {
  cubeMove [i] = 0x00000000;
  }
  cubeMove[16] = initPattern;
  cubeMove[17] = 0x00ffffff;
  for (int i = 0 ; i < 256 ; i ++) {
  GD.sprite(i,450,450,0,0,0);
  }
  level = 0;
} // end resetPlay
```

As with Stop it, the final function is the loop (shown in part 7) sets the play into motion for the game. Other than the names of the functions that are called, this function is nearly identical to the one used in Stop it. To account for the increase in levels and the gimme level, the initial delay has been increased to 120 ms, leaving 18 ms for the player to react at the final level. Because of the increased complexity and the display speeds included with the Gameduino, the program spends a bit more time with the interrupt off.

Listing 11-3. Stack It's Sketch, Part 7 of 7

```
void loop() {
  detachInterrupt(0);
  if (button) {
    checkWin();
  }
  RowShift();
  displaySprites();
  attachInterrupt(0, buttonInterrupt, LOW);
  delay (120 - ( level * 6));
} // end loop
```

Verifying the Code

At this point, the code for Stack it is ready for a trial run. Configure the hardware as per Figure 11-3 (shown earlier in the chapter), and load the sketch onto the Arduino. The game should start immediately after the upload is finished and display four sprites in a row sweeping from side to side above a full row of sprites at the bottom. Once the button is pressed, the current level will stop and move to the next level. Check to see if the game-loss functionality is working by failing to match up the sprites. The game should fully reset when the last sprite is lost. Stack it does not have a convenient developer mode like Stop it has; the final levels have to be reached naturally or the delay has to be increased to check the reset to the beginning from the final win.

▪ **Note** The SPI library is standard and included with the Arduino IDE. Go to the root directory, and then `arduino/avr/libraries`; also remember to fix the reference to `Wprogram.h` to point to `Arduino.h` within `GD.cpp`.

Making Sounds

The Gameduino has the capability to produce stereo sounds via the audio plug. The `voice()` function in the Gameduino library can play two different types of wave functions: a sine wave and noise. The frequency range is about 10 to 8,000 Hz via a 12-bit synthesizer. The Gameduino is capable of 64 different voices that combine to create the output. The total amplitude of all the playing voices' output is a maximum value of 255 per channel—to avoid clipping, keep the total amplitude under 255. The frequency argument of the voices is in quarter-Hertz—for example, a frequency of 880 Hz (an A note) would require an input of 3,520. By adding the sine waves together simulated square and sawtooth waves can be created to better mimic the sound of old game systems. The noise wave in conjunction with sine waves can create sound effects for rockets, car engines, and even fighting games. Once the Gameduino is told to start making a sound, it will continue till told to change. The sound needs time to be heard by the listener, so there will have to be time delays in the code. This can slow down other aspects in the game. Note that changes should happen between running of loops, or in more advanced cases, run in the Gameduino's secondary processor. Sound is a great way to give the player feedback on what is going on (e.g., for losing or completing a level, or to produce a sense of urgency at certain parts of the game).

Adding the first sound effect to Stack it provides an auditory signal when the button has been pressed, add the following code line to the beginning of `buttonInterrupt()` before the loop is entered to have the game make a sound when the button is pressed.

```
GD.voice(0, 0, 5000,254,254);
```

A sound of 1,250 Hz (approximately an E-flat) will start playing from both channels. To get the sound to turn off, add a corresponding call at the end of the `buttonInterrupt()` that would appear just before the `buttonInterrupt()` function returns:

```
GD.voice(0,0, 0,0,0);
```

Listing 11-4 describes three functions that produce more complicated sounds to inform the player of a loss, a big win, and that the game is currently being played.

The first sound function, `moveTone()`, plays three notes: 500 Hz (~B), 750 Hz (~F sharp), and 1,000 Hz (~B + 1 octave). The note timings are based on the delay of the main loop. `moveTone()` generates sound that increases in tempo along with the increase in sweep speed of the sprite. The increase in the tempo as the game approaches the final level provides the feeling of greater urgency. `moveTone()` needs two global variables that are used to count the steps between note changes and to allow other functions to turn the move tone on and off. The variables are an integer and a Boolean declared at the beginning of the code, just after the include section.

```
int movetonecount = 0;
boolean moveToneflag = true;
```

Listing 11-4 is split into three parts. The `moveTone()`, `WinTone()`, and `LossTone()` functions are added to the end of the main sketch after the end of the `loop()` function. The call to `moveTone()` is at the end of the `loop()` function just before `loop()`'s ending curly bracket.

Listing 11-4. moveTone() Sound Functions for Stack It, Part 1 of 3

```
void moveTone() {
  if (moveToneflag) {
    if (movetonecount >= 2) {
    GD.voice(0, 0, movetonecount*1000,127,127);
    }
    if (movetonecount == 5){
    GD.voice(0, 0, 0,0,0);
    movetonecount = 0 ;
    }
    movetonecount++;
  } // end if moveToneflag
} // end moveTone
```

Listing 11-4 part 2 is the WinTone() sound function, and is used to signify the final win. WinTone() plays six tones (750 Hz, 1000 Hz, 1250 HZ, 1000 Hz, 750 Hz, and 500 Hz) twice in a row to give the player a pleasant audio reward for completion. The function should be called from the IncreaseLevel() function just after the call to dispaySprites() within the if statement used to roll the game back to the first level when the player surpasses the game limits.

Listing 11-4. moveTone() Sound Functions for Stack It, Part 2 of 3

```
void WinTone() {
  for (int t =0 ; t < 2 ; t ++) {
    for(int i = 3 ; i < 5 ; i++) {
      GD.voice(0, 0, i*1000,      254,      254);
      delay (150);
    }
    for(int i = 5 ; i > 1 ; i--) {
      GD.voice(0, 0, i*1000,254,254);;
      delay (150);
    }
    GD.voice(0, 0, 0,0,0);
  } // end for loop that plays the tone twice
} // end WinTone
```

In part 3, the third sound function, LossTone(), creates a sound that plays four notes in descending frequency: 1250 HZ, 1000 Hz, 750 Hz, and 500 Hz. This tone is only played once—when the player has missed the last sprite available. This function needs to be called from the checkWin() function inside the if statement that checking for a win before the play resets back to the first level.

Listing 11-4. moveTone() Sound Functions for Stack It, Part 3 of 3

```
void LossTone() {
  for(int i = 5 ; i > 1 ; i--) {
  GD.voice(0, 0, i*500,      254,      254);
  delay (150);
  }
  GD.voice(0, 0, 0,    0,    0);
} // end loss tone
```

Adding a Bit of Splash

After the sound is added to the game a bit of more ambience can be achieved by creating a splash screen so the game can advertise itself when it is turned on and is not being played. Stack it will display anything placed in the cubeMove array when displaySprites() is called. Adding a pattern to the screen is the same as Stop It's method of showing status to the player. The two-dimensional nature of the Gameduino allows for the creation of text using the placement of sprites with a binary pattern loaded into the cubeMove array.

The stackIt() function in Listing 11-5 loads a second array with a binary pattern that represents the words *STACK IT*. The pattern is backward in the logo array because of how the displaySprites() function steps though the cubeMove array. The function copies and displays one row of the logo array to the cubeMove array every 300 μs; then the win tone is played before the game is prepared for play. The StackIt() function can be called in the setup() function, replacing the resetPlay() function call so that when the game starts, the logo will be displayed.

Listing 11-5. A Splash Function for Stack It

```
void StackIt() {
GD.voice(0, 0, 0,0,0);
  long logo[18];
  logo[0]  = 0x00000000;  // hex is revese pattern  1 = # 0 = .
  logo[1]  = 0x00498df6;  // .##.#####.##...##..#..#.
  logo[2]  = 0x002a5249;  // #..#..#..#..#.#.#..#.#.#..
  logo[3]  = 0x00185241;  // #.....#..#..#.#....##...
  logo[4]  = 0x00185e46;  // .##.#..####.#....##...
  logo[5]  = 0x00285248;  // ...#..#..#..#.#....#.#..
  logo[6]  = 0x004a5249;  // #..#..#..#..#.#.#..#.#..#.
  logo[7]  = 0x00899246;  // .##...#..#..#..##..#...#
  logo[8]  = 0x00000000;
  logo[9]  = 0x0003e7c0;  // ......#####..#####......
  logo[10] = 0x00008100;  // ........#......#........
  logo[11] = 0x00008100;  // ........#......#........
  logo[12] = 0x00008100;  // ........#......#........
  logo[13] = 0x00008100;  // ........#......#........
  logo[14] = 0x00008100;  // ........#......#........
  logo[15] = 0x000087c0;  // ......#####....#........
  logo[16] = 0x00000000;
  logo[17] = 0x00ffffff;  // #######################
  for (int i = 17 ; i >= 0 ; i --) {
    cubeMove[i] = logo[i];
      displaySprites();
      delay (300);
    }
  WinTone();
  delay (500);
  resetPlay();
} // end Stack it logo
```

Programming the Game to Play Itself

Most arcade games have a demo mode, which shows the game being played without a human player. Unlike console games, arcade machines are left on during business hours at an arcade. The demo mode entices a player to take part in the game and displays information on how to start playing. Listing 11-6 is split into three parts and demonstrates a method of adding self-play to Stack It. Most games just have a few set patterns that are played before displaying a splash screen; this can be accomplished by creating an array that holds the set patterns. This method would use a lot of program space, however; a procedural method of play, on the other hand, would use less program space and could provide a wider variation on the self-play patters. By utilizing functions used for a human player, Stack it could use random number generation to make decisions on game play. The random numbers could tell the selfPlay() function to call for a check of WinState() to simulate an actual button press.

Listing 11-6, part 1 is the main selfPlay() function, and is called from the loop just before the delay and after the interrupt function is attached. Every time selfPlay() is called, a check is performed to see if the loop has been executed for a sufficient amount of time without player interaction to initiate the self-play mode. The check is based on a count that increments every time selfPlay() is called and not activated; the count has been chosen to be a reasonable amount of time to consider the player inactive.

Listing 11-6. Self-Play for Stack It, Part 1 of 3

```
void selfPlay() {
  if (selfPlayCount >= 300) {
      detachInterrupt(0);
      attachInterrupt(0, exitSelfPlay, LOW);
      GD.putstr(0, 0, "PRESS BUTTON TO PLAY");
      moveToneflag = false;
      if (logoCount >= 51 ){
        StackIt();
        logoCount = 0;
      }
      randomSeed(analogRead(0));
      if (level == 0 && random(10) == 5){
        selfPlayButton();
      }
      else if ((cubeMove[16-level] == cubeMove[17-level])) {
        if (random(2) == 1){
        RowShift();
        delay (120 - ( level * 6));
        displaySprites();
      }
      if (random(2) == 1) {
        selfPlayButton();
      }
      } // end else if level check
  } // end if self play count check
  else {
      selfPlayCount++ ;
  }
} // end self play
```

selfPlay() checks to see if the current level is equal to the last level, and then randomly chooses to push the virtual button by comparing a randomly generated number to a chosen number and when the numbers match the virtual button is pressed. A perfect game will be played if the selfPlay() function can only press the virtual button when the current level is perfectly aligned with the last level even with randomly deciding when to press the virtual button. To add the feel of imperfection to the selfplay() function the same method used as to determine when to press the virtual button to randomly be off by one so that a perfect game is not guaranteed and selfPlay() can lose. When the game is playing, the first level will never equal the foundation level, and the virtual button call will never be activated. selfplay() has to has to trigger the virtual button at a random point to proceed from the first level. The random numbers are generated from seed that is created by reading the Arduino's analog pin 0 while it is not connected and is electrically floating. When a generated random number is checked against a set number, corresponding events will be triggered in the self-play mode.

The move sound is turned off when the game is in self-play mode so that the game does not get irritating to people when it is idle. selfPlay() displays the splash screen every 51 virtual button presses, or about every three to five selfplay() games. The selfPlay() function attaches a different interrupt function to the physical button so that the self-play can be exited and the game can return to a playable state when a player wants to play it. A few things need to be set up in the beginning of the sketch to enable self-play. Two variables need to be initialized so that the program will know when to play the splash screen and to keep track of whether a player is not at the game. One of the variables is incremented when the self-play is called and is initialized to a value of 300 so the self-play functionality starts when the game is turned on. The other variable is incremented when the self-play presses the virtual button. Both variables are reset when a player engages the game. Add the following two variables to the global declarations after the library includes:

```
int logoCount = 0;
int selfPlayCount = 300;
```

A reset of the self-play count (selfPlayCount = 0) is added to the beginning of the buttonInterrupt() function so that the self-play will not be engaged while the player is in the middle of a game. Finally, a call is made to GD.ascii() before the call to StackIt() in the setup() function, allowing the game to use the standard Gameduino font. The font is used so that a string can be printed to the top-left corner of the display to inform a prospective player on how to start a new game.

Part 2 is the virtual button the self-play mode uses to advance the game. A tone is played that is similar when the physical button is pressed. The virtual button makes a call to WinState() to check if the self-play has matched the prior level. The self-play mode uses all the game play mechanisms and mimics an actual player. Self-play will not always win or play the same game every time. logoCount is incremented within this function to signal the splash screen to be displayed.

Listing 11-6. Self-Play for Stack It, Part 2 of 3

```
void selfPlayButton() {
  GD.voice(0, 0, 5000, 254, 254);
  delay (50);
  WinState();
  logoCount++;
  GD.voice(0,0,0,0,0);
} // end self play button
```

The game will return to a normal play mode because the self-play changes the interrupt function. Part 3 is for handling the returning to normal play when a player presses the button while the self-play mode is activated. The string is removed for the top of the screen, play is reset, the move sound is turned back on, and the counts are set to the appropriate states. The logo count is set to 51 so that self-play will execute after the game goes idle.

Listing 11-6. Self-Play for Stack It, Part 3 of 3

```
void exitSelfPlay(){
  GD.voice(0, 0, 5000,254 ,254);
  GD.putstr(0, 0, "                     ");
  while (digitalRead(2)== LOW){
  resetPlay();
  selfPlayCount = 0;
  logoCount = 51;
  moveToneflag = true;
  }
  GD.voice(0, 0, 0,   0 ,   0);
} // end exit self play
```

The Finishing Polish

With Listings 11-4 through 11-6 added to the initial Stack it code and working, the game has moved from a proof of concept to nearing completion. The sprites can be formalized, backgrounds can be created, and coin mechanisms and ticket dispensers can be integrated. The cabinet can be constructed and extras can be added to complete the game for an arcade. By working on small components and adding them to working components one at a time, a fairly complex game can be developed easily.

It is possible for games to quickly outgrow the Arduino Uno hardware by sheer number of pins or memory space. Using other hardware is always a viable solution, but it is always best to make an attempt to create something on less-equipped hardware. This helps developers create efficient code, which can always be ported to different systems. If the Arduino Uno is not capable, the next step for more pins and memory might be the Arduino Mega. If you've outgrown the Gameduino, you can modify the processor and upload it to a bigger Field Programmable Gate Array FPGA. Some clones of the Gameduino have also added extra RAM, such as the MOD-VGA made by Olimex (http://olimex.wordpress.com/).

The Gameduino is an SPI device and can be connected to any master SPI-capable device. Figure 11-7 shows how to connect the Gameduino shield to an Arduino Mega. This set up opens other opportunities for creating interesting gaming platforms for example integrating hardware such as the ADK Mega and Android devices with the graphics capabilities of the Gameduino. Stack It can be uploaded to an Arduino Mega without any changes to the code by selecting the proper board and connecting the Gameduino as per Figure 11-7.

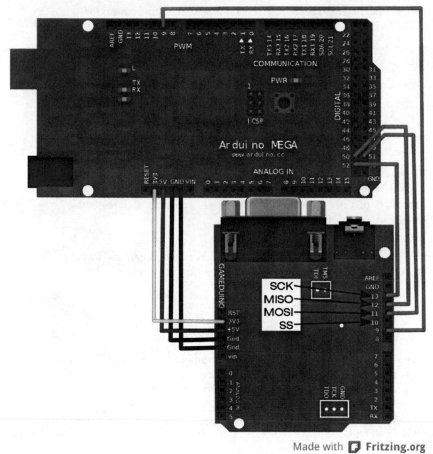

Made with 🄵 Fritzing.org

Figure 11-7. Gameduino to Arduino Mega

Arcade and Game Resources

The following list provides some extra resources that might be helpful for further research into game construction and development. It includes examples of suppliers that handle arcade equipment and supplies. Some professional arcade game development companies are listed to provide an example of arcade games and the industry.

- *www.artlum.com*: This site has a lot of Gameduino projects, including a tutorial on how to connect a classic NES controller to an Arduino.

- *www.brainwagon.org/the-arduino-n-gameduino-satellite-tracker*: This is a wonderful nongame project that uses the Gameduino.

- *www.adafruit.com/products/787* and *www.adafruit.com/products/786*: Provided here are two different coin mechanisms available from Adafruit industries.

- *www.coinmech.com* and *www.imonex.com*: These are two good sources for commercial-grade coin mechanisms.

- *www.deltroniclabs.com*: This company provides commercial-grade ticket dispersers.

- *www.nationalticket.com* and *www.tokensdirect.com*: These supply tickets and tokens for arcade machines.

- *www.uniarcade.com*, *www.coinopexpress.com*, and *www.happmart.com*: These companies offer various replacement arcade machine components, such as main boards and buttons.

- *www.xgaming.com*: This site offers other hardware game development systems, such as the Hydra gaming system.

- *www.bmigaming.com*, *www.benchmarkgames.com*, *www.laigames.com*, *www.universal-space.com*, and *www.baytekgames.com*: These are a few professional arcade game developers; these companies are a great cross section of the arcade games that are currently in use in a majority of arcades.

- *www.iaapa.org*: The International Association of Amusement Parks and Attractions (IAAPA) hosts a few conventions that show off the technology for arcades and amusement parks, and is a great resource for arcade game developers.

- *www.paxsite.com* and *www.gencon.com*: These are couple of large conventions that showcase games from many categories—including board, card, and computer games—from professional and independent developers alike. These conventions are not associated with the IAAPA.

Summary

Developing games of any type is rewarding, fun, and challenging. Game development is a field that combines artistry, storytelling, and many other skills. Starting a game is as simple as having an idea and breaking it down into small components that combine together for a final product. Taking ideas and building them into proofs of concept will help build a game portfolio that can be used to develop more complex games. An increasing number of independent developers are making good games thanks to more outlets for distribution and ease of obtaining skills and knowledge. Arduino development makes a viable platform for developing games because of the unique experience it can provide for any game type.

■ ■ ■

## CHAPTER 12

Writing Your Own Arduino Libraries

Arduino libraries are written in standard C/C++ code and contain either a set of useful functions or an object that is initialized and used in Arduino sketches. The advantage of this is that you can share these libraries across your own projects and with other users. In this chapter, we will create an example "Hello World" library, a Motor control library, and a more complex DS1631 I2C temperature sensor library.

What you need to know to write your own libraries

The choice to program libraries in C or C++ is up to you. Standard C works when using the Arduino library conventions. If you plan to use structs and enum variables you will have to place them in a header file.

C++ gives you the ability to create objects, but since we are working with an 8-bit MCU, there is limited memory space and usually little or no memory management. Make sure to test your code for memory use and heap fragmentation. Remember that not everything must be an object; it is acceptable to have a set of functions that you use as libraries without writing them from scratch for each sketch.

The major difference between Arduino sketches and Arduino libraries is that a sketch is pre-processed, meaning that you do not have to prototype your functions or write a header file for your main sketch. For this reason, a sketch is easy to use and a good starting place for beginners. Libraries, on the other hand, have to conform to the full rules of C/C++. The C/C++ compiler is powerful, but if you use functions, and variables before they are defined, the compiler will indicate an error and ultimately fail. A helpful metaphor is the idea of enrolling a course that has a required prerequisite, but the system cannot identify what the prerequisite is.

A compiler reads from the top of the file to the bottom. If any variables or functions depend on others and one is not defined, an error occurs. These prototypes and header files are a list of all the functions and variables used in the sketch and library code. The only solution is to place a prototype of your function at the top of your sketch or in the header file. For example, let's say you a have a function that adds two integers. The prototype would be:

```
int add(int aa, int bb);
```

The prototype needs only minimal information about return type, function name, and expected types that it will encounter. The implementation, on the other hand, can be done any way that follows the rules set by the prototype.

```
int add(int aa, int bb) {
        int res = aa + bb;
        return res;
}
```

Another valid implementation:

```
int add(int aa, int bb) {
        return aa + bb;
}
```

Preprocessing scans the sketch for functions and libraries that are included in your sketch. This process generates a file that ends in the .h extension—the standard extension for a header file. Arduino does that for you, but libraries require a header file and an implementation file. The header file is a list of all the function signatures, including the return type, function name, and the function parameters. In certain cases, you will need to use in-line functions in order to an optimizing goal. If you are defining your library as a C++ object, you should including the following information in the header file: what the object inherits from, the object class name, when functions are members of the class, and whether these functions are public or private.

■ **Note**   Arduino IDE forces the implementation file to have the *.cpp extension. If you use *.c, you will get errors.

One reason you may opt for a C function rather than a C++ object has to do with the potentiometer. In order to read a potentiometer, you issue a function like analogRead(A0). If all you are doing is reading values from the potentiometer, you are already in good shape. Creating a single potentiometer as an object takes memory and can quite easily overcomplicate a simple read from a device. However, if you are trying to avoid a huge number of global variables, it makes sense to have a single object contain all of the information. If needed, you can create libraries just for a single sketch. If your code starts to take multiple pages and you are writing many helper functions, you can transfer that code into sketch-based libraries. Your project will load with all the library code together, and you'll see multiple tabs. Eventually, you may want to use those libraries in more than one project. To do so, you will need to separate each into their own library area and package them to install easily across the system. Header files can also be used to create hardware profiles. The pins indicate what is used for custom shields, breadboard circuits, and even custom Arduino-compatible boards. This would allow for portable code between hardware devices and configurations.

Figure 12-1 shows the #include "HardwareProfile.h", which pulls in the header file HardwareProfiles.h. In this file, you can define custom variables for a piece of hardware and set their default values.

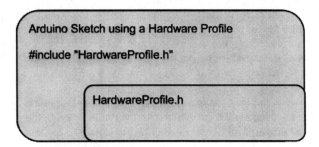

Figure 12-1. *Hardware Profile included into an Arduino Sketch*

Listing 12-1. Example defines in HardwareProfile.h

```
#define motor1Dir 7
#define motor2Dir 8
#define motor1PWM 9
#define motor2PWM 10
#define motor1Enable 11
#define motor2Enable 12
```

Listing 12-1 shows a set of pins defined from the Motor Library example. This guarantees that you use the correct pins every time you work with the same hardware. If you need to change from the default pins, you can redefine the pin numbers in your sketch.

Creating a simple library

There are typically two "Hello World" programs for Arduino. One blinks an LED on and off, and the other sends a "Hello, World!" message over the serial connection. Here, we will convert the sketch into a simple library. Figure 12-2 shows a visualization of the library, implementation, and sketch file that we are creating.

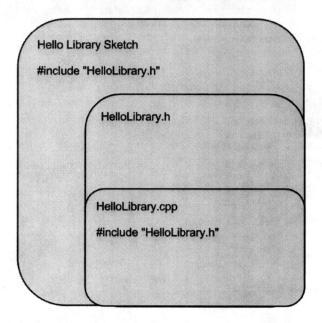

Figure 12-2. SimpleHello.ino sketch and code layout

The starter sketch for this is example is Listing 12-2.

Listing 12-2. Initial sketch code

```
const int LED_PIN = 13;
void setup()
{
  Serial.begin(9600);
  pinMode(LED_PIN, OUTPUT);
}
void loop()
{
  Serial.println("Hello, World!");
  digitalWrite(LED_PIN, HIGH);
  delay(1000);
  digitalWrite(LED_PIN, LOW);
  delay(1000);
}
```

There are several small details in this code that we can clean up and place into a library. The pin can differ between boards, so we will want to define a default pin of 13 and allow for it to be overridden.

■ **Note** Not all boards have the same LED pin. For example the Arduino Ethernet board uses pin 9.

To create libraries, first create a main sketch, and then add the libraries to that sketch. Since the sketch is an auto-generated header file, the library you create cannot have the same name as the sketch. Let's start by creating the library's header file, HelloLibrary.h. In order to create a new library, you have to use a special part of the Arduino IDE. In Figure 12-3, there is a drop down arrow just below the serial monitor button.

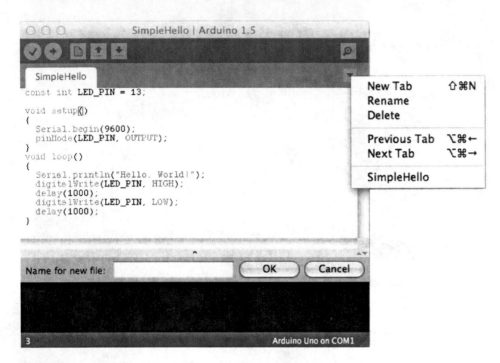

Figure 12-3. *SimpleHello.ino sketch with "New Tab" option*

Make sure your sketch contains the code from Listing 12-2. Then, in Figure 12-3, select "New Tab" from the triangle menu. You will be prompted to create a file. Call this new file "HelloLibrary.h". Once you have created the new file, enter Listing 12-3.

Listing 12-3. HelloLibrary Header File

```
/*
*
* HelloLibrary Header file
*
*/
#ifndef HelloLibrary_h
#define HelloLibrary_h
```

```
#if defined(ARDUINO) && ARDUINO >= 100
#include "Arduino.h"
#else
#include "WProgram.h"
#endif

#define LED_PIN 13
void printHelloLibrary();
void startBlink(int duration);
#endif
```

If you were programming strictly in C, you may want to name the HelloLibrary implementation file as HelloLibrary.c, but the Arduino compiler process will be looking for HelloLibrary.cpp. Normally, it is okay to put C code in the *.cpp file. Next, we will create the HelloLibrary.cpp implementation file. The HelloLibrary.cpp code that we will use for the implementation is shown in Listing 12-4. It is important to note that the implementation file needs to include a reference to the header file. This way, the created functions will conform to the header specification at compile time.

Listing 12-4. HelloLibrary cpp implementation file

```
/*
*
 * HelloLibrary cpp implementation file
 *
 */

#include "HelloLibrary.h"
void startBlink(int duration)
{
  digitalWrite(LED_PIN, HIGH);
  delay(duration);
  digitalWrite(LED_PIN, LOW);
  delay(duration);
}

void printHelloLibrary()
{
  Serial.println("Hello Library");
}
```

The code that causes the actions is now in place in Listing 12-4, and it is almost identical to the code that we made in the main sketch. Once the library is created, the main HelloLibrarySketch.ino sketch resembles Listing 12-5. It includes HelloLibrary.h, as well as the functions and definitions defined in the library that are now available to any application that communicates with the library.

Listing 12-5. Revised main sketch code

```
/*
 *
 * Hello Library Example
 *
 */

#include "HelloLibrary.h"
void setup()
{
}

void loop()
{
  printHelloLibrary();
  startBlink(1000);
}
```

Listing 12-5 outlines the pattern that all libraries follow. Include the library at the top of the file, and the compiler will process the library, and then you can access the functions according to C/C++ principles. In libraries, there is a common pattern for adding enumerations (enum) and structures (struct) to your code. You can use these as types in your code, but only if you write a function that has them as a return type or parameter. Because of the preprocessing, you cannot put them in your main sketch, but you will need to add them to a header file. For example, you may want to keep track of the part of the day—morning, afternoon, evening, or night. It is possible to do this in one of two ways.

- Using #define:

  ```
  #define MORNING 0
  #define AFTERNOON 1
  #define EVENING 2
  #define NIGHT 3
  ```

- Using an enumeration:

  ```
  enum {MORNING, AFTERNOON, EVENING, NIGHT};
  ```

There is an automatic assigning of values starting from 0 and growing by one, until the final one is reached. This can be overridden, and each can be initialized to a specific value.

```
enum {
MORNING = 1,
AFTERNOON = 3,
EVENING = 5,
NIGHT = 7
};
```

For this reason enum sequences are not typically iterated. You should use a different data type for values that you want to iterate.

The other common C feature is structures. Structures are referred to as structs and similarly must be implemented in a header file in order to be used as parameters or return types for functions.

```
struct position {
        int xx;
        int yy;
};
```

This struct would declare a position to have an X and Y value. In strict C, you would have to declare the struct or enum with typedef, but in C++ this is not required. This struct could be added to our Hello Library header file, as indicated in Listing 12-6.

Listing 12-6. Position struct in header file HelloLibrary.h updated

```
/*
*
 * HelloLibrary Header file
 *
 */
#ifndef HelloLibrary_h
#define HelloLibrary_h

#if defined(ARDUINO) && ARDUINO >= 100
#include "Arduino.h"
#else
#include "WProgram.h"
#endif

#define LED_PIN 13
struct position {
        int xx;
        int yy;
};

void printHelloLibrary();
void startBlink(int duration);
#endif
```

Then the Position struct could be used in the main sketch, as shown in Listing 12-7.

Listing 12-7. Code using the Position struct

```
#include "HelloLibrary.h"
void setup()
{
Serial.begin(9600);
position Position;
Position.xx = 20;
Position.yy = 30;
Serial.print("Position X: ");
Serial.print(Position.xx);
Serial.print(" Y: ");
Serial.println(Position.yy);
}
```

```
void loop()
{
}
```

Listing 12-7 uses the struct from the header file in the setup portion of the main sketch. Without using libraries to hold these values, you must prototype them manually in the main sketch, which makes the code less portable to other projects. Using libraries unlocks the real power of C/C++, where function definitions, function parameters and return types can conform to the rules that were defined in your library.

Making a Motor Library

Robots help us get the most out of our movement code. We may have many robots based on the same motor driver chips, so most motor movement can be done from a generic motor library that targets a set of common pin compatible motor control chips. For a more in-depth look, we will create a motor library initially based on the L293D chip. In some cases, like Texas Instruments SN754410, they are pin compatible and need to be modified. However, if a different pin layout were used for a new shield, then the pins would have to be redefined . This project is a based on the IEEE Rutgers motor controller shield, https://github.com/erosen/Line-Following-Robot, with two 5-volt motors. The goal is to convert it to a library that conforms to the Arduino and can be easily distributed for anyone using either chip. In this example, we will create a motor object using the basic C++ features of a class with both private and public methods.

A motor controller needs three types of defined pins: motor direction, the pulse width modulation (PWM), and motor enable. These pins enable the motor behavior—for example: on or off and spin forward or backward. The motor will spin at a particular rate controlled by voltage approximated by the PWM pins. Since these pins can change from board to board, we need a way to set a default set of pins and then an override so that custom pins can be used. For instance, software PWM could be used instead of the physical PWM pins that are indicated by the Arduino type.

The example code we are using in Figure 12-8 already supports many helpful features. You can also write directly to the pins to make the motors move. To enable a motor, set the direction and move it to write:

```
digitalWrite(motor1Enable, HIGH);
digitalWrite(motor1Dir, HIGH);
analogWrite(motor1PWM, 128);
```

Given these basic features, we can control the motor for forward, back, left, right, stop, and various speeds. In a standard Arduino sketch you would end up cutting and pasting them repeatedly, which is not very sustainable. The next step is to create some useful functions that help to avoid cutting and pasting, so we do not end up with code that is difficult to read. The final step is to create a library that organizes these functions so that you can use them in multiple robot or motor projects. The starting sketch is shown in Listing 12-8.

Listing 12-8. Initial motor controller code

```
#define motor1Dir 7
#define motor2Dir 8
#define motor1PWM 9
#define motor2PWM 10
#define motor1Enable 11
#define motor2Enable 12

void initMotorDriver()
{
  pinMode(motor1Dir, OUTPUT);
  pinMode(motor2Dir, OUTPUT);
```

```
    pinMode(motor1Enable, OUTPUT);
    pinMode(motor2Enable, OUTPUT);
    digitalWrite(motor1Enable,HIGH);
    digitalWrite(motor2Enable,HIGH);
    setLeftMotorSpeed(0); // make sure the motors are stopped
    setRightMotorSpeed(0);
}

void setMotorVel(int dirPin, int pwmPin, int velocity)
{
    if (velocity >= 255)
    {
      velocity = 255;
    }
    if (velocity <= -255)
    {
      velocity = -255;
    }

    if (velocity == 0)
    {
      digitalWrite(dirPin, HIGH);
      digitalWrite(pwmPin, HIGH);
    }
    else if(velocity <0)
    { // Reverse
      digitalWrite(dirPin, HIGH);
      analogWrite(pwmPin, 255+velocity);
    }
    else if(velocity >0)
    { // Forward
      digitalWrite(dirPin,LOW);
      analogWrite(pwmPin, velocity);
    }

}

void setLeftMotorSpeed(int velocity)
{
  //Serial.print("Set Left: ");
  //Serial.println(velocity);
  setMotorVel(motor1Dir, motor1PWM, -velocity);

}

void setRightMotorSpeed(int velocity)
{
  //Serial.print("Set Right: ");
  //Serial.println(velocity);
  setMotorVel(motor2Dir, motor2PWM, -velocity);
}
```

```
void setup()
{
  initMotorDriver();
  setRightMotorSpeed(255);
  setLeftMotorSpeed(-255);
  delay(500);
  setRightMotorSpeed(-255);
  setLeftMotorSpeed(255);
  delay(500);
  setRightMotorSpeed(0);
  setLeftMotorSpeed(0);

}

void loop()
{
  //Go Forward 5 secs
  setRightMotorSpeed(355);
  setLeftMotorSpeed(255);
  delay(5000);
  //Stop
  setRightMotorSpeed(0);
  setLeftMotorSpeed(0);

  //loop here forever.
  while(1);

}
```

In the initial sketch, the individual control commands are combined into one function called `setMotorVel`:

```
void setMotorVel(int dirPin, int pwmPin, int velocity)
```

The direction is set by integer velocity, which accepts –255 through 255. If the velocity is negative, then the opposite direction is enabled.

Listing 12-8 code defines the pins that are mapped to control the chip. This defines a motion function that controls all the options, and there are helper functions that make it easy to initiate left and right control of the robot. Now, we are ready to make the library. These functions will move into their own header file, `.h` and their own implementation file, `.cpp`. At this step, we want to create the appropriate project structure.

Listing 12-9. Motor controller header file Motor.h

```
#ifndef Motor_h
#define Motor_h

#if defined(ARDUINO) && ARDUINO >= 100
#include "Arduino.h"
#else
#include "WProgram.h"
#endif
```

```
#define motor1Dir 7
#define motor2Dir 8
#define motor1PWM 9
#define motor2PWM 10
#define motor1Enable 11
#define motor2Enable 12

class Motor
{
 public:
    Motor();
    void begin();
    void setLeftMotorSpeed(int velocity);
    void setRightMotorSpeed(int velocity);

 private:
    void setMotorVel(int dirPin, int pwmPin, int velocity);
};
#endif
```

Here is what the implementation file looks like:

```
#include "Motor.h"
Motor::Motor()
{
  pinMode(motor1Dir, OUTPUT);
  pinMode(motor2Dir, OUTPUT);

  pinMode(motor1Enable, OUTPUT);
  pinMode(motor2Enable, OUTPUT);
  digitalWrite(motor1Enable,HIGH);
  digitalWrite(motor2Enable,HIGH);
  setLeftMotorSpeed(0); // make sure the motors are stopped
  setRightMotorSpeed(0);
}


void Motor::setMotorVel(int dirPin, int pwmPin, int velocity)
{
  if (velocity >= 255)
  {
    velocity = 255;
  }
  if (velocity <= -255)
  {
    velocity = -255;
  }

  if (velocity == 0)
  {
    digitalWrite(dirPin, HIGH);
    digitalWrite(pwmPin, HIGH);
  }
```

```
  else if(velocity <0){ // Reverse
    digitalWrite(dirPin, HIGH);
    analogWrite(pwmPin, 255+velocity);
  }
  else if(velocity >0){ // Forward
    digitalWrite(dirPin,LOW);
    analogWrite(pwmPin, velocity);
  }

}

void Motor::setLeftMotorSpeed(int velocity)
{
  //Serial.print("Set Left: ");
  //Serial.println(velocity);
  setMotorVel(motor1Dir, motor1PWM, -velocity);

}

void Motor::setRightMotorSpeed(int velocity)
{
  //Serial.print("Set Right: ");
  //Serial.println(velocity);
  setMotorVel(motor2Dir, motor2PWM, -velocity);
}
```

Once the implementation code is in place, it is time to work on the main sketch that will use the code. To avoid cutting and pasting the code into every sketch, we can just write #include "Motor.h". The following sketch example shows the code controlling the motor and using features of the library, which is much shorter and cleaner than the original sketch in Listing 12-8.

Listing 12-10. Motor controller main sketch

```
.#include "Motor.h"
Motor motor;

void setup()
{

  motor.setRightMotorSpeed(255);
  motor.setLeftMotorSpeed(-255);
  delay(500);
  motor.setRightMotorSpeed(-255);
  motor.setLeftMotorSpeed(255);
  delay(500);
  motor.setRightMotorSpeed(0);
  motor.setLeftMotorSpeed(0);

}
```

```
void loop()
{
  //Go Forward 5 secs
  motor.setRightMotorSpeed(255);
  motor.setLeftMotorSpeed(255);
  delay(5000);
  //Stop
  motor.setRightMotorSpeed(0);
  motor.setLeftMotorSpeed(0);

  //loop here forever.
  while(1);
}
```

The amount of code for the sketch file is greatly reduced. Now, the sketch is about controlling the robot and less about implementing the low-level motor controlling code. The code can be adapted to be used system-wide across multiple projects.

The anatomy of an Arduino library folder

The previous code shows how to create a library that is available to an individual Arduino sketch, rather than a system-wide sketch that all programs can use. As you continue to develop a set of libraries, you will want to structure them so that other people can use them. This means creating a readme.txt and a keywords.txt, moving examples to their own directory, and placing utility code into a utilities folder, all of which is shown in Figure 12-4.

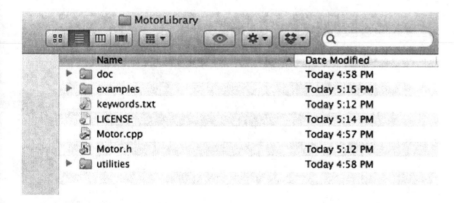

Figure 12-4. Motor library directory structure

- **Library Name:** The folder that contains the motor library will be listed with the library name; for instance MotorLibrary not Motor.h.

- **Examples:** These can be demo programs or test sketches that people will find useful when using your library.

- **Utilities:** A folder for utility code is not needed for main functionality, but provides help code.

- **Doc:** A documentation folder where .pdf, .txt, or .html files go with documentation for the library.

- **Header files**: Our example uses Motor.h, but you may have many other header files in your project. Those would all go in this directory.

- **Implementation file**: This example uses Motor.cpp, but other libraries can have one or more implementation files.

- **License**: The license your libraries will be distributed under, such as the GNU Public License (GPL).

- **keywords.txt**: This contains the formatting to highlight the functions and variables that a user will see in the Arduino IDE.

All of these directories and files need to be compressed into a .zip compressed archive file for download and installation by extracting them into the Arduino libraries folder. Let's examine critical features in more detail.

Examples Folder

The example folder contains all of your example sketches that demonstrate features and instructions. By having examples, your library will appear in the "examples" menu. When your library does not have examples, it will only be found in the "import library" menu. There are occasions where you write several libraries and they all share the same library. In this case, it makes sense to omit additional examples.

■ **Note** New users may be confused and not be able to locate the library if it does not have at least one example.

License

The license file can be anything from GPL to "all rights reserved." If you are building on top of open source software, the license should be compatible. For Open Hardware check out the Open Source Hardware Association (OSHWA) at http://www.oshwa.org/; they maintain the definition of Open Hardware and have helpful information on what licenses are available.

keywords.txt

This file consists of the datatypes, methods, functions, and constants sections. A data type in parenthesis denotes the section. However, a tab character must separate these key and value pairs. Any spaces will cause the parsing to fail, with no indication as to what is wrong.

```
# Datatypes (KEYWORD1)
```

```
Motor    KEYWORD1
```

```
# Methods and Functions (KEYWORD2)
```

```
setMotorVel       KEYWORD2
setLeftMotorSpeed         KEYWORD2
setRightMotorSpeed        KEYWORD2
```

```
# Constants (LITERAL1)
```

```
motor1Dir                 LITERAL1
```

■ **Note**   Even before your code is completed in this format, it is good practice to make it a version-controlled project and enable issue tracking. This is explained in detail in Chapter 2.

Installing Arduino Libraries

The libraries are normally installed in the user sketch folder under `libraries`. Complete libraries are stored there for use in any Arduino sketch. Installation typically consists of extracting the library into the Arduino `libraries` folder.

If you have placed your code in a version control system like GitHub, users can click the download option and extract or clone the project into the default libraries folder. This is a very efficient way to distribute the code and make it communally available.

Using Arduino Libraries

Once a library is extracted and placed, it is ready for use. The code that references the libraries will need to be updated in one of the following formats.

- To look for a system-level library:

  `#include <Motor.h>`

- To look in the project directory for the library:

  `#include "Motor.h"`

The `#include` with caret bracketing (`< >`) indicates a system library, and it will search the library area for your code. This step can be easily overlooked, so be careful and check that you have the correct symbols.

Arduino Objects and Library Conventions

C libraries do not use constructors and destructors. The library simply provides a set of previously created functions and variables. However, in order to use a library, there may be some set-up configuration necessary. This initialization would be in a `begin()` function, where all necessary elements of the library are configured. However, C++ supports objects that typically have a constructor, which is invoked when the object is created. Conversely, a destructor is invoked when the object is removed from memory, which means `begin()` is not always needed.

A destructor would usually be defined as a way to clean up the object on delete. However, delete in the AVR environment is not always available. You can free up pins and clean up after the object is finished, or you can use an `end()` function activated in the void `setup()` portion of an Arduino sketch.

■ **Note**   Destructors are not typically used. The examples have the destructors removed.

The `setup()` function should include all the starting maintenance and object initialization in addition to the constructor. One key reason to use the `begin()` function is that variables, objects, or communications may not be initialized yet. For instance, if you want to use the `Wire` (I2C) library in a library or object, the `Wire.begin()` function must be enabled before your object can use the Wire library. At some point, the user may want to end the use of an object so that the `end()` function can be accessed, which takes care of any necessary cleanup. The recommended Arduino best practice for writing libraries that have some kind of sequential data includes using "read" and "write" functions instead of "send" and "receive".

One common temperature sensor is the DS1631 I2C. It is essential to review the characteristics of the device in order for the code to use these features. This includes going to the data sheet http://datasheets.maxim-ic.com/en/ds/DS1631-DS1731.pdf, on which you can derive the following information.

This is an I2C slave device, which has a pin configurable address for up to eight devices on the same I2C chain as the master device.

This is represented by the 7-bit control byte defined here:

- Bit 0: r/w
- Bit 1: A0
- Bit 2: A1
- Bit 3: A2
- Bit 4: 1
- Bit 5: 0
- Bit 6: 0
- Bit 7: 1

We frequently work with these numbers in hexadecimal format. You will see device configuration that looks like this:

0x90

The way to read it is:

- 9 is 1001
- 0 is 0000

That would mean the device address is 0 and writable. The address corresponds to three bits, A0, A1, A2, and the last bit in the sequence configures if the device is in both write and read mode. So, read-only would look like 0001. The address only needs the 000, so in the implementation, we shift the address by one bit. Then the piece of code looks like this:

_addr = 0x90 >> 1;

Now the address can be used to reference the device. The goal with our code is to put those details into the constructor so that the data sheet can be directly read and the address can be pulled from it without forcing the programmer to make the shift. This also means that the user must wire the DS1631 with a valid address. Then, they must define the address for the library or object. When we configure the object, we require an address. The Arduino I2C master sets the control byte in order to tell the correct DS1631 what command to receive.

Ideally, the programmer will be able to use or hide the commands as needed during the implementation stage. So, startConversion() can be done without the programmer knowing the internal commands, such as the fact that 0x51 means "start conversion". This applies to any of the appropriate and defined commands. For use in the Wire library, these must be converted into a hexadecimal form.

The commands are as follows:

- Start Convert: 0x51
- Stop Convert: 0x22
- Read Temperature: 0xAA
- Access TH: 0xA1

- Access TL: 0xA2

- Access Config: 0xAC

Software POR: 0x54 Registers:

- Temperature, 2 bytes, read only

- Configuration, 1 byte, read/write or set read-only

- Trip point: High, 2 bytes, read/write

- Trip point: Low, 2 bytes, read/write

We will want to obtain and/or set this information. The trigger trip points are very useful because we can set actions to occur if we leave a common boundary. Additionally, we can have interrupts that respond to both high and low conditions.

We will not be using the trip point registers in this example, but they can be found with the website in the final library code.

A typical set of functions would be the getters and setters for those registers:

```
getConfig();
setConfig();
getTemp();
```

The goal for the main Arduino sketch is to print out the temperature at specified intervals. When we distribute the code, this will be moved into the examples folder. We also need to create DS1631.h, and DS1631.cpp in the same sketch folder. Then, we will move the code to its own Arduino generic library. Here's the initial library code, starting with the header file:

Listing 12-11. DS1631 I2C temperature sensor Arduino library DS1631.h

```
/*
 * DS1631 library object.
 * Registers R1, and R2 are used to set 9, 10, 11, 12 bit temperature resolution
 * Between a range of -55C to +125C
 * A0, A1, A2 are used to set the device address. Which is shifted by the library for use.
 * 1-SHOT readings or Continuous Readings can be configured
 * 12 bit resolution can take up to 750ms to be available
 * Temperature is returned in a 16 bit  two's complement Th, and Tl Register
 * The signed bit S, S = 0 for positive, and S = 1 for negative
 */

#ifndef DS1631_h
#define DS1631_h

#if defined(ARDUINO) && ARDUINO >= 100
#include "Arduino.h"
#include "pins_arduino.h"
#else
#include "WProgram.h"
#include "pins_arduino.h"
#endif
```

```
#define DEV0  0x90
#define DEV1  0x91
#define DEV2  0x92
#define DEV3  0x93
#define DEV4  0x94
#define DEV5  0x95
#define DEV6  0x96
#define DEV7  0x97

class DS1631
{
public:
  DS1631(uint8_t _ADDR);
  void begin( );
  byte getConfig();
  void setConfig(uint8_t _ADDR);
  float getTemp();
  void stopConversion();
  void startConversion();

private:
  float calcTemp(int msb, int lsb);
  uint8_t _addr;
  uint8_t _temp[2];
};
#endif
```

Listing 12-11 defines all the valid device addresses that can be used with the object. It is configured so that when reading the data sheet, the hexadecimal I2C address can be used as listed. Since the header file only shows the signature for the functions, we can tell what the class name, constructor, and destructor are for the defined object.

■ **Note**　With the AVR GCC, there is not effective memory management. Objects will not get deleted, so the constructor is not used and can be eliminated from the code.

As there is no effective memory management, the destructor is not used and no memory will be deallocated. The private variables are declared here, and the compiler will enforce them. If you try to directly access _addr, _temp[2], or calcTemp(), the compiler will show an error indicating that you are trying to access private values. By reviewing this code, you can get a quick idea of the functions and the types of parameters that are defined. This information will be used to ensure that the implementation corresponds to the values that are represented in the header file.

It is possible to describe more than one object in a single header file, but this can confuse library users, so it is best to create only one object per header file. If a set of objects will never be used separately from one another, it may make sense to define more than one object in the same header file.

Listing 12-12. DS1631 I2C temperature sensor implementation DS1631.cpp

```
#include <Wire.h>
#include "DS1631.h"
```

```
uint8_t _temp[2];
uint8_t _addr;

DS1631::DS1631(uint8_t _ADDR)
{
  //Cannot use Wire.begin() here because at declaration time it is unavailable.
  //Shift the address so the user can use the address as described in the Datasheet
  _addr = _ADDR >> 1;
}

void DS1631::begin()
{
}

void DS1631::stopConversion()
{
  Wire.beginTransmission(_addr);
  Wire.write(0x22); //stop conversion command
  Wire.endTransmission();
}

void DS1631::startConversion()
{
  Wire.beginTransmission(_addr);
  Wire.write(0x51); //start conversion command
  Wire.endTransmission();
}

byte DS1631::getConfig()
{
  byte config;
  stopConversion();
  Wire.beginTransmission(_addr);
  Wire.write(0xAC); //get configuration command
  Wire.endTransmission();
  Wire.requestFrom(_addr, (uint8_t) 0x01); //The configuration is one byte get it
  while (Wire.available())
  {
    config = Wire.read();
  }

  Wire.endTransmission();
  startConversion();
  return config;
}

void DS1631::setConfig(uint8_t config)//configuration options
{
  stopConversion();
  Wire.beginTransmission(_addr);
  Wire.write(0xAC); //get configuration command
```

```
  Wire.write(config); //configure with options
  Wire.endTransmission();
  startConversion();
}

float DS1631::getTemp() //0xAA command Read Temp, read 2 bytes, one shot temperature read
{
  unsigned char _temp[2];
  int count = 0;

  Wire.beginTransmission(_addr);
  Wire.write(0xAA); // start reading temperature now
  Wire.endTransmission();

  delay(750); //750ms reqiured to get 12 bit resolution temperature
  Wire.requestFrom(_addr,  (uint8_t)2); //get the 2 byte two's complement value back
  while(Wire.available())
  {
    _temp[count] = Wire.read();
    count++;
  }
  float temp = calcTemp(_temp[0],_temp[1]);
  return temp;
}

float DS1631::calcTemp(int msb,  int lsb)
{
  float num = 0.0;
  //Acceptable, but only 2-3 significant digits
   // num = (((((short)msb<<8) | (short)lsb)>>6) / 4.0;
  lsb = lsb >> 4; // shift out the last 4 bits because they are 0
  if (msb & 0x80) // Compare the sign bit = 1, then less than 0;
  {
    msb = msb - 256;
  }
  // Float conversion
  num = (float) (msb + lsb*0.0625);
  return  num;
}
```

The work of implementing the header file is done in the implementation file. Each of the I2C commands needs to be configured exactly to the data sheet. The constructor takes the defined address and shifts it the required one bit in order to be a proper address on the I2C bus. The details of the I2C communication protocol are wrapped inside the functions so that a library user only needs to have some knowledge of the data sheet.

We have a setConfig(uint8_t) and a uint8_t getConfig() that will accept and display the configuration of the temperature sensor.

The datasheet explains that the temperature is in Celsius and is stored in two's complement formats, which mean that the most significant bit is the whole number, and the least significant bit is the decimal place. The float getTemp() function returns the Celsius temperature by calling calcTemp(); this is a private function that the sketch cannot call. There are many ways to do calcTemp(); it could be turned into a virtual function and be overridden by the programmer, but by separating it from getTemp(), it is possible to add flexibility to the library.

Listing 12-13. DS1631 I2C main sketch DS1631Example.ino

```
/*
 * DS1631_CPP Library Example
 */

#include <Wire.h>
#include "DS1631.h"

uint8_t conf = 0x0C;
uint8_t dev1 = DEV0;

DS1631 TempSensor(dev1); //Wire.begin hasn't happened yet
void setup()
{
  Serial.begin(9600);
  Wire.begin();

  TempSensor.stopConversion();
  TempSensor.setConfig(conf);
  byte config = TempSensor.getConfig();
  Serial.print("Config: dev:");
  Serial.print(DEV0, BIN);
  Serial.print(" set: ");
  Serial.print(config, BIN);
  Serial.print(conf, BIN);
  Serial.print(" get: ");
  Serial.println(config, BIN);
}

void loop()
{
  float temp = TempSensor.getTemp();
  Serial.print("TempC: ");
  Serial.print(temp, 4);
  Serial.print(" tempF: ");
  Serial.println((temp*9/5) + 32, 4);
}
```

One key point is that `Wire.begin()` must be initiated for any I2C communication to occur. This explains why `Wire.begin()` is established early in the `setup()` code, before `TempSensor.setConfig(conf)` is called. The Serial library can print float values so the temperature returned as `float` would be printed automatically with two decimal points, but because we have more detail, the code specifies four decimal places.

Lastly, it is possible to have up to eight DS1631 temperature sensors on one Arduino. In this version of the library, the sketch would contain an array of sensors each configured with their own address, as follows:

```
DS1631 TmpSense[8] = {
  DS1631(DEV0),
  DS1631(DEV1),
  DS1631(DEV2),
  DS1631(DEV3),
```

```
    DS1631(DEV4),
    DS1631(DEV5),
    DS1631(DEV6),
    DS1631(DEV7)
};
```

This code initializes all of the possible DS1631 I2C devices and can be used to monitor all eight possible sensors. You can access sensor four by calling TmpSense[4].getTemp(). You can use a for loop to read through the array and obtain all the sensor values. Lastly, in order to get the most from the library, you must document how the device names are defined; otherwise, users of the library will have to examine the header file and deduce all of the features. Another benefit of using libraries is to organize convenience functions like Fahrenheit conversion as shown in the loop code in Listing 12-13. A good follow up exercise is updating the library to support getTempC() and getTempF().

One benefit of using Listing 12-12 is that we abstract away the details of configuring the temperature sensor, making the main sketch code simpler; we only need to configure and use the device. The library and the object contain all the code that are typically cut and pasted into the main sketch. This allows the user to avoid major headaches by using the temperature sensor instead of debugging the code.

Summary

Arduino libraries are powerful tools for sharing code between projects and users. This code is organized for bundling and easy distribution. In this chapter we showed how to create libraries in a specific sketch directory. You can now choose whether to write C style libraries or C++ object based libraries. Then, we explained how to convert that directory into an Arduino wide library. The Motor controller evolved from a single sketch to a powerful library with many helpful commands that control a robot or a set of motors. The other major example shows how to interact with devices using the I2C protocol and makes those devices easier to access and use. We also reviewed the steps necessary to take a library from a single project and make it available to all of your code system-wide. The next steps are to check your library code into GIT and share the project with other Arduino users as we described in Chapter 2.

■ ■ ■

## CHAPTER 13

Arduino Test Suite

Whether you are creating projects, sketches, or examples, testing is a skill that you will need. When you are developing a product to share or sell, it is critical that both your hardware and software behave as expected. Having a test helps people learn about how your project works. The Arduino Test Suite provides a way to prove that your product is functioning correctly. Incorporating tests into a project helps highlight the fixes and improvements that you have made. Additionally, using the social coding principles we described in Chapter 2, users are encouraged to submit issues to http://github.com/arduino/tests, including test examples, to demonstrate problems and verify the resolution of those problems. The more confidence people have in your product, the better.

The Arduino Test Suite library allows you to create a standard test suite for your own software and the Arduino software. This library provides a simple, standard way to build these tests. Each test suite run provides output formatted in the Arduino test result format. This output can be parsed by continuous integration testing software, like Jenkins, which can be found at http://jenkins-ci.org/. These tests can be added to your project's official list of automatic tests, which run every time code is changed in the project's repository.

In this chapter, I will

- Go through the basic features of the Arduino Test Suite

- Show how the built-in tests can be used with a custom test shield

- Provide a basic procedure using the Arduino Test Suite to create a comprehensive test that tests your project and code libraries

- Provide an example of testing memory usage

- Show an example of how to test the Serial Peripheral Interface (SPI) library

You are encouraged to create your own tests and submit them as official tests. They way this occurs is that you would "fork" the project, and create a new tests or modify an existing test for the project in your own repository. Then send a pull request for the change to the Arduino Test project in GitHub. This process is described in detail described in Chapter 2. You can also file issues for the project that suggest changes and improvements.

Installing the Arduino Test Suite

The Arduino Test Suite is located on GitHub in the Arduino Tests project, at http://github.com/arduino/tests. You can download, install, or clone the code into your sketch library folder. In this case, since the Arduino Test Suite is an Arduino library, the code will be installed in your libraries folder.

You can download the library from the http://github.com/arduino.tests download link, or, if you have installed Git, as explained in Chapter 2, you can issue the following command from libraries directory:

```
git clone https://github.com/arduino/Tests  ArduinoTestSuite
```

When you restart Arduino, the Arduino Test Suite will appear in the user-contributed libraries, as shown in Figure 13-1. All of the example tests are in a dedicated folder in the Tests library, and these can be loaded from the Examples drop-down list in the Arduino IDE.

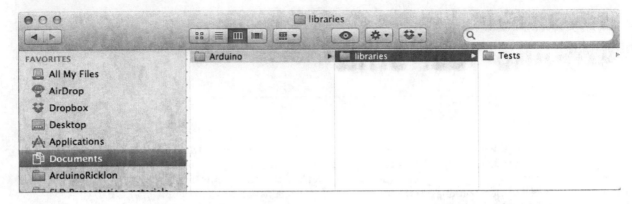

Figure 13-1. *Arduino Test Suite installed in the sketch library folder*

To verify that Arduino Test Suite is working, compile and upload the ATS_Constants example sketch to your hardware, as shown in Listing 13-1. On the serial monitor, you should see each result come back as OK. This indicates a successful test.

Listing 13-1. Arduino Test of Arduino Constants

```
#include        <ArduinoTestSuite.h>

//**********************************************************************
void setup()
{
  Int           startMemoryUsage;

 //Start memory usage must be site prior to ATS_begin
  startMemoryUsage      =       ATS_GetFreeMemory();
  ATS_begin("Arduino", "Test of Arduino Constants");
  /*
   * Test Run Start
   */

  //test true constant
  ATS_PrintTestStatus("1. Test of true constant", true == 1);

  //test false consts
  ATS_PrintTestStatus( "2. Test of false constant", false == 0);

  //Test of HIGH == 1
  ATS_PrintTestStatus( "3. Test of HIGH == 1", HIGH == 1);

  //Test of LOW ==  0
  ATS_PrintTestStatus( "4. Test of LOW ==  0", LOW == 0);
```

```
    ???//Test of INPUT == 1
    ATS_PrintTestStatus( "5. Test of INPUT == 1", INPUT == 1);

    ???//Test of OUTPUT ==  0
    ATS_PrintTestStatus( "6. Test of OUTPUT ==  0", OUTPUT == 0);

    //test decimal
    ATS_PrintTestStatus( "7. Test of decimal constant", 101 == ((1 * pow(10,2)) + (0 * pow(10,1)) + 1));

    //test binary
    ATS_PrintTestStatus( "8. Test of binary constant", B101 == 5);

    //test octal
    ATS_PrintTestStatus( "9. Test of octal constant", 0101 == 65);

    //test hexadecimal
    ATS_PrintTestStatus( "7. Test of hexadecimal constant", (0x101 == 257));

    /*
    * Test Run End
     */
    ATS_ReportMemoryUsage(startMemoryUsage);
    ATS_end();

}

//**********************************************************************
void loop()
{
}
```

Once the code is uploaded to the Arduino, you can connect to the serial port and view the test results. They should look like Figure 13-2.

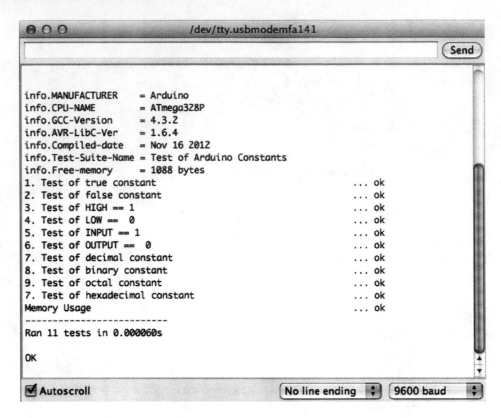

```
● ● ●                    /dev/tty.usbmodemfa141

                                                         Send

info.MANUFACTURER    = Arduino
info.CPU-NAME        = ATmega328P
info.GCC-Version     = 4.3.2
info.AVR-LibC-Ver    = 1.6.4
info.Compiled-date   = Nov 16 2012
info.Test-Suite-Name = Test of Arduino Constants
info.Free-memory     = 1088 bytes
1. Test of true constant                         ... ok
2. Test of false constant                        ... ok
3. Test of HIGH == 1                             ... ok
4. Test of LOW == 0                              ... ok
5. Test of INPUT == 1                            ... ok
6. Test of OUTPUT == 0                           ... ok
7. Test of decimal constant                      ... ok
8. Test of binary constant                       ... ok
9. Test of octal constant                        ... ok
7. Test of hexadecimal constant                  ... ok
Memory Usage                                     ... ok
--------------------------
Ran 11 tests in 0.000060s

OK

☑ Autoscroll          No line ending  ⬍   9600 baud  ⬍
```

Figure 13-2. *Arduino test results*

Figure 13-2 shows the results of 11 tests, all which passed with an OK. If any of these tests fail, something is likely wrong with your Arduino environment, since the constants should always be defined. Now you are ready to run the example tests and create your own tests.

Getting Started with Testing

Testing Arduino helps to verify your hardware configuration and the logic of your software, and ensures that your Arduino-inspired board works exactly as expected. To begin, brainstorm the things that you want to test. Create a list and focus on one area at a time. It is effective to number the tests in your sketch and systematically work through each area. Each test you create should test one condition and verify the pass or fail result. In some cases, a function or a value is supposed to have false value as an expected result to be the success if the output is correct it's considered a success.

Within the Arduino community, it is common to use examples instead of tests. Examples function similarly to tests, but while a test results in either pass or fail, an example allows you to compare what you thought would happen to what actually happens. There are many reasons for testing, including debugging code and observing the behavior of a remote control or line-following robot. Even more importantly, when we create libraries to share with others, we want to ensure that the code works and is easy for people to use. The goal of the Arduino Test Suite is to convert examples into official tests, which you can distribute with your libraries and sample codes, allowing others to learn from them. When someone files an issue against your code, they (or you) can add a test that shows where and how the problem was fixed.

The Arduino Test Suite comes with a test skeleton. This is the smallest test possible, which makes it a good starter sketch. This is shown in Listing 13-2.

Listing 13-2. Minimal Test Sketch

```
#include <ArduinoTestSuite.h>

//**********************************************************************
void setup()
{
    ATS_begin("Arduino", "My bare bones tests");
    testTrue();
    ATS_end();
}
void testTrue()
{
    boolean result;
    result = true;
    ATS_PrintTestStatus("My bare bones test", result);
}
void loop()
{
}
```

Listing 13-2 shows the standard sketch structure. The tests are placed in setup(), so they are only run once. They can also be placed in loop(), which would run them multiple times; this can be useful if you are testing time and repetition issues. You can put your tests in loop() as long as you include while(1){} after the tests are complete.

In order to access the tests, you need to import the Arduino Test Suite with the #include <ArduinoTestSuite.h> line. Remember that tests need a name and an expected result. In this case, we create a Boolean variable called result. Our goal is to show that the result is TRUE. Here's where we begin:

```
 ATS_begin("Arduino", "My bare bones tests");
```

This sets up the test suite run and initializes the starting conditions. Then you can do anything you need to, including setting up variables, calling libraries, and calling any function that you are testing. The test result is set as an outcome of the code, and the status is printed to the serial port:

```
ATS_PrintTestStatus("My bare bones test", result);
```

Finally, once ATS_end() is called, the test is over and you can clean up.

An even better option for testing is to place each test in its own function. That way, it is more clearly isolated from other tests and side effects are largely avoided.

The results of the tests appear in the serial monitor format shown in Listing 13-3.

Listing 13-3. Minimal Test Sketch Results

```
info.MANUFACTURER    = Arduino
info.CPU-NAME        = ATmega328P
info.GCC-Version     = 4.3.2
info.AVR-LibC-Ver    = 1.6.4
info.Compiled-date   = Oct 20 2010
```

```
info.Test-Suite-Name = My bare bones tests
info.Free-memory     = 1464 bytes
My bare bones test                                      ... ok
--------------------------
Ran 1 tests in 1.371s

OK
```

The final OK shows that all tests passed and took a total time of 1.31 seconds. They passed because we created a result variable that held a true value, which was then passed to the ATS_PrintTestStatus() function. It has this function signature:

```
void     ATS_PrintTestStatus(char *testString, boolean passed);
```

This *char *testString* is the test name, and *boolean passed* is the test result.

Arduino Test Result Format

The Arduino test result format is based on the standard test format used by the Nose testing library from Python (https://nose.readthedocs.org/en/latest/). This format uses verbose mode so that all tests are listed with their outcomes. The output of the format is compatible with several different automated test systems. Since memory is limited and we want to preserve it for the tests as opposed to the testing library, this format is not based on an XML format. Each test must be discrete, and if one element fails, the incomplete XML file will be invalid and unusable. However, you can parse the output and change it to an xUnit test structure.

Another common use of the Arduino Test Suite is to use it to test the compiler toolchain to ensure that the compiler, and it's support programs running your code properly. It is important for nonstandard compilers to check if an Arduino compiler upgrade is compatible with the Arduino API. The result format has a set of common data that allows you to know what toolchain your code is being compiled against. This is helpful because you can verify an upgraded GCC compiler or AVR-libc and be assured that your code functions, thanks to a passing test result. Another feature of the format is the ability to identify the manufacturer so you know what platform and microcontroller you are testing against. This way, you can test an entire family of Arduinos and clones and know that they are compatible with your code, libraries, or project. Each test has a date, time, and name, so you can keep track of the different tests.

Test Result Section Format Details

The test result file begins with information data. This is indicated by the info. at the beginning of the line, as shown in Listing 13-4.

Listing 13-4. Test Header Info Fields

```
info.MANUFACTURER    = Arduino
info.CPU-NAME        = ATmega328P
info.GCC-Version     = 4.3.2
info.AVR-LibC-Ver    = 1.6.4
info.Compiled-date   = Oct  4 2010
info.Test-Suite-Name = general
```

The header information section is followed by the test section, which includes the test results.

Test-Naming Structure

The test format is identical for all tests. This makes it easier for other software to parse them. The format includes the following items in the following order:

1. The test name

2. Information about the test (included in parentheses)

3. Ellipsis points (i.e., ...)

4. The test result status

The following line shows an example:

```
name of test (information about test) ... test result status
```

Test Status Options

The tests themselves only have three valid outcomes: success, failure, or error:

```
ok
FAIL
ERROR
```

Test Summary

That last section of the test is a summary. It includes information such as how many tests were run, how long they took, and how many failures occurred. The test result summary is separated from the test by dashes, like so:

```
--------------------------
```

Here's an example of the summary format, followed by final condition:

```
Ran n tests in Secs

OK
FAILED (failures=n)
```

The variable n is replaced by the correct number of tests, and the exact number of failures that occurred in the test run.

Arduino Test Suite Basic Functions

The following functions allow you to start, print, and end tests, respectively. I'll describe them in detail in the following sections.

- ATS_begin()

- ATS_end()

- ATS_PrintTestStatus()

ATS_begin

This is the function signature for `ATS_begin`:

```
void    ATS_begin(char *manufName, char *testSuiteName);
```

Here are some examples of its usage:

```
ATS_begin("Arduino","My test suite.");
ATS_begin("Teensy", "My test suite.");
ATS_begin("Adafruit Motor Shield", "My motor shield tests.");
```

These are all valid examples of beginning statements. You can set the manufacturer of the board or shield and test the suite name. The `ATS_begin` function initializes the serial interface so that you do not have to do this in your test sketches. Once the test starts, it keeps track of the time and other summary test information, such as number of failures.

ATS_PrintTestStatus

You use the test status to return the test result to the user. Here is the syntax of the `ATS_PrintTestStatus` function:

```
void    ATS_PrintTestStatus(char *testString, boolean passed);
```

And here are some examples of its usage:

```
ATS_PrintTestStatus("1. Test result is TRUE test" , true);
ATS_PrintTestStatus("2. Test result is FALSE test (a false result is expected)" , false);
```

In the function, the argument test name is followed by a Boolean test result (`true` or `false`). All tests must pass or fail. You can use a parentheses section to add a note about the test to clarify detail, if necessary. In the `FALSE` test case, we must say that failure is expected, since we want to see the failure case. This is an unusual case so it's important to note it because interpreting the result could cause confusion.

Numbering is not automatic, so if you want to number your tests, put the numbering in the test name, like so:

```
ATS_PrintTestsStatus("1. my numbered test" , status);
```

ATS_end

`ATS_end` completes the test run. Test time and the final count of successful and failed tests are sent in the summary format to the serial port.

```
void    ATS_end();
```

Using the Basic Functions

With these functions, you can create custom test suites and verify your code or project. The code in Listing 13-5 is an example that forces a result to be TRUE or FALSE. It is important to keep track of all test results, but especially failure conditions. This way at a glance the test issue can be found quickly. The failure condition can be described in the test name, and the result would be TRUE, which will appear as OK in the result.

Listing 13-5. Bare-Bones Test Sketch

```
#include <ArduinoTestSuite.h>

//***********************************************************************
void setup()
{
    boolean result;
    ATS_begin("Arduino", "My bare bones tests");
    result = true;
    ATS_PrintTestStatus("My bare bones test", result);
    result = false;
    ATS_PrintTestStatus("1. My bare bones test", result);
    ATS_end();
}

void loop()
{
}
```

Here is the test result:

```
info.MANUFACTURER = Arduino
info.CPU-NAME = ATmega328P
info.GCC-Version = 4.3.2
info.AVR-LibC-Ver = 1.6.4
info.Compiled-date = Oct 20 2010
info.Test-Suite-Name = My bare bones tests
info.Free-memory = 1442 bytes
My bare bones test                      ... ok
1. My bare bones test                   ... FAIL
--------------------------
Ran 2 tests in 1.443s

FAILED (failures=1)
```

Once the test is complete, you will be able to see how many test were run, how long the tests took, and how many failures occurred. You can examine the tests to identify what happened. Additionally, you will get information about how much memory was available when you ran the tests. In this case, info.Free-memory shows that 1442 bytes were free in this test run.

Arduino Test Suite Built-In Tests

The Arduino Test Suite contains several built-in tests. These are very useful, as they standardize some of the basic tests. Running these standard tests will help you confirm that a custom Arduino-derived board has the correct pin numbers and behaves appropriately with the digital, analog, and PWM pins as the serial values are transmitted and received. You will need to test for memory leaks or heap fragmentation if things go wrong. The built-in tests are as follow:

```
ATS_ReportMemoryUsage(int _memoryUsageAtStart)
ATS_Test_DigitalPin(uint8_t digitalPinToTest)
ATS_Test_PWM_Pin(uint8_t digitalPinToTest)
ATS_Test_AnalogInput(uint8_t analogPintoTest)
ATS_Test_EEPROM(void)
ATS_TestSerialLoopback(HardwareSerial *theSerialPort, char *serialPortName)
```

For the Serial port test the RX/TX pins to be wired to one another. This loops the input and output of serial information into each other for reading, and parsing by the test suite. However, the test results are delivered over the first serial port, and the board is programmed through it. Therefore, you can't test the port using this technique on the Arduino Uno, the Arduino Mega has multiple serial so there is extra serial ports that can be tested so you can still get the test results from the default serial.

Since these tests make the assumption that the board is wired for testing, you need to make sure your version of Arduino matches the wiring in Figure 13-3 or 13-4.

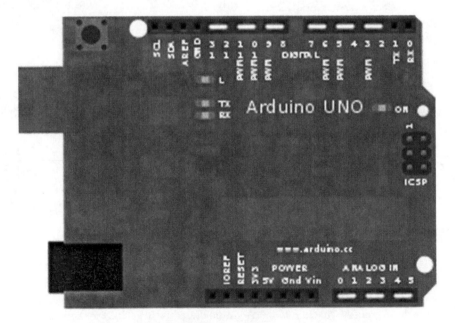

Figure 13-3. *Arduino Uno configured for testing*

You would use the design in Figure 13-4 to test a board similar to the Arduino Mega.

Figure 13-4. Arduino Mega test wiring

Strategies for Testing Your Own Arduino Derivative

The Arduino Test Suite contains all the necessary tests to verify that your board is fully functional. For creating a custom board to be compatible with the Arduino Uno or Mega pin layout, the Arduino Test Suite contains the ATS_General test. This test checks all the features of these two boards, including digital pins, PWM, analog read/write, EEPROM, tone, and serial RX/TX. If your custom board can pass these tests, then the board is pin-for-pin and feature compatible. You can save time and money by identifying problems early.

The ATS_General test requires that you wire the pins in a specific way. The digital I/O pins are tied together, the analog read/write pins are tied together, and serial RX/TX pins can also be tied together. For a board with only one serial port, you will want to skip the RX/TX test. This is detected in the current ATS_General test.

You would use the same wiring options like we've done with the Arduino Uno board in Figure 13-3. You would be configured for testing. You can do something similar for your own board.

Memory Testing

The Arduino Test Suite provides a test for checking the amount of free memory available. This function is particularly useful for checking how much memory is being consumed and if it is being returned after use. You can find out how to use this function by studying the tests. This section will look at a subset of these tests and then demonstrate using this function to track memory usage and create a test that involves memory use. Listing 13-6 shows the code that we will examine. The complete test is part of the ATS examples. We will look at three tests:

- testAllocatingThenDeallocatingPreservesFreeMemory();

- testAllocatingAndDeallocatingSmallerPreservesFreeMemory();

- testRepeatedlyAllocatingAndDeallocatingMemoryPreservesFreeMemory();

Listing 13-6. ATS_GetFreeMemory Tests Example, from Matthew Murdoch

```
#include <ArduinoTestSuite.h>

void setup() {
  ATS_begin("Arduino", "ATS_GetFreeMemory() Tests");

  testAllocatingThenDeallocatingPreservesFreeMemory();
  testRepeatedlyAllocatingAndDeallocatingMemoryPreservesFreeMemory();

  testAllocatingAndDeallocatingSmallerPreservesFreeMemory();

  ATS_end();
}

// This test checks that the free list is taken into account when free memory is calculated
// when using versions of free() which *don't* reset __brkval (such as in avr-libc 1.6.4)
void testAllocatingThenDeallocatingPreservesFreeMemory() {
  int startMemory = ATS_GetFreeMemory();

  void* buffer = malloc(10);
  free(buffer);

  ATS_PrintTestStatus("Allocating then deallocating preserves free memory", startMemory ==
  ATS_GetFreeMemory());
}

// This test checks that the free list is taken into account when free memory is calculated
// even when using versions of free() which *do* reset __brkval (such as in avr-libc 1.7.1)
void testAllocatingAndDeallocatingInterleavedPreservesFreeMemory() {
  void* buffer1 = malloc(10);
  int startMemory = ATS_GetFreeMemory();

  void* buffer2 = malloc(10);
  free(buffer1);

  ATS_PrintTestStatus("Interleaved allocation and deallocation preserves free memory",
  startMemory == ATS_GetFreeMemory());

  free(buffer2);
}

void testRepeatedlyAllocatingAndDeallocatingMemoryPreservesFreeMemory() {
  int startMemory = ATS_GetFreeMemory();

  for (int i = 0; i < 10; i++) {
    void* buffer1 = malloc(10);
    void* buffer2 = malloc(10);
    void* buffer3 = malloc(10);
    free(buffer3);
```

```
    free(buffer2);
    free(buffer1);
  }

  ATS_PrintTestStatus("Repeated allocation and deallocation preserves free memory",
  startMemory == ATS_GetFreeMemory());
}

// TODO MM Currently fails as __brkval is not increased, but the size of the free list is...
// Therefore looks as if the total amount of free memory increases (i.e. negative memory leak)!
void testReallocatingSmallerPreservesFreeMemory() {
  int startMemory = ATS_GetFreeMemory();

  // Allocate one byte more than the space taken up by a free list node
  void* buffer = malloc(5);
  buffer = realloc(buffer, 1);
  free(buffer);

  ATS_PrintTestStatus("Reallocating smaller preserves free memory",
  startMemory == ATS_GetFreeMemory());
}

void testReallocatingLargerPreservesFreeMemory() {
  int startMemory = ATS_GetFreeMemory();

  void* buffer = malloc(1);
  buffer = realloc(buffer, 5);
  free(buffer);

  ATS_PrintTestStatus("Reallocating larger preserves free memory",
  startMemory == ATS_GetFreeMemory());
}

void testAllocatingAndDeallocatingSmallerPreservesFreeMemory() {
  int startMemory = ATS_GetFreeMemory();

  // Allocate one byte more than the space taken up by a free list node
  void* buffer = malloc(5);
  free(buffer);
  buffer = malloc(1);
  free(buffer);

  ATS_PrintTestStatus("Allocating and deallocating smaller preserves free memory",
  startMemory == ATS_GetFreeMemory());
}

void testReallocatingRepeatedlyLargerPreservesFreeMemory() {
  int startMemory = ATS_GetFreeMemory();
```

```
  void* buffer = malloc(2);
  for (int i = 4; i <= 8; i+=2) {
    buffer = realloc(buffer, i);
  }
  free(buffer);

  ATS_PrintTestStatus("Reallocating repeatedly larger preserves free memory",
  startMemory == ATS_GetFreeMemory());
}

void loop() {
}
```

Example: Testing for a Memory Leak

Any new values created inside the memory test will use memory. So, you must declare all the variables that consume memory at the beginning of the setup.

```
startMemoryUsage = ATS_GetFreeMemory();
```

Once this is done, your starting memory is set. Anything that takes without putting back will be counted as a failure. The memory test is over when you call the following:

```
ATS_ReportMemoryUsage(startMemoryUsage);
```

Here are some hints for debugging:

- By putting the memory test at the bottom of the code, you can gradually move it higher into the code and see where the memory was lost.

- An OK indicates that the memory loss occurred below the memory test.

- A binary search will help you find the problem.

Listing 13-7 is a sketch of the testing skeleton.

Listing 13-7. Sketch of the Testing Skeleton

```
#include <ArduinoTestSuite.h>

//**********************************************************************
void setup()
{
    int startMemoryUsage;

    //startMemoryUsage must be set directly before ATS_begin
    startMemoryUsage = ATS_GetFreeMemory();
    ATS_begin("Arduino", "Skeleton Test");
    /*
     * Test Run Start
     * Test one passes because result is set to true
     * Test two fails becuase result is set to false
     * You can test memory for any set of tests by using the ATS_ReportMemoryUsage test
```

```
 * There is also a way to print current memeory for debugging
 */
ATS_PrintTestStatus("1. Test of true test status", true);
ATS_PrintTestStatus("2. Test of false test status, this will fail.", false);
ATS_ReportMemoryUsage(startMemoryUsage);
/*
 * Test Run End
 */
ATS_end();
}
//***********************************************************************
void loop()
{
}
```

Here is the test result:

```
info.MANUFACTURER = Arduino
info.CPU-NAME = ATmega328P
info.GCC-Version = 4.3.2
info.AVR-LibC-Ver = 1.6.4
info.Compiled-date = Oct 20 2010
info.Test-Suite-Name = Skeleton Test
info.Free-memory = 1322 bytes
1. Test of true test status                   ... ok
2. Test of false test status, this will fail.     ... FAIL
Memory Usage ... ok
--------------------------
Ran 3 tests in 1.508s

FAILED (failures=1)
```

Testing Libraries

One of goals of this chapter is to make it possible to test your own libraries. In this section, we will test an Arduino library, which can be used as a model for testing your own. We'll test the SPI library, which is used to communicate digitally with other electronic devices, such as temperature sensors, SD cards, and EEPROM, all of which all support the SPI protocol. To test the SPI protocol of Arduino, we can make two Arduinos talk to each other. We will connect them as a master-and-slave device.

The tests will be from the point of view of the master and ensure that the functions defined in the library work correctly. The tests will be part of the sketch that we load onto the master Arduino. The slave Arduino will be loaded with a sketch that configures it in slave mode and provides a set of information that will return known data to the master.

Figure 13-5 shows the two Arduinos configured in master-and-slave configuration. Pins 10, 11, 12, and 13 are tied together between them. Power and ground are connected so that the slave Arduino is powered by the master.

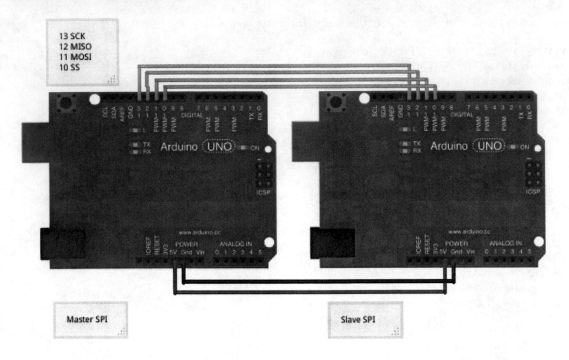

Figure 13-5. *Arduino SPI master-slave wiring*

We will use the Arduino SPI master test sketch and an Arduino SPI slave sketch, which will process the commands, expected returns, and values from the master, and confirm that an action occurred properly. Listing 13-8 shows the configuration of the slave SPI Arduino.

Listing 13-8. SPI_Slave_test.ino

```
/*
* SPI Slave test program
 * by Rick Anderson
 *
 * Set the defaults:
 * MSBFIRST
 * DataMode = SPI_MODE0;
 * Clock divider = SPI_CLOCK_DIV4,
 */

#include <SPI.h>

const byte TESTBYTE = 0b11110000;

void setup()
{
  Serial.begin(9600);
```

```
    //Slave out needs to be enabled by placing the MISO as OUTPUT
    pinMode(MISO, OUTPUT);

    //Use the AVR Code to turn on slave mode
    SPCR |= _BV(SPE);

    //Standard Arduino settings for SPI
    SPI.setBitOrder(MSBFIRST);
    SPI.setDataMode(SPI_MODE0);
    SPI.setClockDivider(SPI_CLOCK_DIV4);

    //Turn on interrupts for SPI
    SPI.attachInterrupt();
    Serial.println("Slave Configured");

}


/*AVR SPI interrupt callback
*Process commands sent to slave
* First transfer is the command value
* Second command pushes the value to the master
*/
ISR (SPI_STC_vect)
{
  const byte cc = TESTBYTE;
  if (SPDR == 0x00) //Only command is 0x00
  {
    SPDR = 0b11110000; // read byte from SPI Data Register
  }
  else
  {
    SPDR = 0b11111111; //Any other command returns 0xff
  }
}

void loop()
{
  Serial.println("SPI Slave Sketch for testing SPI Master.");
  if (digitalRead (SS) == HIGH)
  {
    SPDR = 0;//When not enable set buffer to 0
  }
}
```

This kind of test requires an Arduino to be configured in slave mode. In order to get the slave to be in SPI slave mode, you must use AVR code. SPCR |= _BV(SPE); enables slave mode for AVR SPI. Additionally, the SPI interrupt needs to be enabled. It is worth noting that you can use the Arduino SPI.attachInterupt() or call the AVR code directly. In Listing 13-9, you can see that all the function does is call the AVR code.

Listing 13-9. SPI.h attachInterrupt Code

```
void SPIClass::attachInterrupt() {
  SPCR |= _BV(SPIE);
}
```

Once the interruptions are turned on, you must write the callback function that will run once the SPI interrupt is triggered. This function is

```
ISR (SPI_STC_vect) {}
```

Each function of the SPI library, as well as part of the master Arduino sketch, will need to be tested. The SPI library has defined the following functions:

- begin()
- end()
- setBitOrder()
- setClockDivider()
- setDataMode()
- transfer()

The begin() function instantiates the SPI object. This test will instantiate SPI and determine if the SPI object was created by setting the pin modes for the SPI lines and configuring the hardware SPI feature in master mode.

The end() function disables the SPI configuration using the following AVR code:

```
SPCR &= ~_BV(SPE);
```

This leaves the pin modes as they were: INPUT and OUTPUT.

Given the functions in the SPI library, we can now test them in use. Listing 13-10 is the SPI master test code. The online version provides the full test, https://github.com/ProArd/SPI_Master_test. We will look at a few of the key test cases and examine how they work.

Listing 13-10. SPI_Master_test.ino

```
#include <ArduinoTestSuite.h>
#include <SPI.h>

void setup ()
{
  // Serial.begin(9600);
  ATS_begin("Arduino", "SPI Tests");
  SPI.begin();
  //Run tests
  refConfig();

  testTransfer();
  refConfig();

  testBitOrderMSB();
  refConfig();
```

```
  testBitOrderLSB();

  testDataMode();
  refConfig();

  testClockDivider();

  SPI.end();
  ATS_end();
}

void refConfig()
{
  SPI.setBitOrder(MSBFIRST);
  SPI.setDataMode(SPI_MODE0);
  SPI.setClockDivider(SPI_CLOCK_DIV4);
}
byte SPITransfer(byte val, uint8_t spi_bitorder, uint8_t spi_mode, uint8_t spi_clockdivider)
{
  byte spireturn;
  SPI.setBitOrder(spi_bitorder);
  SPI.setDataMode(spi_mode);
  SPI.setClockDivider(spi_clockdivider);
  digitalWrite(SS, LOW);
  spireturn = SPI.transfer(val);
  delayMicroseconds (10);
  spireturn = SPI.transfer(0x00);
  digitalWrite(SS, HIGH);
  return spireturn;
}

void testTransfer()
{
  boolean result = false;
  byte spireturn;

  spireturn = SPITransfer(0x00, MSBFIRST, SPI_MODE0, SPI_CLOCK_DIV4);

  if (spireturn == 0xf0)
  {
    result = true;
  }
  ATS_PrintTestStatus("1. transfer(0x00)", result);
}

void testBitOrderMSB()
{
  //Sets the bit order to MSBFRIST expects byte 0xf0
  boolean result = false;
  byte spireturn;
```

277

```
  spireturn = SPITransfer(0x00, MSBFIRST, SPI_MODE0, SPI_CLOCK_DIV4);
  if (spireturn == 0xf0)
  {
    result = true;
  }
  ATS_PrintTestStatus("2. setBitOrder(MSBFIRST)", result);
}

void testBitOrderLSB()
{
  //Sets the bit order to LSBFRIST expects byte 0xf
  boolean result = false;
  byte spireturn;

  spireturn = SPITransfer(0x00, LSBFIRST, SPI_MODE0, SPI_CLOCK_DIV4);
  if (spireturn == 0xf)
  {
    result = true;
  }
  ATS_PrintTestStatus("3. setBitOrder(LSBFIRST)", result);
}

void testDataMode()
{
  //asserting the default mode is true
  boolean result = false;
  byte spireturn;

  spireturn = SPITransfer(0x00, MSBFIRST, SPI_MODE0, SPI_CLOCK_DIV4);
  if (spireturn == 0xf0)
  {
    result = true;
  }
  ATS_PrintTestStatus("4. setDataMode(SPI_MODE0)", result);

  result = false;
  spireturn = SPITransfer(0x00, MSBFIRST, SPI_MODE1, SPI_CLOCK_DIV4);
  if (spireturn == 0xf0)
  {
    result = true;
  }
  ATS_PrintTestStatus("5. setDataMode(SPI_MODE1) should fail so reports ok", !result);

  result = false;
  spireturn = SPITransfer(0x00, MSBFIRST, SPI_MODE2, SPI_CLOCK_DIV4);
  if (spireturn == 0xf0)
  {
    result = true;
  }
  ATS_PrintTestStatus("6. setDataMode(SPI_MODE2) should fail so reports ok", !result);
```

```
    result = false;
    spireturn = SPITransfer(0x00, MSBFIRST, SPI_MODE3, SPI_CLOCK_DIV4);
    if (spireturn == 0xf0)
    {
      result = true;
    }
    ATS_PrintTestStatus("7. setDataMode(SPI_MODE3) should fail so reports ok", !result);
}

void testClockDivider()
{
    //asserting the default mode is true
    boolean result = false;
    byte spireturn;

    spireturn = SPITransfer(0x00, MSBFIRST, SPI_MODE0, SPI_CLOCK_DIV2);
    //Slave is CLOCK_DIV4 so this should fail
    if (spireturn == 0xf0)
    {
      result = true;
    }

    ATS_PrintTestStatus("8. setClockDivider(SPI_CLOCK_DIV2) should fail so reports ok", !result);
    result = false;

    spireturn = SPITransfer(0x00, MSBFIRST, SPI_MODE0, SPI_CLOCK_DIV4);
    if (spireturn == 0xf0)
    {
      result = true;
    }
    ATS_PrintTestStatus("9. setClockDivider(SPI_CLOCK_DIV4)", result);
    result = false;

    spireturn = SPITransfer(0x00, MSBFIRST, SPI_MODE0, SPI_CLOCK_DIV8);
    if (spireturn == 0xf0)
    {
      result = true;
    }
    ATS_PrintTestStatus("10. setClockDivider(SPI_CLOCK_DIV8)", result);
    result = false;

    spireturn = SPITransfer(0x00, MSBFIRST, SPI_MODE0, SPI_CLOCK_DIV16);
    if (spireturn == 0xf0)
    {
      result = true;
    }
    ATS_PrintTestStatus("11. setClockDivider(SPI_CLOCK_DIV16)", result);
    result = false;

    spireturn = SPITransfer(0x00, MSBFIRST, SPI_MODE0, SPI_CLOCK_DIV32);
    if (spireturn == 0xf0)
```

```
{
  result = true;
}
ATS_PrintTestStatus("12. setClockDivider(SPI_CLOCK_DIV32)", result);
result = false;

spireturn = SPITransfer(0x00, MSBFIRST, SPI_MODE0, SPI_CLOCK_DIV64);
if (spireturn == 0xf0)
{
  result = true;
}
ATS_PrintTestStatus("13. setClockDivider(SPI_CLOCK_DIV64)", result);
result = false;

spireturn = SPITransfer(0x00, MSBFIRST, SPI_MODE0, SPI_CLOCK_DIV128);
if (spireturn == 0xf0)
{
  result = true;
}
ATS_PrintTestStatus("14. setClockDivider(SPI_CLOCK_DIV128)", result);
result = false;
}

void loop (){}
```

SPI.transfer() Test

SPI.transfer() is the main function of this library. In the past, we've used it to verify that data was sent properly between various configurations. Now we want to test if it sends data as defined in the API. A byte should be sent to the slave device, and a byte will be received as the return value from the slave device, as shown in Listing 13-11.

Listing 13-11. Data Transfer Test

```
void testTransfer()
{
  boolean result = false;
  byte spireturn;

  spireturn = SPITransfer(0x00, MSBFIRST, SPI_MODE0, SPI_CLOCK_DIV4);

  if (spireturn == 0xf0)
  {
    result = true;
  }
  ATS_PrintTestStatus("1. transfer(0x00)", result);
}
```

setBitOrder() Test

The bit order of the device must be matched by the Arduino communicating with it. There are two supported configurations:

- Least significant bit (LSB)

- Most significant bit (MSB)

For the first test, the slave Arduino must be configured for LSB, and for the second test, the slave Arduino needs to be configured to MSB, as shown in Listing 13-12.

Listing 13-12. setBitOrder MSB Test

```
void testBitOrderMSB()
{
  //Sets the bit order to MSBFRIST expects byte 0xf0
  boolean result = false;
  byte spireturn;

  spireturn = SPITransfer(0x00, MSBFIRST, SPI_MODE0, SPI_CLOCK_DIV4);
  if (spireturn == 0xf0)
  {
    result = true;
  }
  ATS_PrintTestStatus("2. setBitOrder: MSBFIRST", result);
}
```

setClockDivider() Test

The clock divider changes the SPI speed to be a multiple of the Arduino clock speed. This way, it is possible to change the speed of the SPI bus to match that of the attached device. For this test, we need to set the clock divider at each of its multiples and ask the attached Arduino for a piece of data that matches the clock speed, as shown in Listing 13-13.

Listing 13-13. setClockDivider Test for SPI_CLOCK_DIV2

```
void testClockDivider()
{
boolean result = false;
 byte spireturn;
  //SPI_MODE0 test 3
  setSlaveClockDivider(SPI_CLOCK_DIV2);
  SPI.setClockDivider(SPI_CLOCK_DIV2);

  spireturn = SPI.transfer(0x02);
  if (spireturn > 0)
  {
    result = true;
  }
  ATS_PrintTestStatus("4. setClockDivider:SPI_CLOCK_DIV2 (failure is OK)", result);
}
```

The test in Listing 13-13 is a testing condition for when the clock divider is set to twice the speed of the slave device. This type of test is expected to fail. The code is written to discover the failure and report a completed test. A true result is reported as a pass. The parentheses are used to indicate that the test is OK even though failure was expected.

setDataMode() Test

The data mode configures the clock phase and the polarity. For this to be tested, each mode must be set, and the slave Arduino must send a piece of data that shows that it was received and returned properly, as shown in Listing 13-14.

Listing 13-14. SetDataMode Test for SPI_MODE0

```
void testDataMode()
{
boolean result = false;
 byte spireturn;
  //SPI_MODE0 test 3
  setSlaveDataMode(SPI_MODE0);
  SPI.setDataMode(SPI_MODE0);
  spireturn = SPI.transfer(0x02);
  if (spireturn > 0)
  {
    result = true;
  }
  ATS_PrintTestStatus("3. setDataMode: SPI_MODE0", result);
}
```

The test in Listing 13-14 will return a TRUE result if you can communicate with the slave device in that mode. If a configuration or communication error occurs, it will fail.

SPI Test Results

In conclusion, the complete set of test runs shows that the expected configuration of the master and slave match. The commands that are issued must be valid configurations of SPI in order to work correctly. If we change the slave configuration, we have to change the master test, or else we will see expected failures due to mismatched configurations.

There are many test cases within each of these variations. The full source for this on the Pro Arduino SPGitHub repository, http://github.com/proardwebsite goes through many more test cases, each with a single change from the last one. Another good challenge for SPI testing would be to reconfigure the slave device to iterate through each of its configurations. Creating these tests proves that SPI is working and simultaneously gives you a chance to learn how SPI works.

Summary

This chapter describes the features and benefits of the Arduino Test Suite. The goal is to show how to move from creating examples that demonstrate your code to creating a test that verifies it. Not only is this good for code quality, but it allows you to make custom circuits, shields, and your own verified Arduino-inspired device. As you share your code and hardware with others, testing provides usage examples and behavior confirmation.

The challenge of creating testable conditions is not simple. The environment of the project must be included, and users are encouraged to submit their tests to the Arduino testing project on GitHub. This ensures that the entire platform is well tested and documented, and provides a high-quality user experience.

Index

CPSIA information can be obtained at www.ICGtesting.com
Printed in the USA
LVOW11s1214290913

354597LV00005B/27/P